TiVo® For Dummies®

D0508288

TiVo Button Shortcuts

Press These Buttons	To Jump to This Screen
TiVo TiVo	Now Playing
TiVo 1	Season Pass Manager
TiVo 2	To Do list
TiVo 3	Search Using WishLists
TiVo 4	Search by Title
TiVo 5	Browse by Channel
TiVo 6	Browse by Time
TiVo 7	Record Time/Channel
TiVo 8	TiVo's Suggestions
TiVo 9	Showcases
TiVo 0	Play the TiVo Animation (except DirecTV TiVos)

Live TV Shortcuts

Press This	To Do This When Watching Live TV
Live TV	Press anytime to view live TV; press again to view Program Guide; press once more to clear Program Guide.
Guide	Press once to display the large Channel Banner; press again to remove.
▷	When Channel Banner is visible, pressing the right arrow cycles between the three banner sizes; leave it set at the one you prefer.
Clear	Remove everything that's not part of the show.
▶▶	Each press fast-forwards at an increased speed (3x, 20x, 60x). When the screen's paused or in slow motion, it advances frame by frame.
◀◀	Each press rewinds at a faster speed (3x, 20x, 60x). When the screen's paused or in slow motion, it rewinds frame by frame.
Record	Begin recording the program you're watching, including any of the show in the buffer, and stop recording at the show's end. (Press again to stop the recording before the show's end.)
Enter/Last	Flips back to the previously viewed channel.
▽	On DirecTV TiVos, this switches between tuners, or when the Channel Banner is visible, displays what's playing on the second tuner.

Now Playing Screen Shortcuts

Press This	To Do This From the Now Playing Screen
Play	Play the highlighted recording immediately.
Clear	Jump to delete screen (also works in To Do list, Season Pass, and WishList).
Chan Page	When viewing a program's description, use this as a Page Up/Down key to read the description of the next or previous program.
Enter/Last	When viewing a program's description, this brings up more show information, including episode number, other actors, and original air date.

For Dummies: Bestselling Book Series for Beginners

TiVo® For Dummies®

Cheat Sheet

Text Entry Shortcuts

Press This Button	To Do This While Entering Text
0	When searching by Title or Actor/Director in a WishList, press this button before entering text to immediately list all shows.
▶▶	Insert a space.
◀◀	Backspace to erase a character.
Clear ○	Clear everything and start over.
▶▶ **Slow**	Enter the wildcard (*) to match any word starting with the previous letters in Keyword and Title WishLists. For example, `natur*` finds *nature, natural, naturally,* and similar words.
❚❚	Enter quotes (") to find exact matches. `"james bond"` weeds out finance shows where James buys bonds.

Enter spaces instead of any hyphens (-), slashes (/), or periods (.) in the name. Ignore apostrophes ('), asterisks (*), and ampersands (&).

Navigation Tips

The little on-screen arrows next to the highlight bar always show your possible directions. Pressing the arrows on the remote moves the Highlight bar in the direction of the arrow.

These arrows show the direction you can move the highlight bar: Up, Down, Left or Right. Pressing Right, for instance, moves to Options. Pressing Left moves back to the previous screen.

Arrows with the little line beneath them mean you can use your Channel Up/Down key to Page Up or Page Down.

For Dummies: Bestselling Book Series for Beginners

TiVo® FOR DUMMIES®

by Andy Rathbone

WILEY

Wiley Publishing, Inc.

TiVo® For Dummies®

Published by
Wiley Publishing, Inc.
111 River Street
Hoboken, NJ 07030-5774

WILEY

About the Author

Andy Rathbone started geeking around with computers in 1985 when he bought a boxy CP/M Kaypro 2X with lime-green letters. Like other budding nerds, he soon began playing with null-modem adapters, dialing up computer bulletin boards, and working part-time at Radio Shack.

In between playing computer games, he served as editor of the *Daily Aztec* newspaper at San Diego State University. After graduating with a comparative literature degree, he went to work for a bizarre underground coffee-table magazine that sort of disappeared.

Andy began combining his two main interests, words and computers, by selling articles to a local computer magazine. During the next few years, he started ghostwriting computer books for more-famous computer authors, as well as writing several hundred articles about computers for technoid publications like *Supercomputing Review, CompuServe Magazine, ID Systems, DataPro,* and *Shareware.*

In 1992, Andy and *DOS For Dummies* author/legend Dan Gookin teamed up to write *PCs For Dummies.* Andy subsequently wrote the award-winning *Windows For Dummies* series, *MP3 For Dummies,* and many other *For Dummies* books.

Today, he has more than 15 million copies of his books in print, which have been translated into more than 30 languages.

Andy lives with his most-excellent wife, Tina, and their cat in Southern California. Feel free to drop by his Web site at www.andyrathbone.com.

Author's Acknowledgments

Thanks to Matt Wagner, Andrea Boucher, Amanda Foxworth, Steve Lionel, and Steve Hayes.

Publisher's Acknowledgments

We're proud of this book; please send us your comments through our online registration form located at www.dummies.com/register.

Some of the people who helped bring this book to market include the following:

Acquisitions, Editorial, and Media Development

Project Editor: Andrea C. Boucher, Carol Sheehan

Acquisitions Editor: Steve Hayes

Technical Editor: Steve Lionel

Editorial Manager: Carol Sheehan

Media Development Manager: Laura VanWinkle

Media Development Supervisor: Richard Graves

Editorial Assistant: Amanda Foxworth

Cartoons: Rich Tennant (www.the5thwave.com)

Production

Project Coordinator: Adrienne Martinez

Layout and Graphics: Andrea Dahl, Michael Kruzil, Kristin McMullan, Barry Offringa, Lynsey Osborn, Jacque Schneider, Melanee Wolven

Proofreaders: Andy Hollandbeck, Carl W. Pierce, Dwight Ramsey, Brian H. Walls

Indexer: TECHBOOKS Publishing Services

Publishing and Editorial for Technology Dummies

　　Richard Swadley, Vice President and Executive Group Publisher

　　Andy Cummings, Vice President and Publisher

　　Mary C. Corder, Editorial Director

Publishing for Consumer Dummies

　　Diane Graves Steele, Vice President and Publisher

　　Joyce Pepple, Acquisitions Director

Composition Services

　　Gerry Fahey, Vice President of Production Services

　　Debbie Stailey, Director of Composition Services

Contents at a Glance

Table of Contents

Introduction

· ·

*W*elcome to *TiVo For Dummies*!

Let's get one thing straight: You're certainly no dummy. Like most people, you specialize in a few chosen areas. And, like the rest of us, you occasionally feel like a dummy when trying to use something unfamiliar. Locating a rental car's windshield wiper switch almost always makes me feel like a dummy, for example.

Because you've picked up this book, you probably know something about TiVo. You may have heard the word or concept, or perhaps seen a friend's TiVo in action. You might own a TiVo, and know how to make it do what you want — sort of.

But you want to know a little bit *more*. This book helps you, whether you're thinking about buying a TiVo, struggling with a TiVo, or just want to use your TiVo a little more efficiently.

What's in This Book?

First, here's what's *not* in this book. This book isn't written for TiVo *experts* — people who want to take apart their TiVo, analyze its software construction and fiddle with its innards. If you're a TiVo tinkerer, pick up Jeff Keegan's *Hacking TiVo* from Wiley Publishing, Inc., and you'll find detailed descriptions of TiVo's inner workings and workarounds.

This book, by contrast, explains things left out by the advanced books. *TiVo For Dummies* starts by explaining the differences between TiVo models, and how to choose the one that meets your specific needs.

You'll find out how to set up a new TiVo with your TV, VCR, and other gadgets clustered around your TV. I explain TiVo's standard tricks like pausing live TV shows and playing Instant Replays. You'll discover ways to record your shows automatically, even if you're not sure when they air.

Computer users will enjoy the chapters on TiVo's Home Media Option, which lets TiVo connect with your computer to play your music files and view digital photos. Plus, I've stuffed in a bunch of tips that let you take advantage of everything TiVo's designed to offer.

And if it's not enough, I even give a step-by-step explanation of how to increase your TiVo's storage space with an easy-to-install hard drive upgrade kit that's made specifically for your TiVo model. (The kit even includes any tools you'll need to do the job.)

How to Use This Book

This book is a *reference* — a collection of informational nuggets, organized logically so you don't have to remember anything. (Some of the most frequently accessed information lives on this book's tear-out "Cheat Sheet.") Don't bother reading this book from cover to cover. Instead, take the pick-and-choose approach, flipping to the particular part or section containing the information you need.

People who haven't purchased their own TiVo yet should start with Part I to discover their options. (TiVo comes in several models, each with their own particular flavor.)

TiVo owners might head straight for the Part of Tens to read tips, all organized into categories like creating recordings, watching live TV, watching recordings, or figuring out error messages.

If you're an advanced TiVo user, jump straight to Chapter 12 to upgrade your TiVo with a larger hard drive. Imagine storing 60 hours of best-quality recordings on your TiVo!

When you find something you like, feel free to dog-ear the page or highlight the section with a marker. Then keep this book near your TiVo or its remote so you can flip to the most appropriate section, read the information, then close the book and keep watching.

Don't Read These Parts

Please stay away from certain parts of this book. Ignore them completely. Should you ever need them, they'll reveal themselves at the right time.

That's because anything marked with the Technical Stuff icon usually contains "engineers" talk. That stuff is for people who pride themselves on taking their TiVo to another level; sometimes by choice, other times because they simply didn't want to pay the repairman.

Sometimes I've added information that only makes sense after you've been using TiVo for awhile. Until you've reached the point where a few key words catch your eye, please feel free to skip right over them.

How This Book is Organized

I've divided this book into five parts, each dealing with a certain theme. I've broken down each part into three or more chapters dealing with specific TiVo information relating to that part's theme. Here's the rundown on what you'll find in each one.

Part 1: Before Buying Your TiVo . . .

Don't have a TiVo sitting by your TV yet? Start here to discover exactly what a TiVo *is* — the concept, the things TiVo can do, why you'd want TiVo to do them, and the things TiVo *can't* do.

After helping you choose the right one, this part of the book guides you through hooking it up to your TV or home theater, weaving the cords through VCRs, telephones, and other audio-visual exotica.

No telephone line jack nearby? I'll even divulge a trick or two to slip you past that requirement, if necessary.

Part 11: Using the TiVo

Once you've connected TiVo to your TV, this part of the book explains how to acclimate TiVo to its new surroundings. It explains how to run TiVo through its Guided Setup, telling it what channels you receive (while weeding out shopping channels and other detritus).

Another chapter lets you start playing tricks while watching live TV, rewinding to catch missed snippets, and watching slow-motion replays of fumbles, explosions, or whatever else flashed by too quickly.

The next chapter guides you through telling TiVo about your favorite programs, actors, directors and subjects, allowing TiVo to automatically grab
them whenever they may air.

Once you grow comfortable watching TiVo's recorded shows, a chapter
explains how to fine-tune TiVo's performance, adjusting recording schedules
so everything fits to best advantage.

Part III: The Home Media Option

People who enjoy their home computer will enjoy TiVo's Home Media Option
(HMO), and this part of the book explains how to connect TiVo to your home
computer. When set up, TiVo's HMO lets you access your computer's good
stuff — your stash of digital photos and music — and play it on your TV or
home stereo. No more crowding around the computer monitor to show off
vacation photos!

This section also explains how to make TiVo record those "can't miss shows"
you just heard about around the office water cooler — even if you're still at
the office (or anywhere there's an Internet connection). Log on to the Internet
from any computer and send TiVo your recording instructions.

If you're not already listening to Internet Radio stations on your home stereo,
you'll be listening to them once you read this part of the book.

Part IV: Upgrading and Fixing Your TiVo

Sometimes your TiVo's *too* good — it finds so much good stuff, it runs out of
room to store it all. A chapter here explains how to order and install a "TiVo-
Ready" hard drive, custom made for your particular model. Upgrade your
TiVo to 200 hours, and avoid future family fallouts.

And although you may never need it, a chapter explains how to fix any odd
problems you may experience. (With TiVo — not yourself. That's a different
book.)

Part V: The Part of Tens

Nothing but tips here — long lists of tips for using TiVo more quickly and efficiently. Flip here on occasion just to make sure you're using TiVo to its fullest.

Icons Used in This Book

This book uses the trademarked "For Dummies" icons you've seen in countless books for the past decade. Here's a look at the ones I've used in this book, and what they mean.

When you spot this icon, look closely at the nearby tip: an informational nugget that helps you use TiVo more quickly or efficiently.

Try to remember these paragraphs, as you'll find yourself using this information repeatedly. (Simply *reading* the rest of this book is good enough.)

My father, a specialist in electronics measurements, built oscilloscopes in the garage. More than a bit of that rubbed off onto me, and now I build robots in my spare time. This icon gives fair warning to lift your eyes from the accompanying TiVo technospeak that follows.

Stop! Please don't do what you're reading about in this paragraph. Anything marked by this icon can damage TiVo, yourself, or the living room carpet. Be *very* careful here.

NOTE: You'll also find smaller icons in the margins that match the buttons found on TiVo's remote. When the paragraph calls for you to press a particular button on TiVo's remote, that button appears in the margin for reference.

Where to Go from Here

Only you know how far down the road you've driven with TiVo. You might want to begin browsing the tips at the very end or jumping to more full-blown explanations referenced elsewhere in the book. If you're relatively new to TiVo, start poking around near the beginning to clear up some common TiVo head-scratchers.

But no matter where you are on your TiVo journey, this book's in the glove box, ready to show you the way.

Part I

Before Buying
Your TiVo . . .

The 5th Wave   By Rich Tennant

"That reminds me — I have to figure out how to get
our TiVo up and running."

In this part . . .

You've probably heard quite a few things about TiVo. Writers mention it in newspapers and magazines. TV characters discuss it while the plot unfolds. You'll even start to notice your friends mumbling about how it changes their life — usually when they're forced to watch commercials at somebody's house. Lucky audience members of Oprah or Rosie O'Donnell even found free TiVos in their "take-home" bags.

What is this "TiVo" that people speak of, and how could it possibly change your life? Does your life *really* need changing? If you take the plunge, which TiVo should you buy? And how do you hook the darn thing up, anyway?

This section answers those questions and many more.

Chapter 1

Knowing the TiVo

*U*ntil you've seen TiVo in action, you can't quite understand all the hubbub. Isn't a "TiVo" just a glorified VCR? Everybody already has a VCR; nothing new here, move along. Yet people aren't moving along. If they're not buying the thing, they're hearing other people talk about it.

Jay Leno and David Letterman talk about "TiVoing" favorite TV shows. The word "TiVo" pops up in newspapers and magazines with increasing frequency. And if you're unlucky enough to meet a TiVo owner at a party, it's time to toddle off to the bar: TiVo owners can't stop themselves from singing TiVo's praises. What's all the fuss about?

Much to the dismay of TiVo's marketing department, it's quite difficult to explain a TiVo in a few short words, or even a 30-second TV spot. To help clear things up, this entire chapter explains what TiVo does well, where it sometimes misses the mark, and just what the darn thing looks like, anyway.

Finally, you'll understand why TiVo owners (myself included) can't seem to stop raving about the darn things.

Pausing Live TV

 Your friends take their seats, the show begins, and, a few minutes later, the pizza man rings the doorbell. Who misses the show to fetch the pizza? With TiVo, nobody misses anything. A press of the TiVo remote's pause button freezes the screen, flicker-free, until you return, pizza in hand.

Pausing a live TV show certainly isn't TiVo's most-used feature, but it's probably the easiest to understand. Armchair philosophers, however, may ask, "How can TiVo *pause* the reality of a live TV show?"

It's easy. TiVo never really displays "live TV." TiVo constantly records whatever channel you're watching. Even when you watch "live" TV, you're actually seeing TiVo's recording, which appears onscreen about one second *after* the show reaches everybody else's TV screens.

✔ Pressing the Pause button merely freezes the display; TiVo continues to record the show in the background. Push the Pause button again, and TiVo starts playing its recording again, right where you left off.

✔ If you paused the show for three minutes, for example, your viewing of the show would extend to three minutes after the *real* show ended.

✔ After returning to watch a paused live TV show, most TiVo users actually *look forward* to the commercials. When the hucksters appear, press the remote's Fast-Forward button to skip quickly through the commercials, eventually catching up to "real time" — one second behind the show's actual broadcast.

✔ Chances are, the pizza delivery guy doesn't miss the show, either. His TiVo records it while he's working.

✔ If you don't return to the paused show within 30 minutes, you begin missing part of the show. After 30 minutes, TiVo starts playing the show from where it paused. If you think you'll be away for more than 30 minutes, and you *really* want to see all of the show, press the remote's Record button before standing up. TiVo courteously saves the rest of the show for you to watch at your leisure.

✔ After owning a TiVo, most people avoid watching live TV. There's just no more use for it. The TiVo's already recorded the good stuff, and you could be watching that, instead.

Controlling Your Own Instant Replays

Sports fans love watching an "Instant Replay." During a football game, for instance, the network's Instant Replay lets everybody see who dropped the ball, why, and who's now lying on top of it. TiVo borrows the power of Instant Replay from the networks and passes it into your own hands. You can see an Instant Replay of anything you're watching, any time you want.

What's the difference between a DVR, a PVR, and a TiVo?

Bobbing in the crowded Sea of Acronyms, the initials DVR stand for *Digital Video Recorder*. PVR stands for *Personal Video Recorder*. Both mean pretty much the same thing: a gadget that records television shows onto a hard drive — just like the ones used by computers — making recordings quick, easy, and much more accessible.

A TiVo is a special breed of DVR/PVR. It records shows onto a hard drive, but it also makes intelligent decisions, saving you a lot of grunt work. For example, TiVo offers things like a "Season Pass," where it automatically seeks out and records all episodes of a TV show, regardless of when they air. Items placed in TiVo's "WishList" — actors, directors, subjects, or titles — can be recorded automatically, whenever they air.

In short, TiVo is a DVR/PVR, but not all DVR/PVRs sport TiVo's intelligent features. Some make you schedule recordings manually, for instance, by entering a show's channel, date, and starting/ending times. TiVo handles those tasks automatically, requiring nothing more than a show's name.

Some technologists pinpoint the difference between DVR and PVR to the machine's IQ. A TiVo is a *Personal* Video Recorder, because it adjusts to your *personal* tastes by automatically recording your favorite shows. A *Digital* Video Recorder, by contrast, merely records shows onto a hard drive: You still need to tell the dumb thing what date, time and channel you want to record, just like a VCR.

 When something exciting happens onscreen, push the TiVo remote's "Instant Replay" button. TiVo instantly rewinds eight seconds and starts playing, letting you watch the past eight seconds again.

Didn't jump back far enough? Push the Instant Replay button *twice* to jump back 16 seconds. If the action happens too fast to see what's going on, push the Pause button, then push the Fast-Forward button to move through the sequence frame by frame.

Although I don't watch much sports, I use Instant Replay after one of my wife's loud belches to catch missed dialogue. It's great for moving through explosions, frame by frame. Movie buffs will enjoy exploring intimate details of a director's composition, figuring out exactly when they cut to a new scene and why.

✔ Fans of movie "bloopers" love TiVo. If you're watching "Titanic," for instance, watch closely to see the guy with the digital watch get into the lifeboat. (The Titanic sank in 1912.)

✔ Instant Reply comes in handy when you return to a paused show. Watching the last eight seconds brings you right back into the action.

✔ You don't miss any of your show by using Instant Replay, even when watching live TV. Pushing the button simply makes the show begin playing again eight seconds from the time you pushed it. (Each time you push the button, your show ends another eight seconds later.)

Putting Your Television to Work

TiVo works as your robotic television manager, constantly scanning upcoming show listings to separate your favorites from the trash. It juggles the recordings to avoid possible overlaps, and it saves the good stuff until you're ready to watch it.

Simply put, TiVo makes *you* the boss of your television. You're no longer at the mercy of the networks, their rigid scheduling, and their loud commercials. You no longer have to watch "whatever's on" when you sit down. Your TiVo insulates you from the bad aspects of TV, catching only the good.

Why buy TiVo when I don't watch TV?

It's easy to see why so many people don't watch TV. There's rarely anything good to watch. Why buy a TiVo when there's nothing to watch?

Look at it this way. Let's say 99.9 percent of TV is awful, leaving just one or two thoughtful, intelligent shows. Most homes have at least 50 channels available. That means 1,200 hours of television programming flows unwatched through your home every day. If TiVo grabs just .1 percent, it's still collecting at least an hour of good stuff every day.

Think about it. You're bound to be interested in *something*. Tell TiVo about it. It doesn't care if it's on some obscure channel during the wee hours. Whenever *anything* flows by that meets your interests, TiVo grabs it.

Then, whenever you decide to watch TV, you'll find something good waiting for you. TiVo found it, bagged it, and has it waiting for when you're ready to watch it.

It's surprisingly easy how TiVo does this. You select names from a list, telling TiVo your favorite show titles, movie titles, actors, directors, or subjects. With a few pokes on the remote, you can even type in subjects like "parrots" or "James Bond." TiVo scours the show listings for the next two weeks, automatically scheduling and recording shows that match your interests.

TiVo immediately tunes to the right channel at the right time — unattended — and records your show. It repeats the process as often as needed to record whatever you want.

When you feel like watching TV, you choose from TiVo's list of recorded shows — shows you *know* you'll enjoy.

- ✔ I explain how to automatically record your favorite shows in Chapter 6.

- ✔ If a sneaky network bumps your favorite sitcom from Wednesday to Thursday for some reason, don't worry: TiVo still grabs it. It knows these things.

- ✔ If the network preempts your show because of a late-running ball game, TiVo grabs the late-running ball game. (Of course, everybody else also missed the show, so you don't feel so bad. TiVo will still catch your unwatched show when it repeats, though.)

- ✔ After awhile, the concept of watching live TV will seem foreign and outdated. You'll forget when your favorite shows air, because you no longer care: That's TiVo's job.

- ✔ If you arrive home 20 minutes after a favorite show started — and you've told TiVo to record it for you — you can watch the show as soon as you walk in the door. TiVo plays the show from its beginning for you, all the while continuing to record the rest of the show.

- ✔ TiVo substantially lowers your movie rental tab. Why rent a movie when your TV is filled with so many movies you already want to watch? It no longer matters that the good films aired at 4 a.m. — TiVo stayed awake to record them for you. (And you no longer must remember to put in a videotape; TiVo never needs them.)

Zipping Past the Commercials

TiVo's remote comes with Fast-Forward and Rewind buttons, just like the ones on a VCR's remote. Unlike a VCR and its slow and awkward tapes, TiVo records everything on its *hard drive* — just like the one inside a computer.

That makes it much faster to fast-forward through those intrusive bits of non-sense called commercials. Whenever a commercial begins, press TiVo's Fast-Forward button. When you spot your show playing on the screen, push the Play button. TiVo backs up a bit, and begins playing your show from when the commercials stopped.

✔ Skipping commercials often reduces a one-hour TV show to just 40 minutes. You don't even need commercials for bathroom breaks: Just pause the show when the need arises. Or when the phone rings. Or the baby cries. Or the cat wants inside. And outside. And inside again.

✔ You can still watch commercials, if you want, especially the funny ones during the Super Bowl. TiVo doesn't edit them out. It just lets you skip past them very, very quickly when you want. (With TiVo's three-speed Fast-Forward button, a 60-second commercial blasts past in a second or two.)

✔ The Fast-Forward button also works great for skipping the boring parts of movies, political debates, and talk shows. When watching Saturday Night Live, for instance, it's easy to zip ahead to the next sketch or musical guest.

My TiVo Spies on Me!

TiVo, Inc. collects something it calls "Anonymous Viewing Information," and that bothers some people. Anonymous Viewing Information means TiVo collects all your remote's actions and sends them off to TiVo, Inc. The corporation, in turn, knows what you've watched, and what you've recorded. It also knows what you've paused, what you've rewound, and what you've watched frame by frame in slow motion.

However, the corporation *doesn't* link these intimate viewing details to your name, household, or address. Instead, they lump everybody's data into general geographic locations — Zip Codes, for instance. That lets TiVo's PR department announce things like, "During last night's Academy Awards, 1,263 TiVo viewers in Dorset, Vermont, used Instant Replay when Madonna tripped."

Although I'm a privacy advocate, I like TiVo's approach. I prefer to let them know *exactly* what I watch. Hopefully, the broadcasters will take notice, stop canceling my favorite shows, and begin scheduling more stuff that matches my interests. I view it as casting an anonymous vote for my favorite TV shows. TiVo already supplements Nielsen's ratings, providing an easy way to gauge a show's popularity.

If you feel this invades your privacy, however, tell TiVo to knock it off by calling (877) FOR-TIVO; they'll remove you from their list. You'll find more information about TiVo and your privacy on the company's Web site at www.tivo.com/privacy.

TiVo's Sweet Little Gifts

After TiVo knows your interests, the friendly box begins leaving you little presents. It works like this: Unless you're recording a weekend marathon of back-to-back *Simpsons* episodes, TiVo usually has some leftover space on its hard drive. Eager to please, TiVo fills that empty space with shows it thinks you might enjoy, based on the shows you're currently recording.

After you watch a Western or two, for example, TiVo may record a few extra cowboy films in the hopes you'll enjoy them. Watching a lot of Audrey Hepburn? You may find several of her other movies on your Now Playing list.

✔ TiVo records suggestions only if there's room. If it's already stuffed full with shows you've told it to record, TiVo stifles its urge to record suggestions.

✔ When your hard drive fills up and TiVo needs more room to record your favorite shows, TiVo starts housecleaning by automatically deleting any suggestions to free up space.

✔ TiVo's remote contains a "Thumbs Up" and a "Thumbs Down" button. If you remember, use these buttons to rate shows you've watched. The more you use the "Thumbs" buttons, the better TiVo knows you, leading to more accurate Suggestions.

✔ If TiVo doesn't seem to know the *real* you, I explain how to nudge TiVo's suggestions in the right direction in Chapter 11.

TiVo and Your Home Computer

Many people try to avoid computers. Others prefer intimate contact, setting up Web sites to constantly monitor their hot tub's temperature. TiVo's happy to oblige computer enthusiasts with its "Home Media Option."

The Home Media Option (HMO), available for an additional fee, lets you connect your TiVo to your computer, often through a wireless connection. With TiVo connected to your computer through HMO, you can settle into your favorite armchair and view all your digital photos on TV, even though they're still stored on your computer. You can hear any computer music files through your TiVo, as well — and the music files sound fantastic when hooked to the home stereo, by the way. If you own *two* TiVos, you can even transfer shows from one TiVo to another.

I explain how to use the Home Media Option to your best advantage — and stretch it to its limits — in Chapters 8 and 9. (No, you can't send shows to a friend's TiVo, just to your *own* TiVos.)

Saving Shows to VCR or DVD Burner

If you and your VCR are inseparable, TiVo teams up with it fairly well. When TiVo records a show that you absolutely *must* add to your videotape cabinet, choose TiVo's Save to VCR option, described in Chapter 6. When TiVo begins playing back your show for the VCR, neatly displaying the show's name in a black stripe along the bottom, press the VCR's Record button.

No, TiVo won't edit out the commercials, but you can do that yourself, if you baby-sit your VCR's Pause button during the recording process.

Sony brand TiVos mind-meld with Sony VCRs: Pressing the Save to VCR option makes TiVo turn on your VCR, automatically record the show, and turn off the VCR when it's through. (You still have to put the tape inside yourself.)

Some TiVo models include a built-in DVD recorder, letting you save your shows to a DVD just as easily. I discuss different TiVo models in Chapter 2. TiVo can send shows to a portable DVD burner just as easily as a VCR; TiVo neither knows nor cares that you're connecting a DVD burner instead of a VCR.

Just What Does TiVo Look Like?

For such a powerful robot, TiVo wouldn't win any battlebot matches. As you can see in Figure 1-1, the typical TiVo is simply a rectangular box, much like a small VCR. Instead of a VCR's slot, clock, and buttons, most TiVo models sport a single pair of tiny lights on the front. The green light means it's currently plugged in; a red light means it's currently recording. You control everything with the remote, shown in Figure 1-2.

Things are more interesting around the back. There, you'll spot a dozen or so connectors sprouting from the case, ready to accommodate a barrage of sound, video, and TV cables. I show more detailed views in Chapter 2 and explain what cable plugs in where.

TiVo is actually *two* things, as described more fully in the next chapter. The *TiVo box*, sold in most stereo stores, and the *TiVo Service*, which supplies your TiVo with the station listings in your area.

The TiVo Service requires a monthly fee to grab and sort through your personalized channel listings. Prices vary according to your particular TiVo model. (Many TiVo models offer "Lifetime" subscriptions where you pay up front to avoid the monthly fee.)

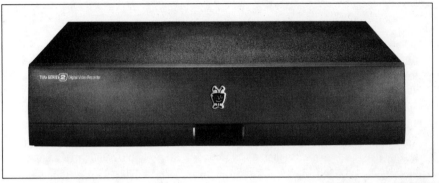

Figure 1-1:
TiVo looks much like a VCR, sans slot and blinking clock.

Figure 1-2:
The remote for many TiVo models resembles a large, elongated peanut.

Chapter 2 holds the dirt on different TiVo models, TiVo Service plans, and which TiVo model works best for your particular television setup, be it a home theater with a satellite dish, or an old "rabbit ears" model from the thrift shop.

What *Can't* TiVo Do?

Although TiVo works very well as your personal television manager, some tasks remain beyond its reach. This should clear up some of the more common TiVo misconceptions.

TiVo can't record TiVo shows from the past. My friend Jim called the other night, asking if I could use my TiVo to watch a show that ran two nights ago. Nope. TiVo can record shows currently airing, and it will schedule recordings for shows airing in the future, but not even a TiVo can pull things out of the past. However, if you enter a few descriptive words about the show — its title, for instance, or the actors' names — TiVo can often catch a rerun.

TiVo can record only channels that you already receive. TiVo isn't a source of television shows. It simply sifts through the shows you already receive, automatically recording the ones you want and ignoring the ones you don't. You still need a TV signal, whether it comes from an antenna, cable, or satellite box.

TiVo can't simultaneously record two TV shows. Unless you're receiving DirecTV satellite broadcasts with a DirecTV model of TiVo, you can't record two shows simultaneously. However, with a bit of installation trickery (covered in Chapter 2), you can record one show while you're watching another live show on a different channel. (TiVo always lets you watch any previously recorded show as it records a new show in the background.)

Not all TiVos record HDTV. Most TiVos can't store High Definition TV signals. At the time of this writing, only a few newer models of DirecTV TiVos can record and play back HDTV programming.

TiVo can't send video to your computer. Even with the Home Media Option, TiVo doesn't provide a way to send your TV shows to your computer. And currently it won't play video from your computer, either. TiVo's new "TiVo to Go" feature, however, plans to add this option. You'll find more information about it at TiVo's Web site (www.tivo.com).

TiVo doesn't work worldwide. Currently, TiVo works only with U.S. and U.K. programming. (TiVos are no longer manufactured for the U.K. market, but TiVo service remains available for customers who bought one.) United Kingdom TiVo information awaits you at uk.tivo.com. TiVo isn't available in Canada, unfortunately, but they still have better beer.

Chapter 2

Buying the Right TiVo Model

· ·

In This Chapter

▶ Knowing the difference between the TiVo box and TiVo Service

▶ Understanding TiVo's service plan

▶ Understanding different TiVo models

▶ Purchasing the right TiVo for your needs

· ·

*T*iVo comes in two parts: the boring box and the service that makes it work. The "TiVo" is simply the boring container. A box harnessed to your TV with cables. Most TiVos have no buttons, slots, or blinking time displays.

The *TiVo Service*, by contrast, does all the work. A combination of software and computer, the TiVo Service automatically fetches and sorts your upcoming TV listings, separating the wheat from the chaff to suit your own tastes. TiVo charges money for its harvesting service. (Hopefully the salesperson explained this fee before you pulled out your charge card.)

This chapter describes the different models of TiVo boxes you're likely to spot on the store shelves. It also reveals intimate details about the TiVo Service and the grunt work it performs behind your back.

What Your TiVo Needs

When you decide to buy a car, you don't simply drive home in a new Porsche convertible. You know to plan ahead for auto insurance, registration fees, gas, and a cool hat with a chin strap.

TiVo also requires a few accessories, but its needs are much more modest. Here's exactly what you'll need to convert fully to the TiVo lifestyle:

- ✔ **The TiVo box.** When you buy a TiVo, this is what you take home. Many places sell TiVos. Some folks buy online directly from TiVo (www.tivo.com). Others shop at major consumer electronics stores (Best Buy, Circuit City), as well as Internet vendors. (I bought mine through Amazon at www.amazon.com.)

- ✔ **The TiVo Service.** Once you've set up your new TiVo, you must buy the TiVo Service directly from TiVo by paying a monthly subscription fee. (Paying a lump sum up front eliminates the monthly payment.) Without the TiVo Service, TiVo sits like a Porsche with no engine: non-functional, yet full of promise. (DirecTV always charges a monthly fee for its TiVos; it doesn't offer a Lifetime Subscription.)

- ✔ **A phone line.** Each day, TiVo briefly phones TiVo headquarters to fetch your region's updated program listings. That means your new TiVo needs a phone jack within 25 feet. (It shares your existing phone line.)

  Computer jockeys with broadband Internet service can connect TiVo to their computer, which I describe in Chapter 8. TiVo then grabs your TV listings through the Internet, bypassing your telephone forever. (DirecTV doesn't offer this option for its own TiVo models.)

- ✔ **A television and television signal.** Television broadcasts enter your house through a satellite service, a cable company, or even an antenna on your TV. (If you can watch shows on your TV now, you already have this, so TiVo will work.)

- ✔ **A power outlet.** TiVo requires electricity, ruling it out for tent campers.

- ✔ **Don't buy any extra cables along with your new TiVo.** The TiVo box includes a thick pack of high-quality cables that meet nearly every configuration. (Avoid those ultra-expensive brand-name cables that commission-based salespeople rave about.) The remote even comes with its own pack of batteries.

- ✔ **Some people fret about finding a telephone jack close enough to their TiVo.** The TiVo's bundled 25-foot phone cord would let a giraffe talk on the phone. Extra tall giraffes, however, can purchase much longer phone cords from Radio Shack, as well as wireless phone jacks designed for computers that work fine with TiVo. (I cover these in Chapter 3.)

Paying for the TiVo Service

The TiVo Service works the same way, no matter what TiVo model you buy. (See the "What's TiVo Basic?" sidebar for the exception.) The TiVo Service automatically grabs the upcoming two weeks of listings for every show your TV can receive. It then compares that list with the shows you want to watch, and magically juggles all the recordings, trying to avoid scheduling conflicts.

Like most juggling magicians, TiVo charges for its service. Signing up for the TiVo Service, also known as "Activating" your TiVo, simply involves typing in your credit card number. Shortly after you plug in your TiVo, it will remind you about the service with the nag screen shown in Figure 2-1.

At the time of this writing, the TiVo Service requires a monthly fee of $12.95. If you own two TiVos, you pay two monthly fees. DirecTV models of TiVo are designed specifically to work with DirecTV satellite service, and their service fee is $4.95 each month, regardless of how many DirecTV TiVos you own. Either way, TiVo places its monthly charge on your credit card.

The wealthy folks can opt for an escape hatch: Paying $299 up front buys a "Lifetime Subscription" for your TiVo. TiVos with "Lifetime Subscriptions" never require a monthly fee.

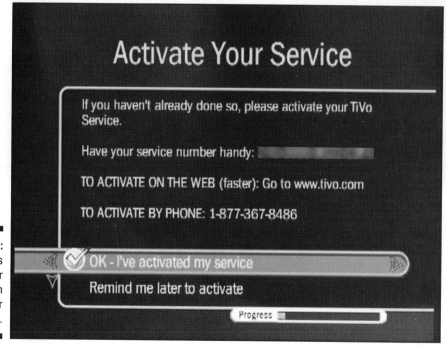

Figure 2-1:
TiVo begins
nagging for
Activation
shortly after
installation.

What's "TiVo Basic" service?

The TiVo corporation lets some companies sell a "watered-down" version of TiVo to include with products like DVD players and recorders. Like its name, TiVo Basic offers basic recording features: Hard drive recording, fast-forwarding, rewinding and pausing live TV, and manually scheduling recordings up to three days in advance.

TiVo Basic users may upgrade to the regular TiVo Service (referred to as "TiVo Plus") by paying the standard subscription fees. Once subscribed, they can search for shows by title or subject, record their favorite shows automatically with a *Season Pass*, receive TiVo's suggestions — the usual fare expected of TiVos.

(TiVo's Home Media Option, covered in Chapter 8, never comes free, no matter what plan or planet you're on.)

Sign up for the TiVo Service by entering your credit card number on TiVo's Web site (www.tivo.com), or by calling TiVo's Customer Support team directly at (877) 367-8486. (The service fee for DirecTV TiVos is part of your monthly satellite bill.)

✔ A few pokes on a calculator show that a $299 subscription fee equals about 23 months of $12.95 payments. If you plan to keep TiVo more than two years (and you will), paying $299 is a better deal: It's completely paid off, and you won't be stuck with monthly fees. If you live paycheck-to-paycheck, stick with the monthly fee.

✔ And if you *don't* pay the Service Fee? Your TiVo won't work. Actually, it still works well at nagging you to pay, but don't expect anything more.

✔ The Lifetime Subscription is tied to the life of your *TiVo*, not you. If you ever sell your TiVo, the lucky buyer receives the Lifetime Subscription along with it. Price it accordingly.

✔ Did your new, Lifetime Subscription TiVo die within warranty? Your heartbreak earns you a break: TiVo lets you transfer the dead TiVo's Lifetime Subscription to your replacement TiVo when repaired through an authorized service center. Make the transfer through TiVo's Web site (www.tivo.com/manage) or by calling TiVo Customer Support (1-877-367-8486).

✔ Bought a second TiVo? You must pay the monthly service fee, or purchase a second, separate Lifetime Subscription for it.

✔ Series 2 TiVos don't work at all without the TiVo Service. But the older "Series 1" TiVos limp along by letting you schedule recordings manually, entering the date, time, channel, and recording length of desired shows. Without a subscription, the "Series 1" TiVo's internal clock slowly loses accuracy, leading to missed recording times. (Telling the Series 1 TiVo to make a daily call often resets the clock, but nothing more.) For more info on the differences between Series 1 and Series 2 TiVos, see the "Standalone TiVo" section, later in this chapter.

✔ A Lifetime Subscription links to the TiVo's *motherboard*. You can replace or upgrade your TiVo's other parts (covered in Chapter 12) and still keep your subscription valid. But if your TiVo's motherboard dies, its Lifetime Subscription dies along with it.

How the TiVo Service works its magic

The TiVo Service tells your TiVo to make a daily call to TiVo headquarters to keep your show listings up to date for the next two weeks or so.

While visiting, TiVo performs the following tasks, usually taking less than five minutes:

✔ It checks your subscription information. Haven't paid? TiVo turns off most of its features until you're paid up again. (You can continue to watch any shows you've already recorded, though.)

✔ It resets its clock. The TiVo needs a very accurate clock in order to record your shows at the correct times.

✔ It grabs show listings up to 14 days in advance, also fetching any software updates or messages from the TiVo company. If a broadcaster has changed a show's air time or date, TiVo takes note and reschedules its recording times accordingly.

✔ After removing any personally identifiable information, TiVo tells the company what you've been watching. (If this strikes you as creepy, Chapter 1 explains how to make it stop.)

When done swapping information with headquarters, TiVo hangs up and its software takes over, sorting all the new show listings and meticulously comparing them with your own list of favorite shows. Finally, TiVo figures out the best way to record them all, trying various combinations to avoid overlapping shows as best as possible.

All this activity happens in the background; you never notice it. Even while performing all these chores, TiVo still manages to record your scheduled shows, play back recorded shows on request, or even record and play back at the same time.

How can I steal the TiVo Service?

It's quite difficult to get the TiVo Service without paying for it. And unlike most taboo items discussed in the Internet's dark alleyways, this topic rarely pops up. That's because most TiVo owners want TiVo to survive as a company. They enjoy what TiVo provides and want to help the company, not harm it.

I researched this subject while writing this book; most people who've tried to fool TiVo into working without a subscription found the process too cumbersome to be worth the effort.

The TiVo Box

Many different manufacturers sell TiVo, each model featuring its own bells and whistles. You'll see older, first-generation TiVos known as "Series 1," the newer "Series 2" TiVos, TiVos designed specifically for satellite reception through DirecTV, and a new mix of consumer gadgets that incorporate TiVo.

Here's a rundown on what you'll find when shopping for TiVo.

The big difference between DirecTV and standalone TiVos

A standalone TiVo works with *any* type of TV signal. It translates the sound and video from the incoming channel into numbers, and it stores the numbers on its hard drive. When you watch a show, the TiVo translates the hard drive's numbers back into the channel's sound and video, and it sends the information to your TV set.

A DirecTV TiVo, by contrast, stuffs a TiVo inside a satellite box. TiVo records the satellite's incoming numbers directly onto the hard drive — there's nothing to convert. Later, when you want to watch a show, the satellite box translates the TiVo's numbers into the appropriate sound and video for your TV. Because the DirecTV TiVo records exactly what the satellite sent, it can preserve Dolby 5.1 surround sound and HDTV broadcasts for your TV.

Standalone models are stuck with the chores of turning the TV signals into numbers for storage and then turning the numbers back into TV signals for your TV. During this extra conversion process, they lose surround sound and HDTV information.

Since DirecTV TiVos aren't as closely linked to the TiVo Corporation as the standalone models, they lack some of the features. They can't use the Home Media Option, for instance, as well as some of the more advanced software found in the standalone models.

Standalone TiVo

A "standalone" TiVo refers to any TiVo that isn't designed specifically for satellite reception with DirecTV. Instead, standalone TiVos work mostly with cable hookups and TV antennas. Actually, these versatile little beasts can *still* work with satellite systems, they just won't take advantage of satellite-specific features. (For more on satellite TiVos, see "DirecTV TiVos," later in this section.)

Series 1 TiVo

No longer sold new, Series 1 TiVos still pop up at garage sales, on eBay, and through other used-goods outlets. Here are the main differences between these older standalone TiVos and the newer models:

- ✔ **Size.** Series 1 TiVos are a little bulky, making them harder to balance atop a TV set or hide on the bookshelf.

- ✔ **Speed.** Just as new computers run faster and more powerfully than their predecessors, Series 1 TiVos are slower than newer models. (Computer people might note that the Series 1 TiVos have a slower CPU and less RAM.)

- ✔ **Software.** Series 1 TiVos lack some popular software enhancements found in Series 2 models. Shows can't be grouped into convenient onscreen folders, for instance.

- ✔ **Networking.** Only Series 2 TiVos offer the Home Media Option (HMO). That option allows TiVo to communicate with your home computer, displaying your digital photos and playing your MP3 files. Once connected, TiVo grabs show schedules through the Internet instead of by telephone.

Without a subscription, a Series 1 TiVo can still pause live TV, fast-forward, and rewind, but it won't record shows automatically. To record a show, you must manually enter the correct channel and recording time.

Some tech-savvy people actually prefer Series 1 TiVos because they're easier to take apart and fiddle with. These tinkerers write their own "add-on" software to make their TiVos do oddball things like display a stock ticker along the bottom of a televised football game. If this stuff appeals to you, check out Jeff Keegan's thick green book, *Hacking TiVo*, from Wiley Publishing, Inc.

All TiVos run the Linux operating system, not the more widespread operating systems like Windows. If you're itching to hack your TiVo, a Linux background comes in *very* handy.

Series 2 TiVo

All TiVos sold today are considered "Series 2" models, as shown in Figure 2-2. Faster, more versatile, and with more features than their predecessors, Series 2 TiVos also contain two USB ports for hooking up to a computer. Only Series 2 TiVos work with TiVo's Home Media Option, described in Chapter 8, which lets users schedule upcoming recordings over the Internet, among other perks.

Series 2 TiVos can't record HDTV broadcasts, and they water down Dolby Digital 5.1 sound to stereo, but they offer more features and recording capacity than their predecessors. You'll probably be much happier with a Series 2 TiVo than a Series 1 TiVo.

DirecTV TiVos

If you receive your TV programs from the DirecTV satellite service, you'll probably want a "DirecTV TiVo," officially known as a *DirecTV Receiver with TiVo Service*. These models record shows in slightly different ways than other TiVos.

For instance, a DirecTV TiVo contains *two* tuners. So? That means you can simultaneously record two live shows on different channels. Or, you can record one channel while watching a different live channel.

Figure 2-2:
The newer, "Series 2" TiVos offer more power and options than TiVo's earlier models.

All DirecTV TiVos can also record shows broadcast with Dolby Digital 5.1 sound; some models record HDTV, as well.

On the down side, DirecTV TiVos work only with DirecTV's satellite source. Standalone TiVos, by contrast, work with *any* signal source. If you stop subscribing to DirecTV's satellite service and switch to cable, your DirecTV TiVo won't work.

Because of their different circuitry and distribution, DirecTV TiVos come with reduced subscription plans.

DVD Player/Recorder TiVos

As the TiVo corporation grows, it stuffs its TiVo Service into a range of gadgets. Toshiba, for instance, wraps a DVD/CD player around a TiVo. Shown in Figure 2-3, the Toshiba's SDH400 plays DVDs, CDs, and MP3 files. Its "embedded TiVo" records up to 80 hours of television on a hard drive. The unit includes TiVo Basic service, upgradeable to standard "TiVo Plus" service. It can be upgraded with the Home Media Option, as well.

Pioneer went further and created a pair of *dream* TiVos that not only play DVDs, but *record* them as well. Owners can create DVD libraries of their favorite shows. The Pioneer Elite DVR-57H, shown in Figure 2-4, stores 120 hours of shows; another Pioneer model stores 80 hours. Both models record shows that will play back on any DVD player.

In addition to burning your favorite shows to DVD, both units can schedule and record programs in the background while you watch a DVD. You can even hook up a camcorder, and copy your vacation videos to DVD. They both come with TiVo Basic service; you need a subscription for the "Plus" TiVo Service that includes the Season Pass, WishList, Suggestions, and other really fun stuff.

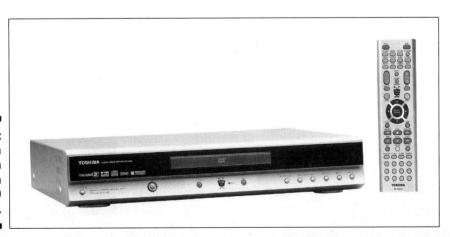

Figure 2-3:
Toshiba combines a TiVo with a DVD/CD player.

Several other companies offer similar TiVo/DVD recorder hybrids, with more models to come.

Figure 2-4:
Pioneer's Elite DVR-57H TiVo stores 120 hours of shows and can copy recorded shows to DVDs.

Choosing the Right TiVo for You

Since TiVo now comes in many different installations, it's may seem more difficult than ever to choose the right one. But actually, it's easier — TiVo fulfills a wider variety of specific needs than ever before.

If you simply want the TiVo Service, just buy a standalone model of TiVo. It hooks up to any TV signal, be it cable, satellite, or an antenna, and lets you automatically record your favorite shows.

If you're using DirecTV satellite service, you'll want a DirecTV TiVo. It's designed specifically for DirecTV's satellite service and preserves your Dolby Digital 5.1 sound. If you watch HDTV channels with your DirecTV, pick up the DirecTV TiVo with HDTV support. (These TiVos don't support Home Media Option for connecting to a computer, however. If that's a must, stick with the standalone TiVos.)

If you don't yet own a DVD player, pick up one of the DVD players with TiVo built-in. Combining the two items means one less box to wedge into your entertainment center.

Finally, if you're the type who enjoys saving TV shows and movies on videotape, pick up a DVD recorder with a built-in TiVo. Storing your shows on DVD is much less awkward than storing them on videotape.

Chapter 3

Setting Up Your TiVo

· ·

In This Chapter

▶ Taking it out of the box

▶ Making room for your TiVo

▶ Understanding different connectors and their quality

▶ Connecting TiVo to your TV

▶ Connecting TiVo to your stereo

▶ Adding your accessories

▶ Recording one show while watching a different live show

▶ Figuring out the complicated setups

· ·

A TiVo lifestyle begins with something unavoidably awful: connecting TiVo to your TV, weaving strands of cables into just the right configuration.

Thankfully, TiVo's installation happens only once. And, for a lucky few, installations are a breeze. Folks with simple television setups merely connect two cables, and TiVo dutifully leaps onto their TV's screen. Other people, usually those of us with a pile of remotes on our coffee tables, have a rougher time.

This section walks you through the process of connecting your TiVo to your TV, and even adding a VCR and other items to the mix, if you desire. First-timers should budget about an hour for this chore.

Throwing in the Towel and Calling a Professional Installer

Pssst. Some people don't bother installing their own TiVo. Just as they let professionals repair their car, plumb their sinks, or mix their martinis, they place their TiVo's installation into more experienced hands. If you're not a do-it-yourselfer, or your TV setup looks imposing, you have several options:

✔ **Installation package with purchase.** If you buy your TiVo directly from DirecTV, Best Buy, or some other stores, you can often order a professional installation package at the same time. Some offer free installation with purchase; others charge more than $100. Some only offer free installations during sales promotions. Never be afraid to ask.

✔ **Installation from TiVo.** TiVo lets you purchase a professional installation from its Web site (https://store.tivo.com/).

✔ **Moonlighting salespeople.** Even if your local store doesn't offer an installation package, ask the salesperson about installation. Many electronics retail "team members" moonlight by installing home theater components. To a person well-versed in S-Video cables, TiVo's a piece of cake.

✔ **Hitting up the neighbors.** Some neighbors or relatives may already own a TiVo, and they just might help install yours. (Some curious folks may also offer to help just to see what all this TiVo buzz is about.)

The Three Steps to Installing TiVo

Although there's no single "right way" to connect a TiVo to your equipment, all installations follow these three steps. The differences depend on the type of connections found on your TV, cable or satellite box, and other accessories. For the best possible picture, always identify and use the highest quality connections available on each piece of equipment.

For the simplest of setups, this short section may be all you need. If something doesn't seem quite right, or you don't understand the cables and connectors on your equipment, the rest of this chapter explains each step in detail.

1. **Place TiVo near your TV.**

2. **Connect TiVo to your phone line.**

   If your TiVo absolutely *cannot* reach your closest phone jack, I offer some alternatives in this chapter's "Connecting TiVo to Your Phone Line" section. Some methods eliminate the need for a long, troublesome phone cord. Others eliminate the need for a telephone line altogether, something quite appealing to today's cell phone generation.

3. **Connect TiVo to your television signal.**

   If you don't have a cable or satellite box, this can be as simple as screwing your cable TV's cable into TiVo's RF In jack and then connecting an identical cable between TiVo's RF Out jack and your TV's RF In or Cable In jack. (Sometimes the TV's jack is simply called "Antenna.") Tune your TV to channel 3 or 4 to see TiVo.

Cable or satellite box users must follow two additional steps to complete the installation:

1. **Set up TiVo to change the box's channels.**

   Depending on your type of cable or satellite box, you need to connect either TiVo's IR Control cable or its Serial Control cable between TiVo and the box.

2. **Connect sound and video cables from your cable or satellite box to TiVo's input ports.**

   TiVo accepts sound and video in several different ways, depending on your needs. Always choose the highest quality connections available. (In an upcoming section, Table 3-2 explains which connections provide the best quality.)

Make sure your TiVo, your TV, and your cable box, if necessary, are plugged into the wall and turned on. (TiVo turns on automatically as soon as it's plugged in.)

That's it. The rest of this chapter discusses these steps in more detail. If you're feeling confident, jump right in with these three steps. Should you run into trouble, want a higher quality picture, or if something doesn't seem quite right, head for the section in this chapter that explains that particular step in more detail.

Consider buying an inexpensive Uninterruptible Power Supply (UPS) for your TiVo (and cable/satellite box). Although TiVo handles power outages gracefully, it doesn't like power fluctuations. (Your computers don't like these, either.) Plugging your TiVo into a UPS (350VA rating or more) protects it and your recorded shows from harm.

Peeking into TiVo's Installation Guide

TiVo comes with a surprisingly well-written and illustrated installation guide. It contains pictures of the connectors you'll use, and clear diagrams showing how to install TiVo with or without a cable/satellite box. Plus, the manual shows how to add a VCR, home stereo, DVD player, and game machine.

If you bought a used TiVo with no manual, download a free copy at www.tivo.com/guides. You'll need a free copy of Adobe Acrobat Reader (www.adobe.com/reader) to view or print the downloaded manual.

Identifying Your Cables and Connectors, and Choosing the Highest Quality

TiVo comes with a thick pack of cables to shuffle information between the connections found on your TV set, VCR, DVD player, home stereo system, and TiVo itself. You won't use all of TiVo's bundled cables; there are *supposed* to be leftovers. Just use the ones that work best with your current television setup.

Table 3-1 helps you identify the cables, their connectors, and their purpose in life. Carefully examine both TiVo and your equipment, identifying the different connectors each has to offer.

Table 3-1	A Cadre of Connectors		
The Cable and its Connectors	*Their Name*	*Their Location*	*Their Purpose*
	Coaxial (RF) cable	TiVo and many audio-video gadgets	Commonly found on nearly all devices, this carries the TV signal itself.
	RCA (composite)	TiVo, some TVs, accessories	These carry sound or video from the currently tuned channel. Yellow cables always carry *video*. Red (right) and white (left) cables carry *stereo sound*.
	S-Video	TiVo, some TVs, some accessories	This cable, usually black, carries high-quality video, but no sound.

The Cable and Its Connectors	Their Name	Their Location	Their Purpose
	Optical/ Toslink	Some DirecTV TiVos and some home stereos, but no stand-alone TiVos	This carries Dolby AC-3 sound (some-times called *multichannel, surround sound,* or *5.1*), but no video.
USB 2.0 plug USB 2.0 port	USB	TiVo, computer	Used with TiVo's Home Media Option (see Chapter 8), this only lets TiVo exchange information with a com-puter. You won't need it for your TV.
	Infrared	TiVo, cable or satellite box	This lets TiVo change channels.
Serial port	Serial	TiVo, some satellite or cable boxes	An alternative to Infrared that also lets TiVo change channels and volume.
Telephone symbol Telephone plug Telephone port	Telephone	TiVo, wall	This allows TiVo to receive show listings and program-ming updates.

TiVo comes with many different types of cables because TiVo can usually connect with your equipment several ways. Today's TV setups vary greatly in quality. Some people are happy connecting TiVo directly to a cheap TV. Others connect TiVo to an expensive home theater. Others take a middle route, perhaps running the TV's sound through a home stereo.

To accommodate all of these different setups, TiVo offers three main ways to connect both video and sound. Table 3-1 explains the connectors you're likely to find on TiVo and your TV (and/or home theater). Table 3-2 explains the quality provided by each type of cable and connection.

Table 3-2	The Best Cables for the Job		
	Good	*Better*	*Best*
Video	The RF connector (the plain ol' cable poking out of the wall) carries both video and sound, but at the lowest quality.	Use the yellow RCA/composite connector and ignore the S-Video.	Use the S-Video cable and ignore the yellow RCA connector. (The HDTV TiVo and some TiVos with DVD recorders have even higher quality "component" connectors with three cables just for video: Red, Green, and Blue.)
Sound	The RF coaxial connector carries mono sound as well as video. Use this only if nothing else fits.	Use the red (right speaker) and white (left speaker) RCA/composite connectors for stereo sound. (If your TV has just one audio connector, use one cable and let the other dangle.)	At the time of this writing, only the DirecTV TiVo (and the Toshiba/ Pioneer DVD integrated TiVos) provide Dolby Digital 5.1 sound. Use the Optical/Toslink cable only between those TiVos and stereos that can handle this multichannel, home theater format.

Before hooking up your TiVo, identify all the connectors available on your TV (and home stereo, if used). Using Tables 3-1 and 3-2, find the connector offering the highest quality. Finally, route the appropriate cable between that connector and the matching connector on your TiVo. That ensures TiVo will provide you with the best quality sound and picture.

Placing TiVo Near Your TV Set

For the easiest installation, TiVo should be within five feet of your television, and within 25 feet of a phone jack. (TiVo's bundled cables only reach that far.) Some folks plop their TiVo atop their large TV set; others sandwich it into their rack of VCRs, DVD players, and stereos.

Once you've set up a standalone TiVo, you'll rarely touch it; just make sure it remains within the line of sight of its remote control. If your TiVo model sports buttons along its front, keep it fairly accessible.

✔ Don't place TiVo *beneath* your TV set; most sets are simply too heavy. TiVo works fine on top of your TV, if you don't mind it staring at you during movies.

✔ TiVo works fine on its side. Just be sure its front faces *toward* you, or the remote might not work.

✔ When positioning your TiVo, be careful not to block its air vents — little slots in the metal casing — especially when positioning it on its side. (Sometimes you can slip little doodads beneath the TiVo to lift it up at least a half-inch above the ground.) Keep TiVo off the carpet, too, as the fibers can block its vents.

✔ If your home theater's cabinetry hides your equipment behind mesh fabric, hide the TiVo in there, as well. Remotes easily penetrate the fabric.

✔ Most TiVos come with a thin strip of protective tape across the front, right over the infrared receiver. Don't forget to peel off the tape once you've positioned your TiVo.

Connecting TiVo to Your Phone Line

TiVo must phone its headquarters every day or so to grab your latest show listings. It also needs to phone its headquarters when you first set it up in your home. Unlike a teenager, TiVo doesn't need its own telephone, or even its own phone line. It's happy to share your home's phone or fax line.

TiVo won't interrupt you when you're talking. And if you happen to interrupt TiVo during its call, just hang up for five seconds. TiVo hangs up, letting you make your call.

How can I set up TiVo *without* a phone line?

TiVo must connect with a land-based phone line to complete its initial Guided Setup. That lets TiVo download its initial software updates, among other things. However, TiVo needn't use *your own* phone line. Carry TiVo over to a friend's or neighbor's house, temporarily connect TiVo to their TV set so you can see its menus, and let TiVo borrow their phone line for its Guided Setup.

Once your new standalone TiVo has made its initial phone call, hook it up to your home network and let it piggyback on your broadband Internet connection, as described in Chapter 8.

Older, Series 1 TiVos don't have the luxury of connecting through home computers. They must be connected to a telephone line. (If you're handy with computers, however, check out network cards offered by companies like 9th Tee (www.9thtee.com) in Chapter 13. They allow Series 1 TiVos to connect with broadband home networks.)

DirecTV's official policy requires DirecTV TiVos to be hooked up to a phone line. However, some users report that their DirecTV TiVos work fine without a phone line, as long as they ignore the nag screens and don't try to order Pay Per View events from their DirecTV TiVo menus. (DirecTV TiVos receive their guide information directly from the satellite.)

To connect the phone line, attach one end of TiVo's bundled 25-foot phone cable into TiVo's phone jack, and plug the other end into a nearby phone jack in your house.

If your telephone already hogs the closest phone jack, use TiVo's bundled "phone line splitter," shown in Figure 3-1. Plugging the splitter into a phone jack gives you two jacks — one for your phone and the other for TiVo.

Figure 3-1:
Plug TiVo's phone line splitter into a phone jack to create two phone jacks — one for TiVo and one for your phone.

✔ A household phone line works fine, but a digital "PBX" phone line — like the multiline systems found in many offices and hotels — will *not* work and may damage your TiVo.

✔ Conceal a long phone cord by pressing it into the edge where your carpet meets with your walls.

✔ If your phone jack is too far away from TiVo, or it leaves an ugly dangling cord, you have several options:

• **Leave the phone cord unplugged.** Then, every few days, plug in the TiVo and use TiVo's Setup menu option to make TiVo "call now." (I describe this in Chapter 11's "Solving phone problems" section.) When TiVo finishes, unplug the phone cord and stash it. Repeat once a week.

• **Connect TiVo to your computer's broadband connection.** Computer savvy folks can connect to their computer's broadband connection through a wired or wireless network, described in Chapter 8. That lets TiVo grab your information from the Internet, eliminating the need for a telephone line altogether. (You need a wired network or a phone line to run TiVo's initial Guided Setup, covered in Chapter 4.)

• **Buy a wireless phone jack.** You'll find them at Radio Shack, Amazon, Home Depot, and TiVo's online store (https://store.tivo.com/), as well as at some of the TiVo accessory stores listed in Chapter 13. These plug into a phone jack and "beam" the signal through the air or your power lines to a receiver, which plugs into TiVo's phone jack. Make sure the wireless phone jack works *specifically with modems or fax machines*, and not just voice.

Connecting TiVo to Your Television Signal

Is TiVo placed near your TV? Connected to the telephone line? Then you're ready to connect TiVo to your television signal. The signal usually enters your house in one of two ways: through a single cable protruding from the wall, or through a satellite or cable box.

If you don't use a cable box or satellite box, you qualify for the simplest installation of all, described in the next section.

If you *do* have a cable or satellite box, the installation's a little more difficult, so it's described in an upcoming section.

Hooking Up TiVo without a Satellite or Cable Box

If you currently have a single cable poking out of a wall and running into your television — with no cable box or satellite dish — everything's easy. Follow these six steps, and you're through. When finished, head to Chapter 4 and run TiVo's onscreen Guided Setup.

1. **Make sure TiVo is sitting next to your TV set and is plugged into the phone line.**

   Don't plug TiVo's power cord into the wall quite yet.

2. **Unplug or unscrew the cable from your TV and plug it into TiVo's RF In jack.**

   Keep track of where the cable came out of your TV; you'll need to reattach a cable to that spot in the next step.

3. **Plug a second cable from TiVo's RF Out jack to your TV's Antenna, Cable, or RF In jack.**

   This second cable comes packaged with TiVo, and it looks like the one you unplugged in Step 3. (The two cables may be different colors.)

   When connected this way, your TiVo and TV should resemble the setup shown in Figure 3-2.

4. **Plug in your TiVo, and turn on your TV tuned to channel 3 or 4.**

   Your TiVo remote won't yet control your TV. (I explain how to do that at the end of Chapter 4.) But TiVo turns itself on as soon as you plug it in, and you'll see it on either channel 3 or 4 of your TV set.

   Flipping the little 3|4 switch near TiVo's RF Out jack lets you choose whether to tune your TV to channel 3 or 4 to watch TiVo.

That should do the trick; you're through with this chapter. If you have a cable or satellite box, however, or you want to add a VCR or other accessories, you'll need to check out this chapter's upcoming sections.

Save all of TiVo's cables in a safe place, even if you don't need them today. You'll probably need them in the future, if you add other equipment, change TV providers, or buy a new TV.

To improve picture quality, see if your TV offers composite or S-Video connectors. If so, connect the composite or S-Video cables between the TV and TiVo's connectors. (Don't use the RF cable.) You'll need to tune into your TV's "Line Input" to watch TiVo.

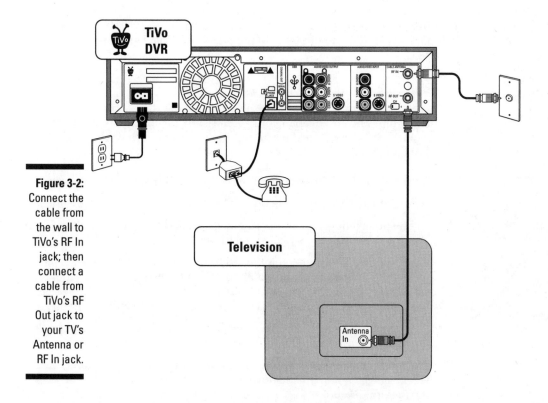

Figure 3-2:
Connect the cable from the wall to TiVo's RF In jack; then connect a cable from TiVo's RF Out jack to your TV's Antenna or RF In jack.

Connecting TiVo with a Cable or Satellite Box

TiVo works fine with your satellite or cable box, if your television signal flows through one. The biggest obstacle is letting TiVo change the box's channels. TiVo also needs a way to grab sound and video from the box. The next two sections show how to accomplish both tasks.

Letting TiVo change channels on a cable or satellite box

When watching TV through a cable or satellite box, you change channels with the box's remote. That presents a problem for the fingerless TiVo, because it must change the box's channel to record your shows. How can TiVo change the channels without being able to push buttons on the remote?

TiVo resorts to one of two tricks: a strange "Serial Control" cable used by some satellite boxes, or an even stranger "mini-remote on a string" called an "IR (infrared) Control" cable that works with both satellite and cable boxes. I explain each method below; choose the one that works best with your particular box.

Hooking up a Serial Control cable

A few satellite boxes let you plug in this special cable so TiVo can change its channels. Here's how to eyeball your satellite box for the right connector, and, if your box is one of the lucky ones, how to connect the right cable. (It comes bundled with TiVo.)

1. **Examine the back of your satellite box for a "serial port" connector.**

   Seen in the margin, this little oblong bump has either 9 or 15 tiny holes.

   If you spot a 9-hole connector, rummage around for TiVo's bundled Serial Control cable with the 9-pin connector and proceed to Step 2.

   If you spot a *15*-hole connector, head to Radio Shack and buy a "15-pin male to 9-pin female" adapter and push it onto the end of TiVo's included serial port connector. TiVo's Web site (https//store.tivo.com) sells the same adapter, as do some TiVo accessory stores listed in Chapter 13.

2. **Push the larger end of the TiVo serial cable into the plug on the back of your satellite box.**

   The plug's pins should align perfectly with the holes. If they don't, you're plugging it in upside down or you need the adapter discussed in the previous step.

3. **Plug the cable's other end into TiVo's Serial Connector port.**

Tell TiVo to use the "serial" connector for changing channels when you run TiVo's onscreen "Guided Setup" (described in Chapter 4).

- ✔ Once you've connected TiVo to your satellite box, *hide the box's remote*. TiVo's now responsible for changing channels, so stick with TiVo's remote exclusively. If you accidentally press a button on the satellite box's remote while TiVo's recording a show, you might accidentally change channels in the middle of your recording.

- ✔ Some RCA satellite receivers use a "Home Control" connector that looks a tad smaller than a phone connector. If your RCA-brand satellite box has a Home Control cable (not included with TiVo), plug one end into its jack and the other end into TiVo's Control Out/Serial jack. Don't have the right cable? Either buy one at TiVo's Web site (https://store.tivo.com) or use TiVo's Infrared (IR) Control cable, instead, as described in the next section.

- ✔ The Motorola DCT2000 cable box also uses a serial connection, but not all cable companies enable the serial port. If you have that particular model of cable box, give it a try by following the same steps above.

✔ If this section sounds too complicated, or you can't find those connectors, don't worry. Just use the IR (Infrared) Control, described next. It works for all boxes, but sometimes needs a little extra adjustment.

Hooking up an Infrared Control cable

"IR Control cable" is a fancy name for the "mini-remote on a string" that TiVo uses to change channels on your cable or satellite box. When you fasten TiVo's little IR Control cable in the right place on the front of your cable or satellite box, TiVo uses it to beam signals telling the box to change stations.

Follows these steps to set it up:

1. **Locate the IR Control (Infrared Control) cable packaged with your TiVo.**

   Shown in Table 3-1, the IR Control cable is black; one end sports a little pointed connector, the other has two angular plastic doodads. (You might spot a little "bulb" on the end of each doodad.)

2. **Locate the infrared receiver on your cable or satellite box.**

   The thing's almost invisible, but it's always on the box's front, usually behind a semi-transparent plastic window. Grab a flashlight, and peek through any suspicious semi-transparent plastic areas on the box. Eventually, you'll spot the flat little receiver inside, usually square or rectangular. (It's right next to the digital clock on our cable box.)

3. **Fasten TiVo's infrared controls above and below the cable or satellite box's infrared receiver.**

   Let the two doodads hang about 1.5 inches past the box's edges, as shown in Figure 3-3. Use the bundled pieces of double-sticky tape to fasten each control to the box.

Figure 3-3:
Put the TiVo's IR controls above and below the box's Infrared receiver, extending about 1.5 inches.

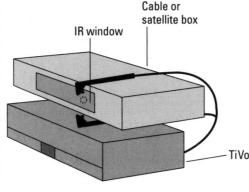

4. **Plug the cable's other end (usually purple) into the TiVo's IR jack.**

You'll test your work later when running TiVo's onscreen Guided Setup (covered in Chapter 4). You may need to make a slight adjustment in positioning.

Routing the sound and video to TiVo and your TV

Once TiVo's connected to your telephone line and your cable or satellite box's channel changer, you've completed the hard stuff. Now TiVo needs to grab the sound and video sent by your satellite or cable box. Finish up by connecting TiVo's audio and video outputs to your television.

Follow these steps to send the box's information to TiVo and let TiVo send information to your TV set:

1. **Examine your cable or satellite box's Video Out connectors.**

Table 3-1 identifies the connectors.

2. **Connect the best video cable connection between the box's Video Out jacks to TiVo's Video In jacks.**

Use S-Video if your box offers it; otherwise, use the yellow RCA/composite cable.

3. **Examine your box's Audio Out jacks.**

You'll probably use the red and white RCA/composite cables.

Only a DirecTV TiVo can record in Dolby 5.1 Surround Sound. Standalone owners should ignore Surround Sound outputs on their cable box, no matter how tempting, or else their sound won't match the video.

4. **Connect the appropriate sound and video cables between TiVo's Audio Out and Video Out jacks to your TV's Audio In and Video In jacks.**

Red is for the *right* channel, and white is for the *left*. If your TV doesn't have stereo sound, plug in one of the two jacks and leave the other dangling.

If your TV offers S-Video, connect an S-Video cable between it and TiVo's S-Video Out. (Leave the yellow cable dangling.) No S-Video? Then use the yellow RCA/composite cable.

If your TV only offers an Antenna or RF In jack, connect a cable between that and TiVo's RF Out jack. (Only one cable will fit, and it carries both sound and video.) Tune your TV to channel 3 or 4 to see TiVo.

Depending on your brand of cable or satellite box and TV, your setup will probably resemble the one shown in Figure 3-4.

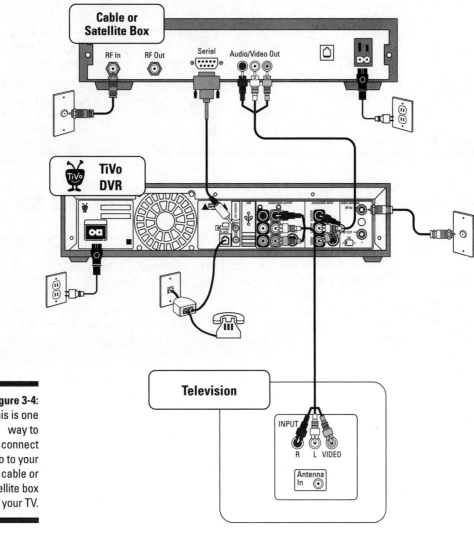

Figure 3-4:
This is one way to connect TiVo to your cable or satellite box and your TV.

TiVo and tuners

When your television stream flows straight into TiVo — with no cable or satellite box in between — TiVo changes channels using its own built-in tuner. To record programs, TiVo automatically tunes to the right channel at the right time. TiVo's internal tuner can tune channels 2 through 99, which works fine when hooked up to an antenna or most other analog feeds.

But if your television service sends any *digital* broadcasts, encrypted shows (HBO, for instance,

and other pay channels), or channels numbered higher than 99, then you probably need a box, typically provided by your cable or satellite service. The TV stream enters the cable or satellite box, which decodes the digital channels to analog, and uses its internal tuner to route the appropriate channel to TiVo for recording.

Finally, DirecTV TiVos come with a built-in satellite box that contains *two* tuners, letting TiVo record two different channels simultaneously — something standalone TiVos can't handle.

Connecting TiVo's Sound to Your Stereo

Televisions work best for displaying video. And stereo systems work best for playing sound. So it's only natural that many people connect their TiVo to their *home stereo* as well as their TV. The hard part is figuring out which place to plug it in on your home stereo.

The simplest way is to leave TiVo's video cable hooked up to your television. But connect the red and white audio cables from TiVo's Audio Out jacks to your stereo's Line In jacks. (Leave your TV's sound turned down or off, if possible.)

To listen to your TiVo, turn on your stereo and turn the knob to "Line Input." Turn on your TV to see the picture.

Depending on your stereo, you can often route the video through your home stereo, too. I route our TiVo through our stereo's "Video Input 3" connector, which offers a pair of audio connectors and a video connector. Then I run an S-Video cable from the stereo's S-Video OUT to the TV's Line In connector.

To watch TiVo, I turn the stereo to Video Input 3. Simple. Well, it is once all the cables are connected.

No matter how you hook it up, leave appropriate sticky notes on the knobs for your spouse.

Connecting a VCR and Other Accessories between TiVo and Your TV

Although TiVo quickly replaces the VCR for most folks, some people just can't let go of their stacks of archived Simpson's episodes. TiVo's perfectly willing to oblige both camps. TiVo even shows a "Save to VCR" option (explained in Chapter 6) on the menu of every recorded show. You can even connect a DVD recorder instead of a VCR, as TiVo won't know the difference.

Although your setup options will vary according to the number of inputs on your television, these steps usually work when connecting your VCR (or DVD recorder) to TiVo and your TV.

1. **Set up your TiVo and television.**

   Make sure TiVo's connected to your phone line, cable or satellite box (if necessary), and television, as explained earlier in this chapter.

2. **Find your VCR's Input jacks.**

   You'll find several jacks on the back of your VCR. Look for its red and white Audio In jacks and the yellow Video In jack.

   If your VCR doesn't have those, look for its RF In connector.

3. **Connect a cable between the TiVo's Sound and Video Out jacks to the VCR's Sound and Video In jacks.**

   TiVo has two Sound and Video output jacks (One set goes to your TV). Connect the unused jacks to your VCR. The yellow cable goes between the Video connectors, the red cable goes to the Audio Right, and the white cable goes to the Audio Left.

   Or, connect an RF cable between TiVo's RF Out and your VCR's RF In jacks.

4. **Connect a cable between the VCR's RF Out jack and your TV's Antenna or RF In jack.**

   Tune your TV to channel 3 or 4 to watch your VCR; tune your TV to Line Input to watch TiVo. When installed this way, TiVo's connections will resemble the ones shown in Figure 3-5.

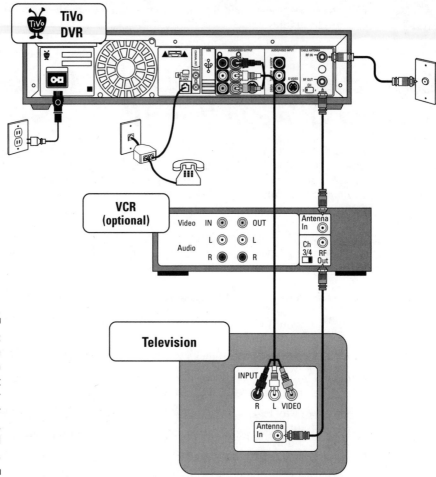

Figure 3-5:
This is one
way to
connect
TiVo to your
cable or
satellite box,
your TV, and
your VCR.

✔ The amount of items you can connect depends mainly on the amount of input jacks available on your TV. Fancy TVs offer four, which provides a connection for TiVo and three accessories. Cheaper TVs may offer only one or two input jacks.

✔ TVs with only one or two inputs limit your options, unfortunately. One solution is to buy a "switchbox," available at most electronics or stereo stores. Connect a cable between the switch box's Out ports and your TV, and connect your other gadgets to the switchbox's In ports. By selecting different inputs on the switchbox, you can "switch" between items and choose what is sent to your TV.

✔ If you have the cash, invest in an audio/visual receiver with enough Line Inputs to handle all your devices: VCRs, TiVos, DVD players, game machines, and fog machines. Plug each device into its own connector and turn a knob on the audio/video receiver to choose between each device.

✔ A switchbox is a less-expensive option for hooking up several different items to your TV. Buy a switchbox that has an input for each of your gadgets.

✔ Richard Parker's TiVo Wiring Guide Web site (`www.electrophobia.com/tivo`) contains illustrations of how to connect TiVo in more than 20 ways, allowing for many combinations of hi-fi goodies.

Recording One Show While Watching Another Live Show

You can always watch a recorded show while TiVo records a live show in the background. TiVo simply tunes to the channel of the live show and records it, playing back your recorded show all the while.

Problems flare when you want to watch a *live* show while TiVo records a different live show. TiVo needs to "watch" the channel that it's recording, so that prevents you from changing that channel to something else.

The simplest way to record one channel while watching another comes to people without a cable or satellite box. (This also works for people who use a cable box but don't have pay channels or digital cable.)

Tenting your cable or satellite box

Sometimes you'll want to give TiVo its own cable or satellite box to control, while you use a second one to watch live TV uninterrupted. To do this successfully, you must cover the front of TiVo's dedicated box; that keeps the second box's remote from interfering with the first box.

Some people place a strip of tin foil or thick black cloth along the box's front, as shown in Figure 3-7, covering TiVo's IR transmitter and the box's receiver. Others go so far as to place the cable or satellite box completely inside a cardboard box where no light can reach it.

Once you've covered the box, test it by trying to change its channels using the second box's remote. If you're successful, you won't be able to change its channels at all. Only TiVo will, ensuring that it works correctly.

That simple solution is to use a *splitter* — an inexpensive gadget found in electronics and hardware stores that splits a single cable into *two* cables. Once you've split the cable into two, connect one cable to TiVo and the other straight to your TV. Figure 3-6 shows an example.

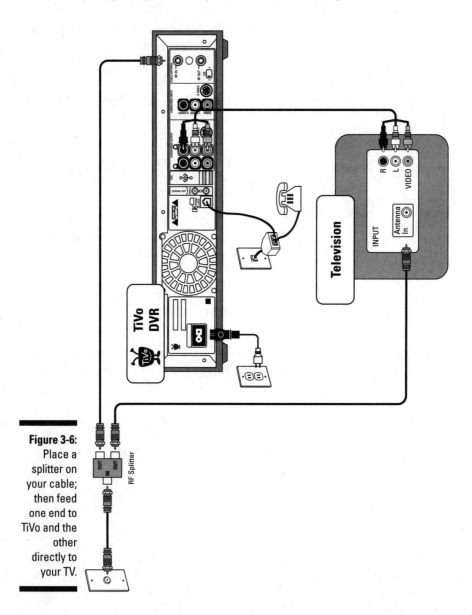

Figure 3-6:
Place a splitter on your cable; then feed one end to TiVo and the other directly to your TV.

To watch TiVo, select the Line Input. To watch live TV, turn the TV to the channel you want. The splitter gives TiVo and your TV their own direct connection to the TV source, keeping them from getting in each other's way.

- ✔ DirecTV TiVos used with the DirecTV satellite service don't experience this problem. They come with two tuners, letting you watch one live show while recording another live show in the background.

- ✔ If you have a digital cable box, however, and you want access to all your channels, your best solution is to ask the cable company for a *second* digital cable box. Use a splitter to connect each cable box to the cable. Connect one cable box to TiVo, and connect the second box straight to your TV, letting you watch live TV unobstructed. Be sure to "tent" the cable box connected to TiVo, as described in the nearby sidebar and shown in Figure 3-7.

- ✔ If you have a digital cable box and don't mind just watching channels 2–99 live, you can make do with the splitter described above.

- ✔ If your TV's two inputs are already used up by both TiVo and your VCR, use the splitter to connect a second cable feed to your VCR. Switch the TV to watch your VCR, and use your VCR's tuner to switch to the live channel you want to watch.

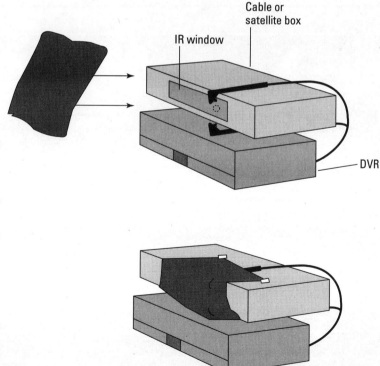

Figure 3-7: Cover the infrared receiver of TiVo's dedicated cable or satellite box so the remote from your second box won't interfere with it.

Part II
Using the TiVo

The 5th Wave   By Rich Tennant

"Oh, I'll get us in – I had every episode of 'Touched By
An Angel' AND 'Highway To Heaven' on TiVo."

In this part . . .

When first hooked up, TiVo is the worst sort of houseguest: all demands and no gifts.

For instance, TiVo immediately demands money in the form of subscription fees. Then it demands to know what TV channels you receive, and how they enter your house. Then, it demands to know your favorite shows, so it can begin recording them.

Even after you fulfill these first few requests, don't expect much from a new TiVo for the first few days; TiVo can only record your shows when they air. That means TiVo usually takes a week to transform from a demanding houseguest to a humble servant that rewards you with gifts whenever you turn on your television.

This part of the book serves as your training manual through these rough few days of teaching your TiVo exactly how you want it to behave in your home. When you're through, TiVo will perform amazing tricks that you'll love to show off to visiting friends and neighbors.

Chapter 4

TiVo's Remote and the Guided Setup

A newly installed TiVo doesn't go out of its way to be friendly. After you've spent an afternoon connecting cables to take care of its physical needs, your newly powered-up TiVo offers a token "Welcome" message. And when the Welcome screen disappears, TiVo presents you with yet *another* chore: completing its onscreen Guided Setup.

This chapter walks you through TiVo's Guided Setup, where you navigate menus with the remote, telling TiVo everything you've done in Chapter 3 — and then some.

Budget about an hour for this chore. When done, feel free to kick back and start watching live TV through TiVo. For the next three to six hours after you've finished setting it up, TiVo will work in the background, sorting through its newly downloaded TV listings. TiVo places everything into its massive digital filing cabinet for easy access, eagerly preparing for your upcoming TV nirvana.

You probably won't return to this chapter, except, perhaps, to read the section on programming your remote control to control your TV's power switch and volume. (This oft-delayed task makes life much easier.)

Preparing for TiVo's Guided Setup

Place these items within easy reach before turning on TiVo and running its onscreen Guided Setup. Each one lowers your frustration level a few notches for the upcoming installation tasks.

- ✔ **Your latest cable or satellite bill.** TiVo needs to know who provides your television signal, the company's name, as well as what channels you receive. (Premium channels? Special packages? Foreign language channels?) A peek at the bill helps you select your lineup from TiVo's onscreen list.

- ✔ **Your phone book.** TiVo calls its headquarters daily, so one setup menu lists nearby phone numbers. A phone book lets you weed out any long-distance numbers from the mix.

- ✔ **A recent TV Guide.** A local TV Guide helps you match station names with their content. When TiVo lists "KGTV Channel 15," for instance, you'll remember the station, as well as whether you ever watch it.

- ✔ **A beverage.** TiVo's Guided Setup takes from 30 minutes to an hour. Stay refreshed.

- ✔ **TiVo's remote.** You won't get far without it. (I explain how to make TiVo's remote control the power and volume of your TV or home stereo later in this chapter.)

Knowing Your Remote

Different models of TiVo use slightly different remotes, but they all resemble a VCR's remote, with a few special keys tossed in to confuse you. (If you forget a key's purpose, check out Figure 4-1 or the handy tear-out "Cheat Sheet" near the front of the book.) You'll probably use only the Arrows and Select buttons in this chapter, but here's a rundown on them all:

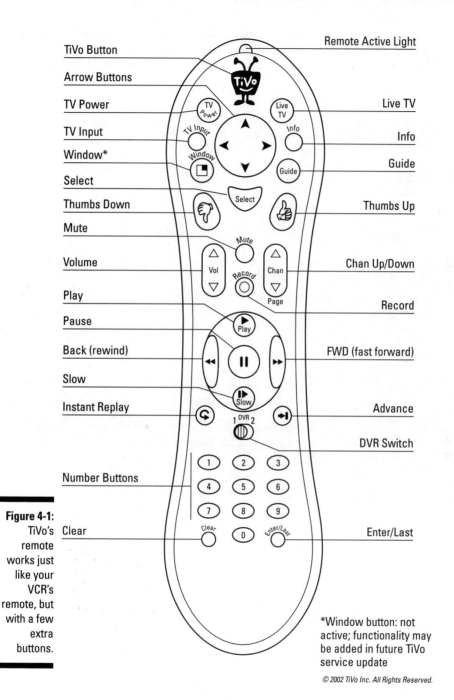

TiVo Button

Arrow Buttons

TV Power

TV Input

Window*

Select

Thumbs Down

Mute

Volume

Play

Pause

Back (rewind)

Slow

Instant Replay

Number Buttons

Remote Active Light

Live TV

Info

Guide

Thumbs Up

Chan Up/Down

Record

FWD (fast forward)

Advance

DVR Switch

Enter/Last

Figure 4-1:
TiVo's
remote
works just
like your
VCR's
remote, but
with a few
extra
buttons.

Clear

*Window button: not
active; functionality may
be added in future TiVo
service update

Arrows: This round button with the four arrows works just like the Arrows knob on a DVD player. Push the arrow in the direction you want to move the onscreen cursor. (Some remotes replace the round button with individual Arrow buttons.)

Select: When you've highlighted your desired option, press the Select button to tell TiVo to carry out that option.

 Number: Just as with your TV remote, press Number buttons to type in channel numbers.

TV Power: Turns your TV (or stereo, if that handles TiVo's sound) on or off.

TiVo: Jumps to the TiVo Central screen, the starting point for all menus.

Live TV: Jumps to live television.

TV Input: Switches between different inputs on your TV. (Some TVs let you plug the VCR into one input, for instance, and a DVD into another. By switching between the two inputs, you choose which one to watch.)

Info (Information): Brings up a screen with the currently playing show's name, channel, and show description. (The button on DirecTV TiVos says "Display" instead of "Info.")

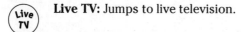 **Select:** Chooses the currently highlighted item.

Thumbs Up: Press this button to tell TiVo you enjoyed, really enjoyed, or *loved* a show. (Can be pressed up to three times to rate your enjoyment level.)

Thumbs Down: Press this button to tell TiVo you disliked, were irritated by, or absolutely hated a show. (Can be pressed up to three times to emphasize disgruntlement level.)

Mute: Turns off the volume; press again to turn back on.

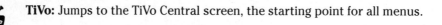 **Volume:** Press top portion of button to raise volume; press lower portion to lower volume.

Channel: Press top portion of button to advance one channel; press lower portion to move down one channel. On some menus, this does double-duty as a Page Up/Down button.

 Record: Press to begin recording the show you're currently watching.

 Play: Plays the currently selected show. (This immediately plays the show, even if you're paused, rewinding or fast-forwarding.)

 Rewind: Rewinds the currently viewed show. (Can be pressed up to three times to increase speed.)

 Fast-Forward: Fast-forwards the currently viewed show. (Can be pressed up to three times to increase speed.)

 Pause: Pauses the currently viewed show; press Play to resume.

 Slow: Slows down the current playback speed.

 Instant Replay: Immediately jumps back eight seconds and plays again.

 Advance: This acts as a sort of "jump to end" button. When pausing live TV, for instance, press this to catch up to the current action. When watching recorded TV, this jumps to the end of the recorded show.

 DVR Switch: Only used if you have two "Series 2" TiVos; this lets you assign a different remote to each TiVo.

 Clear: Clears the screen of any TiVo menus. Or, from the Now Playing list, press Clear to delete the currently highlighted show.

 Enter/Last: Used occasionally to display additional options from certain menus. It also flips between two channels when watching live TV.

 Window: Not currently used, but this feature may be added in the future.

- TiVo makes a congratulatory beep sound whenever you press a key. Some owners find this reassuring, others annoying. (I explain how to turn off the beep or change its volume — as well as adjust other settings — in Chapter 7.)

- Don't forget to place batteries into your remote. (It uses AA batteries, slipped in through a slide-off cover on the back.)

- Fumbling with a remote in the dark? My wife discovered that one end of our remote is heavier than the other, so we point the lighter end at the TiVo. With experience, you'll identify your remote by shape and weight, too. (Or, try sticking a piece of thick tape under the front end of the remote where you don't normally hold it. That provides a clue when you're holding it the wrong way.)

- When I tell you to use one of the remote's buttons, its picture appears alongside the text.

Completing Onscreen Guided Setup

Different brands and models use slightly different Guided Setups, so I won't use a numbered, step-by-step explanation. Instead, I describe the general areas you'll encounter when completing TiVo's Guided Setup with a "stand-alone" Series 2 TiVo. Described in Chapter 2, standalone TiVos work with any type of TV signal: cable, satellite, or antenna.

The Guided Setup lets TiVo understand how you receive your channels and how it's hooked up. TiVo's Guided Setup asks fairly intelligent questions, saving time by basing its next question on your previous answer.

If you answer something wrong, all is not lost. Press the Back arrow to back up and change your answer. Or, if TiVo insists on trudging forward, you may change most of these answers in its Settings area, which I cover in Chapter 7. You can also repeat the Guided Setup, covered in Chapter 11.

Press the remote's Select button to choose an answer and move to the next screen. Sometimes you merely need to read a screen, press the Select button, and advance to the next screen.

- When turned on for the very first time, most TiVos come to life with the words "Welcome. Powering up," as shown in Figure 4-2. That's a good sign; your TiVo has passed the first step. If this screen never appears, don't give up yet: Some cables may simply need tweaking. I explain how to track down and fix TiVo problems in Chapter 11.

- The Welcome screen is soon replaced by "Almost there. A few more seconds, please . . . ". After about a minute of hesitation, TiVo shows that everything is okay by displaying its official blue "Welcome!" screen, as shown in Figure 4-3.

Figure 4-2:
When turned on for the very first time, TiVo displays the "Welcome. Powering up . . ." screen.

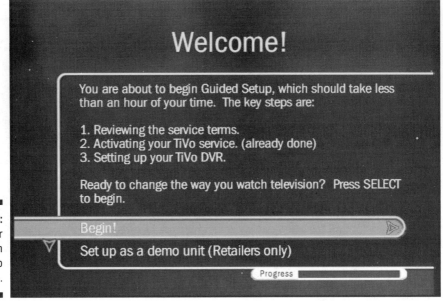

Figure 4-3:
Press Enter to begin setting up your TiVo.

Agreeing to TiVo's terms

Before using nearly any computer-related product these days, you're asked to agree to its legalese- and jargon-filled terms of agreement. TiVo's no exception, as you can see in Figure 4-4. TiVo's manual lists the agreement, and the most up-to-date versions appear on TiVo's Web site at www.tivo.com/privacy. (Actually, TiVo's service agreement and privacy policy are far less offensive than the 50-page agreement Microsoft tacks onto Windows XP.)

Basically, TiVo says that you must pay for the service, and that it collects information about shows watched by the TiVos in your general area. No, they don't know what *you* watch. They simply collect anonymous statistics from TiVos in your Zip code, similar to a US Census Report.

If you object, simply tell them to stop, as described in Chapter 1. Personally, I enjoy telling the networks what I watch. It's not as good as sharing my opinions with the studio head on the golf course, but it's probably the closest I'll get.

Select

Press the remote's Select key to nod your head and move onward.

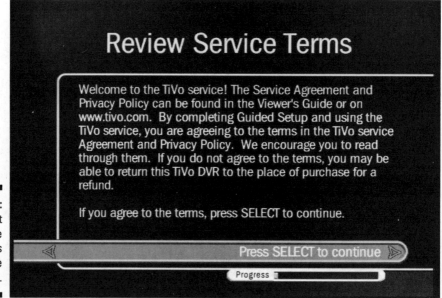

Figure 4-4: Press Select to approve TiVo's Service Terms.

Review Service Terms

Welcome to the TiVo service! The Service Agreement and Privacy Policy can be found in the Viewer's Guide or on www.tivo.com. By completing Guided Setup and using the TiVo service, you are agreeing to the terms in the TiVo service Agreement and Privacy Policy. We encourage you to read through them. If you do not agree to the terms, you may be able to return this TiVo DVR to the place of purchase for a refund.

If you agree to the terms, press SELECT to continue.

Press SELECT to continue

Progress

Activating the service

TiVo wastes no time in asking you to Activate your service, as shown in Figure 4-5.

Choose "OK, I've activated my service" if you've already activated TiVo. If you haven't activated, choose "Remind me later to activate" and continue setting up the TiVo.

TiVo makes its next phone call seven days after you finish the Guided Setup. If it discovers that you *still* haven't activated, it stops recording your shows. If it discovers that you *have* activated, it displays "Activated" status on its Status screen (covered in Chapter 7).

But until TiVo makes that phone call to see if you've activated, it nags you daily to activate. To stop the nagging, force TiVo to make its daily call by following these steps:

1. **Choose TiVo Messages & Setup from TiVo Central.**
2. **Select Settings and choose Phone & Network Setup.**
3. **Select Connect to the TiVo Service Now.**

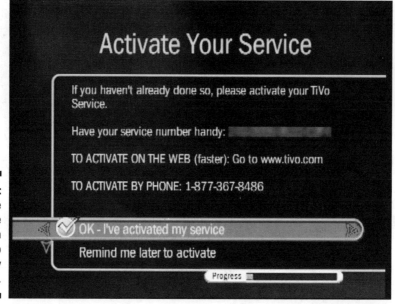

Figure 4-5:
Activate
your service
through
TiVo's Web
site or by
phone.

TiVo will discover that you've activated, stop nagging you, and continue with business as usual.

Note the Progress status bar at the screen's bottom in Figure 4-5. The little green line creeps further to the right with each step, letting you gauge your progress.

Telling TiVo about your location

When a new TiVo wakes up in your home, it needs to know a few specifics about its location and hookup. How do you receive your TV channels, for instance? Does your particular area observe Daylight Savings Time? These answers help TiVo tackle the work that lies ahead.

Choose your broadcast source

After the Activation screen, TiVo explains why it needs a connection to a telephone line. (I explain that in Chapter 3, if you'd rather hear it from me.) Give it a virtual head nod by pressing the Select button.

Next, tell TiVo how you receive your current TV channels, as shown in Figure 4-6.

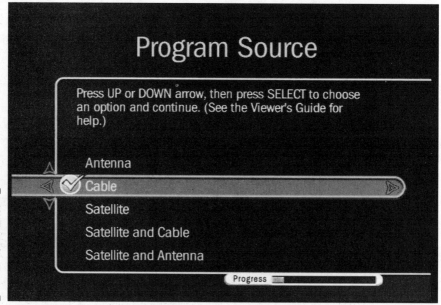

Figure 4-6:
Tell TiVo
how you
receive your
television
broadcasts.

To select an option, press the remote's Arrow buttons until you see your chosen option highlighted; then press Select. (If you're unsure how you receive your television signal, check your monthly bill or ask your landlord.)

Enter your Zip code

TiVo asks for your Zip code, as shown in Figure 4-7, to figure out your area's available channels. Enter your Zip code by pressing the Number buttons on your remote and then pressing Select to continue.

You can also enter the numbers using the Arrow buttons: Up and Down change the selected number; Right and Left move back and forth between spaces.

Choose your Time Zone and Daylight Savings Time status

On the next page, tell TiVo your Time Zone so it can adjust its clock accordingly.

Although TiVo resets its internal clock with every phone call, it takes more than an accurate clock to grab shows at the right time. So, the next page asks if your area observes Daylight Savings Time. Make sure you answer this one correctly so TiVo still grabs your shows on schedule. (Although TiVo automatically remembers to adjust its clock for Daylight Savings Time, some states and communities wisely ignore Daylight Savings Time buffoonery; if so, TiVo needs to know.)

Figure 4-7:
Tell TiVo your Zip code so it knows your area's available channels.

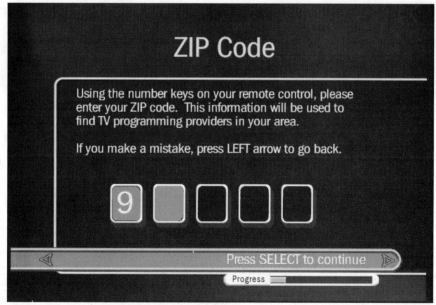

If you give the wrong answer, or if TiVo misses your shows by an hour once Daylight Savings Time begins, I explain how to return to this screen in Chapter 11.

Enter area code and prefix for phone

Because TiVo needs to call headquarters every day or so, it needs to know your exact phone setup. The area code is simple enough. But to accommodate more elaborate phone setups, it needs to know if you must dial "9" or disable call waiting before making a call, as shown in Figure 4-8.

Disabling call waiting usually involves placing *70, before the phone number. Enter the comma by pressing the Pause button; enter an asterisk by pressing Clear. (If you don't disable call waiting, the "beep" signaling an incoming call will throw TiVo off the line.)

Highlight your choice with the Arrows and press Select.

Letting TiVo make its first setup call

Now that TiVo knows some rudimentary details, it's ready to look up the channels you currently receive. TiVo's first setup call, shown in Figure 4-9, takes about 15 minutes.

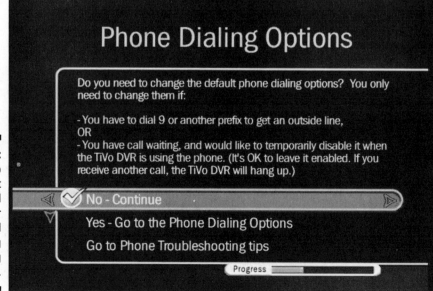

Phone Dialing Options

Do you need to change the default phone dialing options? You only need to change them if:

- You have to dial 9 or another prefix to get an outside line, OR
- You have call waiting, and would like to temporarily disable it when the TiVo DVR is using the phone. (It's OK to leave it enabled. If you receive another call, the TiVo DVR will hang up.)

✓ No - Continue

Yes - Go to the Phone Dialing Options

Go to Phone Troubleshooting tips

Progress

Figure 4-8: Tell TiVo whether it should dial "9" or disable call waiting when using the phone.

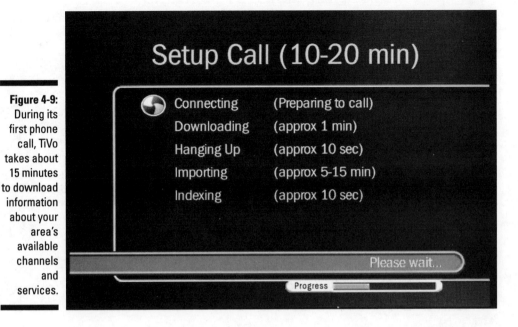

Use the Arrows button to highlight your choice, and press Select to choose.

During its toll-free call, TiVo also fetches a current list of TiVo Service phone numbers local to your area and performs some other maintenance chores.

Choosing your dial-in number

When TiVo returns from its first call, it displays its first batch of retrieved goods: a list of available phone numbers in your area. TiVo can make its future calls through any one of these numbers. Whereas TiVo's first Setup Call always uses a toll-free number, some of *these* numbers, shown in Figure 4-10, may not be free.

To avoid mysterious long-distance charges next month, grab your local phone directory to check its "local area codes" list. Most people can quickly spot a local number for TiVo's future daily calls. (TiVo's "daily" calls, made every 30 hours or so, typically last five to ten minutes apiece.)

When you spot a suitable number, press the Up and Down Arrow buttons until you've highlighted it, and then press Select.

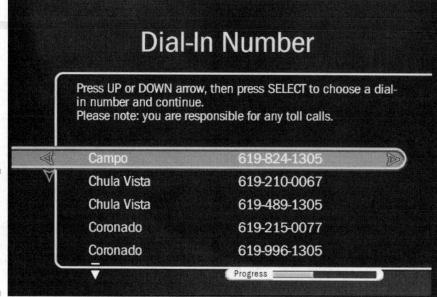

Dial-In Number

Press UP or DOWN arrow, then press SELECT to choose a dial-in number and continue.
Please note: you are responsible for any toll calls.

	Campo	619-824-1305	
	Chula Vista	619-210-0067	
	Chula Vista	619-489-1305	
	Coronado	619-215-0077	
	Coronado	619-996-1305	

Progress

Figure 4-10: Make sure you choose a local number for TiVo's daily phone call.

To accommodate different phone setups, TiVo also asks whether you need to dial the number only, the prefix followed by the number, or add a 1 before the prefix and the number. Choose the format your phone company prefers, and press Select.

If you're having trouble finding a free number, check online for the most recent list at http://www3.tivo.com/tivo-misc/popfinder.do. You may want to call your local phone company to make sure a number is *really* local. Also, TiVo adds new numbers fairly often. When it adds one for your area code, it lets you know through a message, available through TiVo's opening screen. Finally, depending on your calling plan, an out-of-state number may be less expensive than an in-state number.

If you can't find a local number — but you have a broadband (always "on") Internet connection — I explain how to connect TiVo to your computer, piggyback on its Internet connection for free, and bypass phone calls altogether. See chapter 8.

Telling TiVo your television setup

With the phone call setup squared away, TiVo now needs to know about its living conditions: Is it connected to a cable box, for instance? Antenna? Satellite dish?

Most of these questions involve choosing Yes or No answers and selecting your provider from the list. If you choose Cable, for instance, TiVo lists the providers in your area and lets you choose yours from the list.

Choosing your package

Here's where a copy of your cable or satellite bill comes in handy. Do you have Digital Service? Regular? Any special or premium packages? None of those? Without my bill in front of me, I never would have known to choose "Digital Extended Basic," as shown in Figure 4-11.

If you're not sure and don't have a monthly bill within grasp, choose None of the Above. You can figure it out later by choosing your channels manually in the next step.

Choosing your received channels

Why, some readers may ask, do you have to choose your channels from a list when you've just told TiVo exactly what service you receive? Shouldn't TiVo be able to figure them out?

Actually, TiVo *does* figure them out, and it presents you with a fairly customized list, shown in Figure 4-12. (Note the checkmarks next to each station, meaning TiVo assumes you receive those channels.) However, not everybody watches all of their available channels — especially the *really* boring ones. Here's your chance to remove the boring stuff.

Figure 4-11:
Choose your
type of
television
package
from TiVo's
list of
options
offered in
your area.

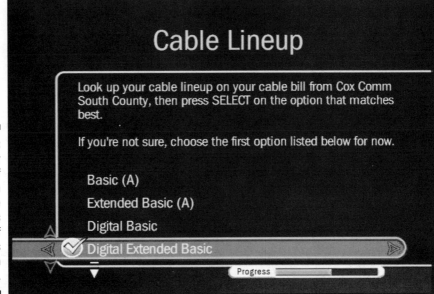

Cable Lineup

Look up your cable lineup on your cable bill from Cox Comm South County, then press SELECT on the option that matches best.

If you're not sure, choose the first option listed below for now.

Basic (A)

Extended Basic (A)

Digital Basic

Digital Extended Basic

Progress

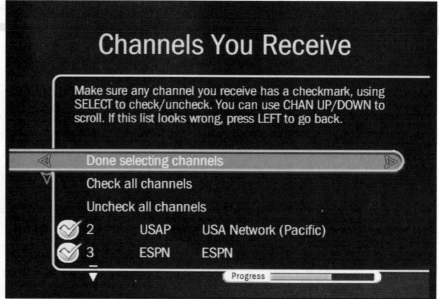

Channels You Receive

Make sure any channel you receive has a checkmark, using SELECT to check/uncheck. You can use CHAN UP/DOWN to scroll. If this list looks wrong, press LEFT to go back.

◁ Done selecting channels ▷

Check all channels

Uncheck all channels

☑ 2 USAP USA Network (Pacific)

☑ 3 ESPN ESPN

Progress

Figure 4-12: A checkmark by a channel means TiVo assumes you receive it.

If the channels look unfamiliar, press the Back Arrow button and choose a different service package until you find the right match.

When the channels finally match what you receive, you have three options:

- ✔ **Done selecting channels:** Choose this if TiVo guessed all your channels correctly and you're itching to move forward.
- ✔ **Check all channels:** Choose this when you've made a mistake and want to select them all. TiVo places a checkmark next to each option.
- ✔ **Uncheck all channels:** This removes all the checkmarks.

Surprisingly enough, "Uncheck all channels" sometimes works out best. This option lets you pick and choose among the listed channels, checking only the channels you watch. That weeds out the channels you'd never watch, keeping them from cluttering your onscreen show listings.

- ✔ Uncheck channels dedicated to shopping, foreign language broadcasts, 24-hour soap operas, children's programming, college stations, courts, government, or any other topic you never watch. Some premium packages dedicate blocks of channels that play different categories of music, for instance; make sure those are unchecked.

✔ Don't remember which channel is which? Search your cable/satellite company's Web site for its list of channel numbers, station names, and descriptions of their programming. Or, just type in the channel's numbers to view it immediately; press the Left Arrow button to return to this menu and make your decision.

✔ Don't check a channel unless you're *sure* you actually receive it. After being set up, TiVo will display show descriptions for every channel you've checked on this list. If you choose to record a show on a channel you don't receive, TiVo will record a black screen.

✔ If you accidentally check a channel you *don't* like, TiVo might record some of their programming as Suggestions. (I explain Suggestions in Chapter 6.) If you spot this happening, come back here and remove the channel from your list.

Telling TiVo about your box and connections

You're almost to the end of the Guided Setup; don't lose hope. TiVo needs to know which cables you've connected to it and where those cables come from. If you told TiVo earlier that you receive channels through a cable box, for example, it asks which cables you used. Eager to please, TiVo even shows a friendly picture of possible cable combinations, as shown in Figure 4-13.

Figure 4-13: Press the Up and Down Arrows, and TiVo tests its different connections for incoming sound or video signals.

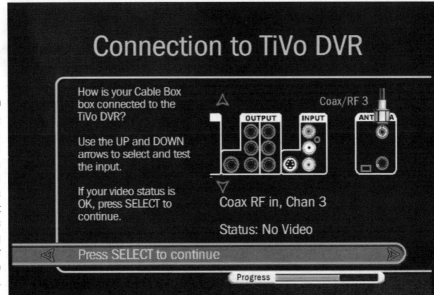

Press the Up or Down Arrow to move between potential hookups; for each hookup you select, TiVo checks for an incoming TV signal. In Figure 4-13, TiVo checks for incoming video on its Coax connector. Because it didn't find any, it reported "No Video."

Press the Up or Down Arrow until TiVo reports that the connection is "OK." Then press Select to continue.

Connection not working? Better head back to Chapter 3 for a recheck of your cables.

Channel changing

If you're hooked up to a cable or satellite box, TiVo needs to know whether you used the little "tape-on" Infrared connectors or connected a serial cable between TiVo and your cable or satellite box's serial port. (I cover this in Chapter 3.)

Press the Up or Down Arrow to make your choice; then press Select to move to the next step.

Choose type of cable/satellite box

TiVo works with a wide variety of cable and satellite boxes. Check the box for its manufacturer's name, usually written across the front or back. Then use the Arrow buttons to select your box's manufacturer from the list (as shown in Figure 4-14), and press Select to continue.

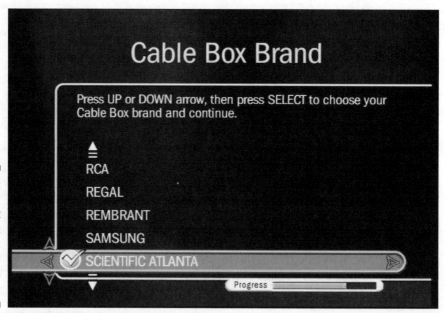

Figure 4-14:
Choosing
the right
brand of box
ensures
TiVo knows
how to talk
with it.

TiVo needs to know your box's manufacturer so it can mimic the language the box uses to talk with its remote control. You'll control both the TV and cable/satellite box through TiVo's remote, so you won't need those remotes anymore. (Two less remotes for the coffee table!)

Choose two- or three-digit displays

Even when TiVo knows the specific brand of your cable/satellite box, it doesn't know the exact model. Some boxes only have a two-digit display, meaning you never have to press more than two numbers to change a channel. Other boxes, typically digital boxes, let you press *three* digits. (These boxes typically let you enter channels like "200.")

Choose whether you see two or three digits on your box's display, and press Enter.

Sometimes TiVo needs to know whether your box expects you to press Enter after typing in the numbers, or if the box automatically jumps to the correct channel when you press the last number of its channel. If you press Enter after entering a channel number, choose Yes; otherwise, choose No.

Choose speed of channel changing

This one can make a lot of difference, so be careful. When you enter a channel on TiVo's remote, TiVo translates that channel into the language of your cable/satellite box. Then, it sends the channel request to the box. This extra bit of translating and sending causes a short delay whenever you change channels.

To reduce that delay, TiVo wants to send the signal as quickly as your box can receive it. The only way to discover your box's channel changing speed is to test it. So, after asking you to double-check your cable connections, TiVo asks you to try different codes used by your particular box, as shown in Figure 4-15.

Highlight a code by pressing the Up or Down Arrow; then test the code by pressing the TiVo remote's Channel Up button. (Feel free to press it several times, to make sure it's *really* working reliably.) Each time, TiVo displays the currently selected channel.

Depending on your model of box, TiVo may ask other questions — whether you need to press "Enter" after entering a channel's numbers, for instance.

✔ Spend some time with this part of setup, especially if you watch a lot of live TV. You might try rearranging the little TiVo remotes you fastened to the cable/satellite box for optimum speed. Most people find the "Medium" speed to work best, and it isn't really much slower than "Fast."

✔ Be sure to hide your old remote, the one that belonged to the cable/satellite box. If you accidentally use it, you might inadvertently change the channel while TiVo's recording a show.

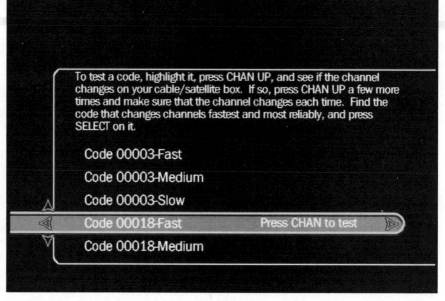

Figure 4-15:
Try each of the channel changing codes supported by your box and select the fastest one that still works reliably.

To test a code, highlight it, press CHAN UP, and see if the channel changes on your cable/satellite box. If so, press CHAN UP a few more times and make sure that the channel changes each time. Find the code that changes channels fastest and most reliably, and press SELECT on it.

Code 00003-Fast

Code 00003-Medium

Code 00003-Slow

Code 00018-Fast   Press CHAN to test

Code 00018-Medium

Letting TiVo make its first Program Call

When you finally finish TiVo's Guided Setup, it doesn't toss you much of a cookie. That's because TiVo needs about a half hour to download details about each show received by each of your channels for the next two weeks.

And after hanging up the phone, TiVo then needs to index that mammoth chunk of new information, cataloging all the actors, directors, themes, ratings, and other handy informational tidbits.

Simply put, your TiVo will be very busy for the next four to eight hours, as shown in Figure 4-16. Feel free to watch, pause, and rewind live TV, but you won't be able to record anything until TiVo finishes sorting its new information.

✔ Leave TiVo plugged in during this session to avoid serious problems. In fact, you should *always* leave TiVo plugged in so it can record shows no matter when they're on. (Whenever TiVo is plugged in, it's automatically turned on.) Only unplug TiVo when you need to move it. If your TiVo does lose power during this stage, restart the Guided Setup. After that, TiVo can handle power outages on its own.

✔ This long delay only happens during TiVo's initial setup, fortunately. For the rest of its calls, TiVo merely grabs a single day's programming information, and it retains full functionality all the while.

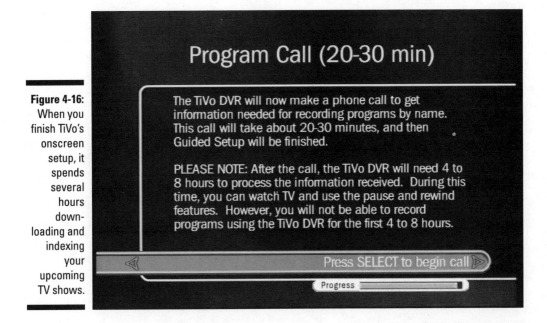

Figure 4-16: When you finish TiVo's onscreen setup, it spends several hours down-loading and indexing your upcoming TV shows.

✔ When TiVo finishes its call, it asks you to press the remote's TiVo button to move to its opening screen, TiVo Central. (You may see an animation in between.) Press the remote's Live TV button to begin watching live TV; you can still watch live TV while waiting for TiVo to finish indexing.

✔ Feel free to spend this time testing TiVo's tricks for live TV, which I cover in Chapter 5. When TiVo tells you it's finished, head to Chapter 6, where I explain how to record your favorite shows.

Fine-Tuning TiVo's Remote

You're able to change channels using TiVo's remote immediately after completing TiVo's onscreen Guided Setup. But if you invest a little more time, TiVo's remote can also control your TV's volume level and mute button, as well as its power switch.

Or, if you've routed TiVo's sound through your home stereo, TiVo's remote can control that, instead. The rest of this section explains how to program TiVo's remote to handle these additional tasks.

Making TiVo's remote control the power, volume, and mute switch of your TV (or stereo)

Introducing TiVo's remote to your TV works much like hooking up friends at a party; let them know a little about each other, then wait to see if they hit it off. To make things comfortable between TiVo's remote and your TV (or stereo), sometimes the remote just needs to know the brand name.

Follow these steps to help the two become friends:

1. **Go to TiVo's Remote Control Setup screen.**

   Press the TiVo button to go to TiVo Central (the main menu). Next, select TiVo Messages & Setup, then Settings, then TiVo DVR Setup, then finally, Remote Control Setup.

2. **Choose Remote Control – TV (power, volume, mute).**

3. **Select your TV's brand from the onscreen list.**

   TiVo lists code numbers popular for your brand of TV, as shown in Figure 4-17, for you to test.

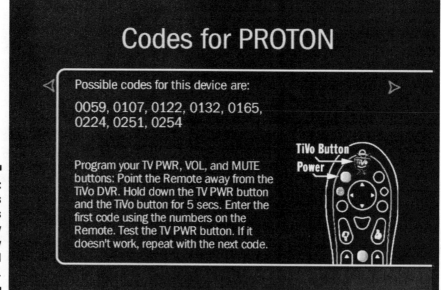

Figure 4-17: TiVo lists codes commonly used by your brand of TV.

Codes for PROTON

Possible codes for this device are:

0059, 0107, 0122, 0132, 0165, 0224, 0251, 0254

Program your TV PWR, VOL, and MUTE buttons: Point the Remote away from the TiVo DVR. Hold down the TV PWR button and the TiVo button for 5 secs. Enter the first code using the numbers on the Remote. Test the TV PWR button. If it doesn't work, repeat with the next code.

TiVo Button

Power

4. Enter one of the listed codes into TiVo's remote.

During this two-step process, you tell the remote which button to program; then you assign a "code" to that button.

First, cover the remote's front end with your hand, blocking any signals while you punch buttons. While blocking the remote, simultaneously hold down the remote's TV Power button and TiVo button for five seconds. (The light on TiVo's remote stays lit when it's ready for you to enter codes.)

Next, type the first listed code into the remote. (That assigns the code to the remote's TV Power button.)

5. Test the TiVo remote.

Aim TiVo's remote at the TV and press the TV Power button. If the TV turns off, you're done; you've programmed the remote to control your TV. (Make sure the Mute and Volume controls work, as well.) If it doesn't work, repeat Step 4 and try the next listed code.

✔ If your TiVo's hooked up through your stereo, you don't need to fiddle with your TV's volume or mute. Instead, control your stereo's volume by using almost the same procedure. Just choose the "Remote Control – AV Receiver" option in Step 2, and select your brand of stereo in Step 3. Then see if it works in Step 4. Repeat until done.

✔ If none of the listed codes work, TiVo can still try to guess the right code for your remote control (if you're up to the challenge). I describe the process in the next section.

✔ To accommodate TVs with several inputs, program your remote's "TV Input" control to switch between them. To do that, repeat these steps, but choose Remote Control – TV Input in Step 2. Also, simultaneously hold down the TV Input and TiVo buttons for five seconds in Step 4.

Searching for remote codes

If your TV or home stereo won't embrace any of TiVo's suggested codes, TiVo lets you search for them semi-automatically, trying every combination in the hopes that you'll stumble across the right one by accident.

The good news: You might uncover the secret code that cures your remote's problems.

The bad news: The process is dreadfully boring, and, depending on your luck, could consume 20 minutes of your life with absolutely nothing to show for it.

If you're ready to chance it, here are the steps:

1. **Enter the code to tell the remote what you want.**

   Hold down the button combination that tells the remote what action to take. Table 4-1 explains what buttons to hold down for each action.

Table 4-1	Remote Code Search Buttons			
To Control:	*TV Power, Volume, and Mute*	*TV Input*	*Stereo Power, Volume, and Mute*	*Stereo Volume and Mute Only*
Hold down these buttons:	TV Power and TiVo buttons	TV Input and TiVo buttons	TV Power and TiVo buttons	Mute and TiVo buttons

2. **Enter the search code.**

   To begin searching either of the two TV codes, press 0999. To begin searching for either of the two home stereo codes, press 1999.

   (Once you've entered the initial code, the remote's red light remains lit to show you it's ready for action.)

3. **Point the remote at the TV or stereo and press Chan Up.**

   If pressing Chan Up worked, you're in luck! Quickly press the Enter button; your remote assigns that code to the button you pressed with the TiVo button in Step 1.

   If nothing happened, repeat Step 3. Then again. And again. Don't move too quickly, or you might miss your chance to push Enter when a code works.

   When the remote's red light finally turns off, it has given up. You're out of luck. (I was out of luck with our aging Proton NT-333 television. However, the listed code worked fine with our Sony stereo, so everything worked out fine.)

Chapter 5

Watching and Recording Live TV

• •

In This Chapter

▶ Watching live TV

▶ Recording live TV

▶ Understanding the Status bar

▶ Pausing and restarting live TV

▶ Watching Instant Replays

▶ Viewing the Channel Banner

▶ Viewing the Channel Guide

▶ Recording live TV

▶ Weaning yourself from live TV

• •

Although TiVo's talents lie mainly in finding and recording your shows automatically, it also enhances live television. This chapter covers all your new live TV tricks: pausing the action, creating Instant Replays, and slowing everything down for detailed frame-by-frame analysis.

With TiVo, you rarely need your TV's remote, nor the remote for your cable or satellite box. Stuff them both under the couch, *quickly*. Thanks to all your hard work in Chapter 4, almost everything now happens with TiVo's remote — even live TV.

Turning On and Watching Live TV

TiVo offers several magic hat tricks with live TV; some to be expected, others a pleasant surprise. When you first turn on your TV, for instance, you usually see live TV on the screen, just like before TiVo arrived.

Press the TV Power button on your TiVo's remote to turn on your TV; the TV displays whatever channel it's currently tuned in to.

Or, if your TV's already turned on, press the Live TV button from any TiVo menu to jump quickly to the currently playing channel.

The first truly pleasant surprise comes with the Rewind button: When first turning on the TV and seeing live TV, feel free to hit TiVo's Rewind button a bit to catch up. Because TiVo's always recording *something*, it constantly records up to the last half hour of the currently tuned live show, just in case you might want to watch it. Quite a thoughtful robot, that TiVo.

As you watch live TV, TiVo won't forget your scheduled recordings. In fact, when it needs to record one, it lets you know a few minutes beforehand: TiVo explains what show it needs to record and asks permission to change the channel, as shown in Figure 5-1.

If you don't press any button at all, TiVo assumes you've nodded off and it's expected to record your show as scheduled. So, when the recording time begins, TiVo changes the channel automatically and records your scheduled show.

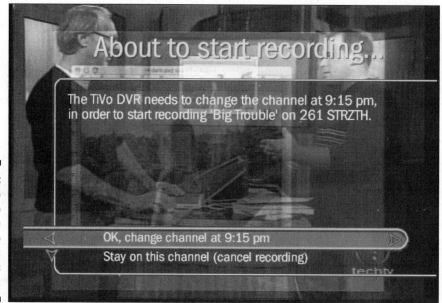

Figure 5-1: When TiVo needs to change the channel to record a show, it lets you know.

But if you're so deeply engrossed in live TV that you simply *must* keep watching, choose the "Stay on this channel (cancel recording)" option and press Select. TiVo won't change the channel, and you can finish your live TV show. However, because TiVo wasn't allowed to change the channel, you lose your originally scheduled recording.

✔ If you demand full access to live television — without TiVo interrupting you when it needs to record a different show — you must hook up your TiVo and TV set a little differently. I explore several options in Chapter 3 that let you watch live TV uninterrupted while TiVo dutifully records your shows in the background.

✔ You may also jump to live TV by selecting Watch Live TV from the TiVo Central menu.

✔ Pressing the Rewind or Fast-Forward button speeds up the action three-fold in the appropriate direction. Pressing again increases the speed 30 times faster; one more press increases 60 times faster. (Pressing a fourth time reverts to three times faster, as punishment for the greedy.)

✔ Is TiVo's remote having problems turning your TV on or off? It's time to program TiVo's remote, a task I describe at the end of Chapter 4. (If you pipe your TV's sound through your home stereo, the same section describes how to control the stereo with your remote.)

Recording Live TV

 If you've suddenly stumbled across an intriguing live show that you wish you'd recorded, it's not too late. Just press the Record button; TiVo brings up the menu shown in Figure 5-2.

To record immediately, press Select. TiVo immediately grabs as much of the show as it currently holds in its "buffer" (up to a half hour), tosses the show onto your Now Playing list, and then continues to record the show until it ends. You won't miss a single second.

To create a Season Pass that records the entire series, select Season Pass & other options. From there, you may record that individual show, as well as choose options for your Season Pass. (I cover Season Pass in Chapter 6.)

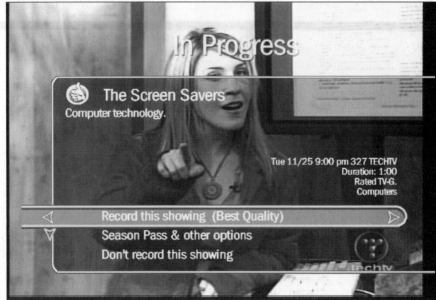

Figure 5-2:
Press the
Record
button to
record your
currently
viewed live
show.

Finally, if you pressed the Record button by mistake, choose the third option: Don't record this showing. TiVo quickly removes its menu and pretends it didn't notice your fumbled fingering.

✔ The simplest option is the first: Press Select to record immediately. After TiVo has begun recording your newfound show, mosey off to the Season Pass area and tell TiVo to record all the episodes, if you want.

✔ When you record live shows with the Record button, TiVo uses Best Quality. (I explain recording-quality settings in Chapter 6.) Because TiVo *always* displays live TV at Best Quality, it simply keeps those settings when recording the rest of the show.

✔ If you're waffling on whether to grant a Season Pass to a newly discovered live show, press the Record button and choose Season Pass & other options. From there, choose View Upcoming Showings to peek at future shows in that series. That helps you decide whether the show warrants an entire Season Pass, or whether the current episode is enough.

✔ When you record from live TV, you'll find your newly recorded show waiting on TiVo's Now Playing list, which I cover in Chapter 6.

What's TiVo's buffer?

TiVo records live television, 24 hours a day. When TiVo isn't recording something you've requested, or a show it thinks you may enjoy, TiVo simply records your currently tuned channel. It stuffs the incoming video into a constantly updated, 30-minute-long pouch called the *buffer*.

When the buffer fills up with 30 minutes of video, TiVo begins deleting as quickly as it records. It pushes the oldest stuff out of the buffer to make room for the new. TiVo's buffer — that 30-minute holding tank of Best Quality video — comes in handy in several ways.

When you switch to live TV, feel free to press Rewind: TiVo dips into its buffer, letting you view the last half-hour of that channel. Or, if you press Record, TiVo grabs any part of that show from the buffer and saves it along with the rest

of the show. By grabbing the buffer, TiVo can save part of the live show you may have missed.

The buffer has one important oddity: Whenever the channel changes, TiVo empties its entire buffer and begins filling it with fresh recordings from the *new* channel. Because TiVo emptied the buffer, there's nothing for you to rewind after a channel change. Change channels again — even back to the first show — and TiVo empties its buffer yet again.

TiVo doesn't need to change channels when you watch a recorded show, or when you head to a different menu, so the buffer remains intact. But when TiVo needs to record a show on a different channel — or when you switch to live TV and change the channel — TiVo dumps its buffer from the old channel and starts afresh.

Pausing and Restarting Live TV

TiVo's Pause button works just like the one on a VCR: To pause a TV show, press the remote's Pause button. To begin playing the show from where it's paused, press the Pause button again. (Or press Play.)

Unlike a VCR, though, TiVo can pause *live* TV as well as recorded shows. While the live show's paused, TiVo continues to save the rest of the show in its buffer for up to 30 minutes.

If you don't return within 30 minutes, TiVo assumes you've given up; it begins playing back the show from where you paused it. (You'll probably hear the TV's sound blast back on, alerting you of your neglect.)

If you ever think you'll be away more than 30 minutes — which is *quite* some time, if you think about it — press the Record button to record the show for later viewing.

Instant Replays and Slow Motion

 The much-heralded Instant Replay button is really just a mini-Rewind button. It makes TiVo skip back eight seconds and begin playing again, instantaneously. But, gosh, is it handy.

With each subsequent press, it jumps back another eight seconds. Press four times, for instance, to jump back about a half-minute.

 Press the Slow button, and TiVo slows down the action for greater detail. When watching in Slow motion — or paused — press the Fast-Forward or Rewind button to move back and forth, frame by frame.

 When returning to a paused show, press the Instant Replay button to start the action again. TiVo jumps back eight seconds and instantly begins playing the show from that point. Eight seconds of replay is usually enough to remember where you left off.

Finding Your Place in the Status Bar

When watching live TV on TiVo, it's easy to lose track of reality. With all that pausing and rewinding, where are you in relation to "real" time? Are you watching something that aired five minutes ago? Is the show really "over?" Or have you caught up with real time? How can you figure it all out?

TiVo tosses you a bone with its Status Bar — a green bar riding along the screen's bottom, shown in both Figures 5-3 and 5-4. (Pressing Play or Pause always brings up the Status Bar.) The Status Bar provides a visual timeline, quickly pointing out your current location during your time travels.

The long Status Bar always represents one full hour of live TV. The light-colored block inside the Status Bar represents TiVo's recorded portion of the live show. By looking at the size of the block — and its location within the hour time slot — you can gauge how much of the show has been recorded, what hour you're watching, and which portion of the show you're currently viewing.

In Figure 5-4, for instance, the numbers straddling the Status Bar reveal that you're viewing an hour-long block of live time between 10:30 and 11:30. To help judge your point in time, little white lines separate the bar into four quarters of 15 minutes each.

Figure 5-3:
The green
Status Bar
places a
visual
perspective
on your
location
within a live
TV show.

Note the light portion of the bar, directly beneath the numbers 11:14. That light-shaded block (it's green, when seen onscreen) represents how much of the live show TiVo has recorded. (The light block keeps growing longer as you watch.) The block's right end represents the place where you catch up with live TV. Its left end, by contrast, shows where TiVo began recording.

Figure 5-4:
The light-
colored
block in the
Status Bar
shows the
amount of
live show
TiVo has
recorded,
as well as
your current
viewing
position.

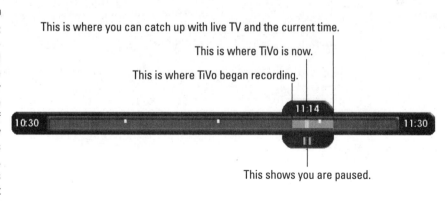

See the little white line near the middle of the recorded section? That line shows you the exact portion of the live show you're currently viewing. In Figure 5-4, for instance, you're watching the recorded portion that originally aired at 11:14. Got it?

- Press Play to view the Status Bar; press Play again to clear it.

- The larger the block within the Status Bar, the greater the amount of show TiVo has recorded. The block never covers more than half of the Status Bar, though, because TiVo only saves a half hour of live TV.

- The "Paused" symbol in Figure 5-4 means you've paused the show, viewing a single frame onscreen. When you press Play to see the show again, the Paused symbol becomes a single triangle that faces forward. When fast-forwarding or rewinding, two or three triangles appear, depending on the speed. (The triangles always point in the direction you're moving.)

- These concepts sound a little confusing, but that's why TiVo uses the Status Bar to let you see the action in progress. After you've paused, fast-forwarded, and rewound a little bit, the Status Bar's meaning will become quite clear — a visual *CliffsNotes* explaining the size of TiVo's buffer and the portion you're currently watching.

Viewing Information about the Show You're Watching

When you jump to live TV, TiVo normally displays a banner explaining the current time, the channel, show name, and description. Press Clear to clear the banner, or wait for it to disappear after about five seconds.

The banner also appears whenever you change channels. If you find it too large, feel free to experiment with its size. When the banner appears, press the Right Arrow to toggle between the banner's three possible sizes: large (Figure 5-5), medium (Figure 5-6), and small (Figure 5-7).

Feel free to leave the banner at the size you prefer. TiVo subsequently uses that banner when you change channels or jump to live TV.

✔ Whenever the banner's *not* visible, press the Right Arrow to bring it back to the screen. Press the Left Arrow to clear the screen and go back to your show.

✔ The Right Arrow brings up the banner in the *same size* it last appeared. Pressing the Info (or Display) button, by contrast, always brings up the *full-sized* banner. Stick with whatever method you prefer.

✔ You can shorten the length of time the Channel Banner stays onscreen in TiVo's Setup menus, which I cover in Chapter 7.

✔ Pressing Clear immediately rids the screen of any TiVo menu overlays, letting you see what you're trying to watch.

✔ When the full-sized Channel Banner appears, a press of the Down Arrow reveals other options: Record sits at the top; below it, Parental Controls let you place the current channel on the children's "restricted" list (covered in Chapter 7). The bottom icon (rarely used) jumps to TiVo's messages.

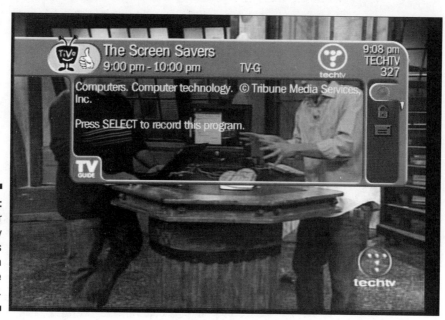

Figure 5-5: The banner normally displays this information about a live show.

Figure 5-6:
Press the
Right Arrow
to change
the banner's
size.

Figure 5-7:
Press the
Right Arrow
a second
time to
change the
banner's
size again.

Changing Channels

You change channels with TiVo's remote just as you did with your old
remote — the one that came with your TV or cable/satellite box.

Just press the Channel button toward the top to advance a channel; press the
lower part of the button to move down a channel. TiVo dutifully changes the
channel accordingly.

The only time you may run into something odd is if TiVo's currently recording
the show you're watching. TiVo must stay tuned to the current channel in
order to record the show, so TiVo fills you in on its dilemma, as shown in
Figure 5-8.

If you don't want TiVo to finish its recording, choose "Change the channel,
stop recording." TiVo stops recording, saves the portion it has already
recorded, and lets you change channels all you want.

Figure 5-8:
If you're
watching a
show while
TiVo's
recording it,
changing
the channel
prevents
TiVo from
finishing its
recording.

But if you want TiVo to finish recording the show, press Select to abandon your channel change. TiVo will continue recording the current show.

> ✔ If you want full access to live television — without interrupting TiVo's recordings — head back to Chapter 3. There, I explain different ways of connecting TiVo to your TV that let you watch live TV while TiVo records other shows on different channels.

> ✔ TiVo normally changes channels more slowly than your old TV or cable/satellite box remote. But if TiVo's not changing channels properly, check out the section "Connecting TiVo with a Cable or Satellite Box" in Chapter 3. You may need to adjust TiVo's setup.

Viewing and Recording through the Channel Guide

When you browse through live TV, ignoring TiVo's recorded shows, the burden of finding a decent show plops squarely into your own lap. To help out during your time of need, TiVo offers a hand with its Channel Guide.

TiVo's Guide resembles the TV listings found in newspapers and magazines, but it's much more fun: TiVo lets you record upcoming shows simply by highlighting their names and pressing the Record button. Here's how it all works.

 Press the Guide button while watching live TV to bring up TiVo's Channel Guide: a handy list of channels and their current offerings, shown in Figure 5-9.

When the Guide appears, the left side highlights your currently viewed channel; the right side places your current show at the list's top. In Figure 5-9, for instance, I'm watching a show called "The Screen Savers" on TECHTV.

Beneath "The Screen Savers," the Guide lists upcoming shows: "Anime Unleashed" will air immediately after "The Screen Savers."

Press the Up or Down Arrow, and TiVo moves to the next channel, automatically updating the Guide's right side to show that new channel's upcoming shows. Feel free to browse the left or right side of the list, looking at different channels or reading descriptions of a channel's upcoming shows.

Spot something good? Highlight the name and press Select to tune to that channel's currently playing show.

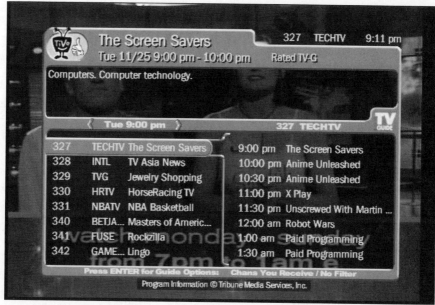

Figure 5-9: TiVo's Channel Guide lists your channels along the left, with the highlighted channel's list of scheduled shows along the right.

Spot something so good you want to record it when it airs? Highlight the show's name, and press the Record button. When the Record menu appears, press Select to record the show. Pushed Record by mistake? Then choose "Don't record this showing" to cancel the recording.

If you receive a lot of channels, all those show listings can be overwhelming. Pressing Enter while viewing the Channel Guide lets you customize the list in several ways, as shown in Figure 5-10. That lets you filter out shows that don't interest you, making it easier to spot the ones that do.

Here's the rundown on customizing the Guide for your immediate needs:

Channels: This selection allows three options. Choosing Favorites tells TiVo to list only your Favorite channels, making it easier to find good shows. Haven't set up your Favorite channels? Just leave the Channels selection set to channels "You receive." (Only the insatiably curious select "All." That lets them see *every* available channel, whether they receive them or not.)

Day: Change this to browse shows airing on different dates.

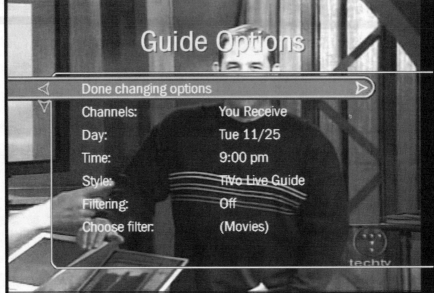

Figure 5-10:
Press Enter
to customize
TiVo's
Channel
Guide in
different
ways.

Time: Usually used in combination with the Day option, this lets you view shows playing at different times.

Style: TiVo normally displays the "TiVo style" guide shown in Figure 5-10. Switching to the "Grid Guide" displays a *TV Guide* magazine-style layout, shown in Figure 5-11. (I find the TiVo style faster and more manageable than the Grid Guide.)

Filter: This narrows the lists to display specific show categories. Choose Movies, for instance, and the Guide "grays out" everything but movies from the list. That makes it easier to see what movies are currently playing or will be airing soon. (TiVo offers filters down to the most miniscule category.)

 ✔ If the Guide suddenly looks weird, and you can't see all your shows or your channels, you've probably accidentally turned on a filter. Press Enter while viewing the Guide, and change Filtering to "Off." Everything should reappear.

 ✔ Press the Fast-Forward or Rewind buttons to advance or reverse the guide by 90 minutes; press the Channel Up/Down buttons to move up or down page by page.

 ✔ Several TiVo options, including the Guide, let you limit your lists to Favorite channels. That cuts out channels you rarely watch, clearing lists of clutter. I explain how to put channels on a Favorites list in Chapter 7.

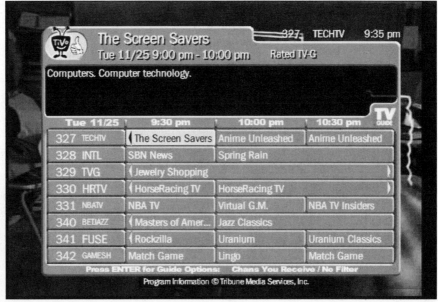

Figure 5-11:
The Grid
Guide
displays a
TV Guide-
style layout.

Weaning Yourself from Live TV

Watching TiVo's recorded shows looks the same as watching live TV. There's no visible difference on the screen. The biggest difference between the two is what's *missing* from live TV:

- ✔ You can't fast-forward through commercials.
- ✔ You can't fast-forward through the boring parts.
- ✔ Live TV makes you watch TV whenever your show airs. If you're not home, you miss the show.
- ✔ Biggest of all, though, live TV carries no promise that you'll find something worth watching.

TiVo offers these things only when you're watching recorded TV. That's why most TiVo owners eventually stop watching live TV. Their TiVo lets them control their TV, and it's frustrating when that feeling disappears.

The point? Although TiVo lets you watch live TV, try to wean yourself away from it. After you've owned TiVo for a few days, it will begin stockpiling your favorite shows. Don't keep watching live TV out of habit. Instead, head straight for the recorded shows on TiVo's Now Playing list. Not only will they be worth watching, but they let you skip commercials.

Whenever you turn on your television, press the TiVo button twice. That immediately takes you to your Now Playing list.

With a TiVo, you never need to watch live TV again.

Live TV Remote Shortcuts

Here are the most common things you'll do with the remote when watching live TV. Some tricks involve pressing a single button several times or pressing several buttons in sequence:

Info Press Info (called Display on DirecTV TiVos) to display the full-sized Channel Banner; press again to remove. When the banner *isn't* visible, press the Right Arrow to bring up the banner in your favorite size; press the Left Arrow to remove it.

Guide The Guide button brings up a list of your channels, their upcoming shows, and a description of the current show.

Pressing the Right Arrow while the banner is displayed presents a small, medium, and large version of the banner. Press the Left Arrow at the size you prefer; the banner remains that size during channel changes.

Clear Use Clear to remove any TiVo menus from the screen so you can see what you're trying to watch. (Works great for examining paused scenes in detail.)

Record Record the program you're watching, ending the recording at the show's end. (Press Record again to stop recording before the show ends.)

Pause the action.

Jump back eight seconds and begin playing again.

Fast-forward more quickly with each key press. When pressed while the screen is paused or in slow motion, TiVo moves forward, frame by frame.

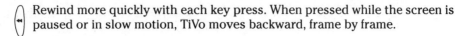 Rewind more quickly with each key press. When pressed while the screen is paused or in slow motion, TiVo moves backward, frame by frame.

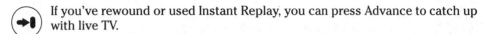 If you've rewound or used Instant Replay, you can press Advance to catch up with live TV.

Jump back to the last channel you viewed.

DirecTV TiVo owners can press the Down Arrow to jump to the box's second tuner.

Chapter 6

Recording and Watching Favorite Shows

• •

• •

*T*iVo frees you from your TV's "be there or miss it" scheduling. TiVo makes you the boss and enforces *your* rules. But how do you tell TiVo — a little robotic box — exactly what your rules *are?* As this chapter shows, it's refreshingly easy.

You'll create a "Season Pass" that makes TiVo scurry through the airwaves, capturing every episode of your favorite TV series, no matter when it flies by.

Want to capture more than just a TV series? Create a "WishList" that tells TiVo to grab every appearance of your favorite actor, everything created by your favorite director, or even shows about your favorite subjects, no matter how esoteric.

TiVo will even fetch that unforgettable movie with its forgettable title — something with the word "schoolhouse" in the title, perhaps? That single word is enough for a TiVo WishList to hunt it down when it airs.

Once TiVo begins grabbing your shows, you'll no longer watch TV. You'll be watching *TiVo*, as it customizes your television viewing around your schedule.

Creating a Season Pass to Record a Series

TiVo's Season Pass catches every episode of your favorite show, no matter when it airs. If a sneaky network moves your show to a different day or time, TiVo still grabs it. You no longer need to track down your shows.

TiVo's Season Pass automatically records shows that have a recurring title: "Friends," "The Sopranos," or "I Love Lucy," for instance.

Although the word "season" often implies something temporary, TiVo's Season Pass captures *all* seasons of a show: past, present, and future. (A Season Pass can record new episodes exclusively, if you wish, but it doesn't restrict you to them.) A Season Pass also limits that show's recording to a single channel; that keeps TiVo from recording reruns of old shows aired on different channels. (If you want those episodes, too, create a WishList, instead, described later in this chapter.)

When navigating any of TiVo's menus, the Right Arrow moves to the next TiVo menu, letting you fine-tune your previous selection. To back up to a previous menu, press the Left Arrow. (Little onscreen arrows in each menu point to the directions you may travel.)

1. **Press the TiVo button to bring up the TiVo Central screen.**

   TiVo Central, shown in Figure 6-1, provides a launching pad for all TiVo operations. When in doubt, head here and select your general task; each subsequent menu lets you fine-tune your request.

2. **Choose Pick Programs to Record.**

   Start here to schedule any recording or search for upcoming shows.

3. **Choose Search by Title.**

   Season Passes apply mostly to a TV series with a title. To record "Frasier," for instance, you'd select Search by Title.

   To choose shows to record based on something other than a recurring title — all shows with actress Uma Thurman, for instance — create a WishList, instead, described later in this chapter.

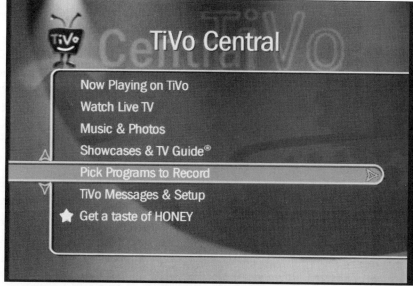

Figure 6-1:
Press the
TiVo button
twice to
bring up
TiVo Central.

4. Choose the show's category.

Feel free to narrow down the search by choosing a specific category, as shown in Figure 6-2.

I'm *much* too impatient, so I always choose the first option, All Programs, and dash to the next option.

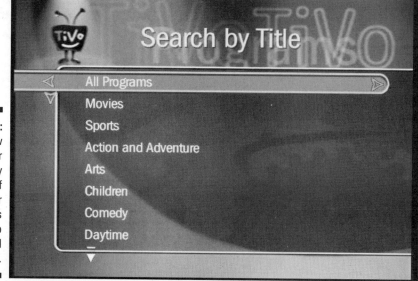

Figure 6-2:
Narrow
your
choices by
category, if
you want, or
just press
Select to
choose All
Programs.

5. Select the show's title.

Press the Arrow keys to begin spelling out the show's name: Highlight each letter, and then press Select. After you enter a few letters, TiVo begins listing possible matches along the right, as shown in Figure 6-3, narrowing down the list with each entered letter.

Typed the wrong letter? Erase it by pressing the remote's Rewind button. If you're quick, your guests won't notice.

When you spot your show's title on the list, stop pressing letters, press the Arrow keys to highlight your show, and press Select.

6. Choose Get a Season Pass.

As shown in Figure 6-4, TiVo located the "Frasier" series; it displays a description of the first upcoming show and offers five options:

Watch now: Rarely seen, this option appears only if your show's currently airing. Choosing this abandons your Season Pass quest, quickly jumping to the live show.

Record this episode: TiVo offers to record *only* the upcoming episode listed in the show description. This also abandons your Season Pass quest and jumps to the next step.

Figure 6-3:
As you select the first few letters, TiVo quickly brings up a list of matching shows.

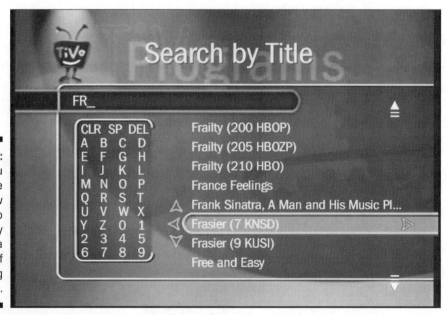

Figure 6-4:
Choose Get
a Season
Pass to
immediately
set up your
pass.

Get a Season Pass: This no-nonsense option immediately creates your Season Pass with the default options. To see or change those options, select Options, which moves you to the next step.

View upcoming episodes: Not sure if the series merits an entire Season Pass? This option displays descriptions of episodes airing in the next ten to 12 days. (If the series looks promising, press the Left Arrow to select a Season Pass.)

When viewing show descriptions, press the Channel Up or Down button to move quickly to the next description.

Don't do anything: An "out" for finger fumbles, this cancels everything, quickly returning to TiVo Central.

7. **Choose your Recording Options.**

Experienced TiVo users often tailor a new Season Pass by changing its Recording Options, as shown in Figure 6-5. Recording Options appear whenever selecting any program for recording, whether through a Season Pass, a WishList, or individually.

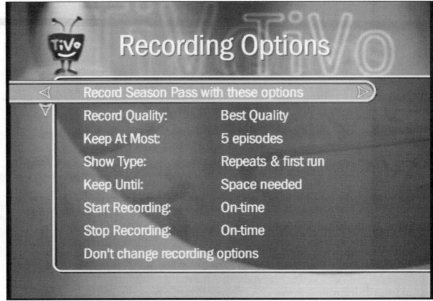

Figure 6-5:
Adjust the
Recording
Options to
meet your
special
needs.

Record Quality: TiVo offers four types of recording quality, from Best to Basic. Best quality looks best onscreen, of course, but hogs the most recording space. Try lower quality levels, should your TiVo be tight on space.

As a general guide, choose Best for fast-paced action films and sports, High for movies, Medium for talk or cooking shows, and Low for news and some animation. You won't know which works best on your TV until you experiment. (When you've found one you like, Chapter 7 explains how to set it as a default, letting you skip this setting in the future.)

Keep At Most: How many shows should TiVo keep available before deleting the old to make room for the new? Save every episode? Just 10? Five? One?

Selecting Two often works well, allowing time to catch a missed show. Raise or lower the number depending on your viewing habits.

When you only want a show's *latest* episode — the evening news, for instance, or last night's David Letterman — set the recording options to "First Run Only" and set "Keep At Most" to one episode. As TiVo dutifully records the newest version, it deletes the old. Whenever you turn on your TV, TiVo presents the most current episode.

Show Type: This covers how TiVo deals with reruns. Some love 'em, some hate 'em.

> **Repeat & First Run:** The best choice by far, this records the latest shows, as well as repeats that TiVo hasn't already grabbed in the past 28 days. That weeds out duplicate recordings, but allows for reruns you haven't seen in a while.

> **First Run Only:** This records shows the very first day they air, then never again.

> **All including Duplicates:** Rarely used, this records *all* instances of a show, including duplicates.

Keep Until: Here, you decide how long TiVo keeps an episode before deleting it to make room for newer requested shows.

> **Space needed:** The best choice, TiVo saves your show for at least two days and then deletes it only if it needs room for your newly requested recordings. (You'll be surprised how long old shows linger before being deleted.)

> **Keep until I delete:** If you absolutely *must* see a show, choose Keep until I delete. This works well to save shows for visitors.

Start Recording: Does your network traditionally start that particular show a little early? Start TiVo's recording a few minutes early to compensate. (Don't overuse this option, though, as your "padding" could keep TiVo from recording the show that airs directly before this one.)

Stop Recording: Handy for recording live events that often run late, this tells TiVo to add from one minute to three hours to the show's scheduled ending time. (Great for sporting events and Academy Awards.)

Don't change recording options: An escape hatch, this option bails out without making changes and simply uses the default options. (The Left Arrow does the same thing.)

✔ To delete or edit an existing Season Pass, visit the Season Pass Manager, described later in this chapter.

✔ After you've created more than one Season Pass, you should prioritize them so TiVo knows which one to record if the shows — gasp — air at the same time. Prioritize them in the Season Pass Manager, covered later in this chapter.

✔ Don't go wild with the "Save until I delete" option, especially for shows that air frequently. This option hogs storage space, leaving TiVo with less room to schedule other recordings.

Where does TiVo gather its show information?

To schedule upcoming shows, TiVo relies mainly on the information supplied by the networks. The networks usually label each show with an episode number, description, length, the stars' names, and other information. TiVo buys the data information from Tribune Media Services and tweaks it for its own use. (You'll find much of TiVo's same data posted online at www.zap2it.com.)

Whenever TiVo displays a show's description, press the remote's Enter button to see *everything* about the show. (You'll probably have to press the Page Down button to see it all.)

If a lazy network doesn't supply a complete show description, TiVo has difficulty separating the first runs from the reruns, causing much hand-wringing. Before damaging your hands, try solving the dilemma with the Manual Recording option, covered later in this chapter.

Entering Letters and Numbers Using the Remote

Only a handful of hip cell phone users enjoy spelling out names on a small keypad. To accommodate the rest of us, TiVo provides a fairly intuitive way to enter names by choosing letters and numbers from an onscreen grid (refer to Figure 6-3). TiVo also employs a few helpers throughout the process.

For instance, if you manage to peck out a few letters, or perhaps complete a word, before a slipped thumb sends you dancing off to a different menu, don't worry. TiVo remembers what you'd typed — your earlier efforts remain when you return to the entry menu.

Plus, most items rarely require more than a few letters before TiVo displays the entire name on the list. You'll encounter shows that include numbers or symbols in their names. Table 6-1 shows how to handle those and tosses in a few tricks for maneuvering the keypad more quickly.

Table 6-1	Remote Shortcuts for Entering Show Names
Press This Key . . .	*. . . To Enter This.*
Number keys	Inserts a number to find shows like "60 Minutes."
(⏩)	Inserts a space between words — the space between "60" and "Minutes", for example.

Press This Key . . .	. . . To Enter This.
⏪	Erases the previously entered character.
Clear ◯	Erases *everything* and starts over.
⏩ Slow	Enters a "wild card" symbol to match any word starting with the previous letters or words. For instance, Gidget* captures any show with "Gidget" as the first word.
⏸	Adds quotes that limit searches to certain phrases: "James Bond," for instance, stops a WishList from locating financial shows where James discusses bonds.
Hyphens (-), slashes (/), and periods (.)	When a show's name contains these symbols, replace them with a space (the Fast-Forward key).
$	Use the letter S for a dollar sign.
The letters "a", "an", and "the"	Leave out these words when creating WishList entries.
Apostrophes ('), asterisks (*), and ampersands (&)	TiVo ignores these symbols within a show name. So should you.

Creating WishLists to Record Favorite Things

Some shows don't qualify for a Season Pass because they lack a specific title. For instance, you might want to record every movie with Katie Holmes, or all films directed by Akira Kurosawa. Circus confection lovers may crave shows discussing "cotton candy."

That's where a WishList comes in handy. Created much like a Season Pass, they're just as easy to set up.

1. **Press the TiVo button to bring up TiVo Central, the starting menu for most TiVo operations. Then select Pick Programs to Record.**

2. **Select Search Using a WishList.**

   The Search Using a WishList screen appears, as shown in Figure 6-6. Below the menu, TiVo lists your previously created WishLists.

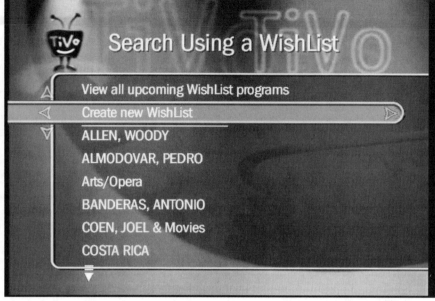

Search Using a WishList

View all upcoming WishList programs

Create new WishList

ALLEN, WOODY

ALMODOVAR, PEDRO

Arts/Opera

BANDERAS, ANTONIO

COEN, JOEL & Movies

COSTA RICA

Figure 6-6:
The Search
Using a
WishList
menu lists
your current
WishLists,
and lets you
create new
ones.

Feel free to highlight an existing WishList to edit or delete it.

3. **Choose Create new WishList.**

The other option, View all upcoming WishList programs, displays every show matching your existing lists, letting you pick the ones you want to record.

4. **Select the type of WishList you want to create.**

TiVo lets you automatically record any show featuring a certain Actor, Director, Category, Keyword, or Title. Here's the rundown:

Actor: TiVo locates any show where that actor participates: movies, TV shows, talk shows, comedy shows — anything.

Director: TiVo locates movies created by your favorite director.

Category only: This jumps to Step 5, letting you locate shows fitting a specific category — animated children's shows, for instance, or specific types of sporting events.

Keyword: The most versatile search, this records shows containing certain words in their description. Enter "James Bond," for instance, to catch any James Bond movie, no matter who starred.

Title: Can't remember a movie's entire title? Enter the words you *do* remember to see a list of matches.

Always enter a person's last name first, followed by a comma, a space, and their first name.

5. **Select the Category.**

Narrow your search, if you want, to certain categories: Kevin Bacon's Historical Drama Movies, for instance.

Or, if you chose Category Only in Step 4, here's your chance to grab cooking, mystery, or romance shows, or shows from hundreds of other categories. (Sports fanatics can choose among 93 subcategories, including football, baseball, arm wrestling, and table tennis.)

6. **If desired, tell TiVo how to record your new WishList.**

Automatically grabbing every show your WishList locates can be risky. A particularly prolific actor could fill up your TiVo's hard drive in a single day. To control the amount of shows TiVo records, choose between several options, shown in Figure 6-7.

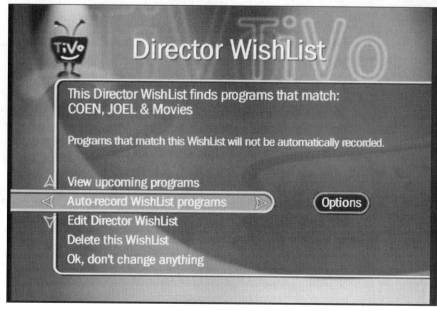

Figure 6-7: Tell TiVo how to record your new WishList.

View upcoming programs: The safest option, this lists every show found by your new WishList. This not only confirms that your WishList catches what you want, but it also lets you pick and choose, weeding out the awful Gregory Peck movies and seizing the ones you're after.

When viewing a list of show descriptions, press the Channel Up or Down button to move quickly from one description to the next.

Auto-record WishList programs: A dangerous option, this tells TiVo to automatically record every show matching your criteria. (TiVo then places that new request at the bottom of your Season Pass list.)

Edit Actor or Director WishList: This lets you adjust an existing WishList to meet different needs.

Delete this WishList: After a WishList grabs everything you want, feel free to delete it.

Ok, don't change anything: Finished? Select this to wrap it up.

✔ After creating a new WishList, always choose "View Upcoming Shows" to make sure the WishList works the way you intended.

✔ Choosing to Auto-record a WishList item lets you select its Recording Options, just as for Season Passes. I explain Recording Options, shown in Figure 6-5, earlier in this chapter's "Creating a Season Pass to Record a Series" section.

✔ Visit your WishLists often to see what they've turned up. Select an individual WishList, or choose View all upcoming WishList programs to see *everything* ferreted out by all your WishLists. When you spot something good, select its name to record it.

✔ If a newly requested show conflicts with other scheduled recordings, choose Cancel. Then select the View Upcoming Episodes option to find a rerun of the desired show. Most networks repeat their shows several times throughout the week, and choosing to record a rerun often resolves the conflict.

✔ If TiVo's Now Playing list shows too many shows with the same actor, director, or category, an Auto-recording WishList may be the culprit. They're particularly susceptible to "marathon" programming, where a station runs episodes or thematically linked films continuously for a day or two.

✔ When you create an Auto-recording WishList, TiVo places it at the bottom of your Season Pass list. To give it a higher priority, see the upcoming section "Handling Scheduling Conflicts with the Season Pass Manager."

✔ Add upcoming travel destinations to WishList to prepare for your trip.

✔ Unlike Season Passes, WishLists are made to be deleted. When TiVo has granted your wish — found all the shows you wanted — feel free to delete the WishList without remorse.

✔ The WishList's Auto-record option has nothing to do with the Save to VCR feature. I explain how to save a recorded show to your VCR in the "TiVo's Now Playing List" section, later in this chapter.

Handling Scheduling Conflicts with the Season Pass Manager

Nobody enjoys deciding between two TV shows that air simultaneously. Yet TiVo faces that thorny issue whenever it encounters a scheduling conflict. Which show gets recorded and which gets the boot? Sometimes TiVo can catch both simply by catching a repeat a day or two after it first airs.

When a conflict can't be solved by that little trick, TiVo turns to you for guidance in the form of a *Season Pass Manager*.

That's a fancy name for a simple list of all your Season Passes — and any Auto-recording WishLists, too. When faced with a recording conflict, TiVo records the one with the highest position on the list. Here's how to manage your Season Passes, making sure you've ranked your shows in order of importance.

1. **From TiVo Central, select Pick Programs to record.**

2. **Select Season Pass Manager.**

   TiVo displays your Season Pass Manager, shown in Figure 6-8.

Figure 6-8:
The Season
Pass
Manager
prioritizes
your
automatic
recordings,
letting TiVo
choose your
favorite
during a
scheduling
conflict.

3. Arrange your shows in order of importance.

To rank a show higher or lower, highlight its name with the Arrow keys and press the Right Arrow key. Then press the Up or Down Arrow keys to change the show's list position. Done? Press the Left Arrow to lock it in place.

As soon as you're done rearranging your Season Pass order, TiVo begins recalculating all its scheduled recordings to make sure they comply. Depending on the amount of shows, TiVo might take a few minutes to finish recalculating and update its To Do list.

✔ Place your "just gotta see it" favorites at the list's top. Place shows with constant reruns — old sitcoms, for example — near the list's bottom. Currently running shows belong closer to the top, especially the ones that don't repeat a day or so later.

✔ Visit your Season Pass Manager often. Your viewing habits will change through the months, and you'll probably want to move new Auto-record WishLists from their initial ranking at the bottom.

✔ Whenever you rearrange your Season Passes, TiVo recalculates its entire recording schedule, adjusting it accordingly. Depending on the list's length, this can take a few seconds or a few minutes.

✔ DirecTV TiVos come with two tuners, so they can record two shows simultaneously. Standalone TiVos, which all have single tuners, can record only one show at a time. I discuss different TiVo models in Chapter 2.

Managing Your Recording Space

TiVo packs all your recorded shows into its built-in suitcase, known as a *hard drive*. When TiVo's hard drive fills up with recorded shows — and TiVo needs to record a newly requested show — TiVo must delete something to make room. Here's how it makes the agonizing decision.

First, TiVo deletes any Suggestions that it automatically recorded for you. In fact, a lack of Suggestions on your Now Playing list warns that TiVo's probably running short on recording space.

Second, TiVo looks at the "Save until" date of each show on your Now Playing list, taking note of the shows with the oldest "Save until" date. (Any show saved past its "Save until" date has a yellow icon with an exclamation point inside.)

TiVo then begins clearing the decks by axing the show with the oldest "Save Until" date. (If you haven't been fiddling with a show's "Save until" date or the Now Playing list's sorting options, it's usually the oldest show on your list, often the one sitting at the list's bottom.)

✔ Alarmed? Don't worry about it. Think about how many shows you missed *before* TiVo arrived; you survived. Besides, TiVo constantly brings in fresh new shows. (And if you miss that particular show desperately, TiVo can probably pick it up on a rerun, given enough time.)

✔ To increase storage space, try lowering your recording quality. Instead of recording everything in Best, try High or Medium quality for some shows.

✔ Upgrade your TiVo with a larger hard drive, allowing it to hold more shows. This can be surprisingly simple, and I walk you through the easiest do-it-yourself hard drive upgrade in Chapter 12.

Checking TiVo's List of Upcoming Recordings

Using TiVo requires a leap of faith — a suspension of disbelief — that a mechanical object can *really* capture all your favorite shows. Your faith in TiVo will eventually increase as you watch it in action. But the doubters find relief in TiVo's "To Do" list.

Found at the bottom of the Pick Programs to Record option, TiVo's To Do List shows TiVo's recording schedule for the days ahead. TiVo's To Do List in Figure 6-9, for instance, shows the next scheduled recording is "The Simpsons," slated for 7 p.m. on channel 6.

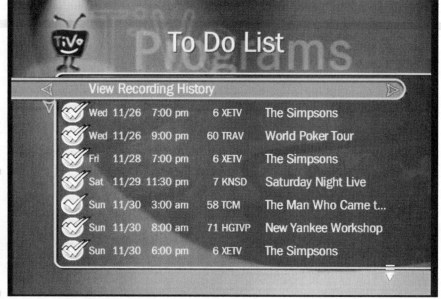

Figure 6-9:
TiVo's To Do
List shows
all of its
upcoming
scheduled
recordings.

Highlight any listed recording and press Select to view the show's description, change its recording qualities, or cancel it completely.

✔ TiVo's To Do List is always up-to-date except when you've recently changed a Season Pass or WishList. TiVo sometimes takes a minute or two to reflect the changes.

✔ Curious folks can view TiVo's upcoming Suggestions by choosing TiVo Suggestions from the Pick Programs to Record menu. (You may only view Suggestions; you can't cancel or edit them.)

✔ Sitting atop TiVo's To Do List lies the View Recording History option. Here, TiVo explains why shows were deleted or not recorded, along with its reasoning. If a recording is suddenly missing, for instance, head here to read things like, "This program was deleted because someone in your household removed it." (It provides the time and date of removal so you can track down the guilty party.)

Manually Recording by Time, Day, and Channel

TiVo's Manual Recording feature offers a last resort option for grabbing particularly problematic shows.

For instance, the "Comedy Central" channel sometimes neglects to describe its "South Park" episodes. Instead, the description offers the generic, "Four boys living in Colorado." Without a show description, TiVo doesn't know if it's a new episode or not, and TiVo won't save it as a "First Run" show.

But because I know the exact day and time each new South Park episode airs, I set up a manual recording telling TiVo to record the episode from that particular timeslot. That always brings in the new episode, even without a correct description.

Manual recordings also come in handy for recording *parts* of shows. Grabbing the last 15 minutes of "The Tonight Show," for instance, often catches the musical guest, skipping the rest.

A press of the Left Arrow backs up to correct mistakes.

1. **Choose Pick Programs to Record from TiVo Central.**

2. **Choose Record by Time or Channel.**

3. **Choose Manually Record Time/Channel.**

4. **Select the type of recording, and then press the Right Arrow.**

   As shown on the left side of Figure 6-10, TiVo offers two choices: One Time and Repeating. Selecting One Time creates a temporary, single-use recording. Repeating, by contrast, repeatedly captures that same time slot.

Figure 6-10:
When necessary, TiVo can record a certain time slot on a certain channel, regardless of what's playing.

5. **Choose the day or days for the recording, and then press the Right Arrow.**

   Press the Up or Down Arrows to select the correct Day. If you chose Repeating in Step 4, choose when the recording should repeat.

6. **Choose a channel for the recording, and then press the Right Arrow.**

   Enter the channel number with the remote's keys, or press the Up or Down Arrows to display the channel.

7. **Select the recording time, and then press the Right Arrow.**

   Using the Up and Down Arrows, choose the hour, minute, and AM/PM setting for the recording's Start and Stop times.

8. **Press Select to schedule your recording.**

   TiVo presents one last screen, listing your recording's Start and Stop times, Channel, Duration, and Quality. Everything correct? Then press Select and TiVo slips your new recording into its queue.

Although manual recordings sometimes come in handy, they lack the intelligence of a Season Pass. TiVo won't know if a show has been rescheduled, for instance, to adjust the schedule as necessary.

However, they still remain powerful weapons in TiVo's arsenal for hunting down shows that elude capture any other way.

You still need a subscription — an Activated TiVo — in order to record manually by time and date. The older Series 1 TiVos can still record manually without a subscription, but that leads to clock accuracy problems described in Chapter 2.

Finding Interesting Shows to Record

When completely ignored, TiVo won't record much. After all, it can't find and record your favorite shows unless it knows what to look for. But after you toss TiVo a few scraps, it sure knows how to run.

Here are some quick and easy ways to toss some tidbits to your TiVo. After confiding a few show titles, subjects, or actors, your Now Playing list will swell with shows you'll enjoy.

This takes a small effort on your part, but TiVo's doing all the major work, tracking the shows down and making sure they're available when you're ready.

Recording movies you missed at the theater

Everybody has postponed a trip to the theater until it's too late: That movie that everybody's seeing is no longer anywhere to be seen. Instead of waiting for the DVD, place the movie's title on your WishList, and forget about it. WishLists work continuously in the background, scouring upcoming show listings and pouncing at the right moments.

When that must-see movie finally flies through the airwaves (or cable, or satellite), TiVo will serve it up on your Now Playing list.

Making WishLists work for you

Creating WishLists is a little like buying stock. You place a few good bets and then sit back to see what pays off. The more patient you are, the better your chances of success.

Drop by your WishList area once a week or so to check up on your portfolio. Choose View Upcoming Programs, and TiVo presents a list of what it can capture within the next 10 days or so. Select the interesting items to read more about them; if they still sound worthwhile, push the Record button so TiVo captures them for future viewing.

Because TiVo's doing all the grunt work now, you can record *anything*. You don't have to fiddle with the TV Guide, set the VCR, or even be home. Take advantage of this. Whenever you come across an interesting show from a newspaper, magazine, Web site, friend, or at the office water-cooler, write it on a scrap of paper. When you get home, enter the show on a TiVo WishList. TiVo tracks it down, records it, and leaves it waiting for your return.

People with TiVo's premium "Home Media Option" don't need a scrap of paper. They can schedule recordings from the Internet, as I explain in Chapter 9.

Feel free to create WishLists describing upcoming events in your life: "remodel," travel destinations, or upcoming holidays. If that hot new date seems interested in a certain subject, add it to your WishList, finding shows for conversation fodder.

Browsing TiVolution Magazine for shows

TiVolution Magazine, found in TiVo Central's Showcases & TV Guide area, sorts many shows into convenient categories. Each Monday, TiVolution presents its latest results, highlighting upcoming new shows for quick, one-button recording.

1. **Choose Showcases & TV Guide from TiVo Central.**

   A box-like grid appears, displaying several flashy items, most of them ads or paid promos for upcoming shows. Feel free to ignore them, of course, and head straight for "TiVolution magazine."

   Press the Left or Right Arrow to navigate the grid of boxes; press the Up and Down Arrow to see boxes that may be hidden below or above your current view.

2. **Select TiVolution magazine.**

   The magazine, shown in Figure 6-11, contains an assortment of show listings sorted into tidy categories:

Figure 6-11: TiVolution magazine highlights upcoming shows of interest, breaking them into categories for easy browsing and recording.

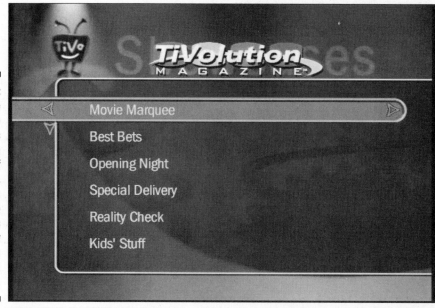

Movie Marquee: My favorite by far, this lists a large assortment of movies, complete with "star" ratings, for just about every category: Favorite Genres, Award Winners, Top 20 Actors, Top 10 Directors, Classics, and B-Movie Theater. Like most TV fare, most movies are at least a year old, some up to 60 years.

Best Bests: This offers a sampler from many categories, usually movies that created or still create a buzz.

Opening Night: These shows are airing for the first time. New shows often appear here first, the majority at the start of a new TV season.

Special Delivery: Documentaries and seasonal specials often show up here.

Reality Check: TV reality show fans find the latest crop here.

Kids' Stuff: Two separate categories cater to pre-schoolers and older children.

3. **Highlight a show's name and select Record this Show to grab it.**

   TiVo quickly sends you to the Recording Options area, just as with a Season Pass or WishList, and then nestles the newly scheduled recording into its To Do list.

✔ Film buffs should visit TiVo's Movie Marquee every week or so. (I drop by the Classics section to browse for movies that are well-aged yet well-preserved.)

✔ Occasionally TiVolution will list a show, but say there are no upcoming showings or it's on a channel you don't receive. This happens if the show ran a few days before you visited TiVolution or if it's airing on a channel you don't receive. (Hey, at least you know what you're missing.) Feel free to add that show to your WishList to catch future showings.

Watching Recorded TV with TiVo

After TiVo automatically gathers and records your favorite shows and subjects, it lines them up in plain view, ready for you to watch. That list of shows appears on TiVo's Now Playing list.

This section describes how to watch TiVo's recorded shows. It explains the Now Playing list's hidden details, how to fast-forward through commercials, how to save shows to a VCR tape (if you choose), and other TiVo tricks and tips at your disposal.

TiVo's Now Playing list

Press the TiVo button twice to jump to TiVo's Now Playing list and see your list of recorded shows, shown in Figure 6-12. TiVo normally lists the shows by recording date, with fresh shows at the list's top and the oldest near the bottom. At the very bottom sit TiVo's Suggestions — shows TiVo guesses you'll enjoy based on past viewing habits.

To see any show's description, highlight it with the Arrow button and press Select. The show's description appears, as shown in Figure 6-13.

To see even more information about the show than revealed in Figure 6-13, press Enter. TiVo shows *every* detail it knows about the show, as shown in Figure 6-14. (Press the Chan Up/Down button to see details that won't fit on one screen.) Pressing Select brings you back to the show's shorter description.

To play a show, highlight its name and push the remote's Play button. Or, if you're viewing the show's description in Figure 6-13, highlight Play and press Select. TiVo begins playing the show.

Figure 6-12: The Now Playing screen lists all of TiVo's currently recorded shows.

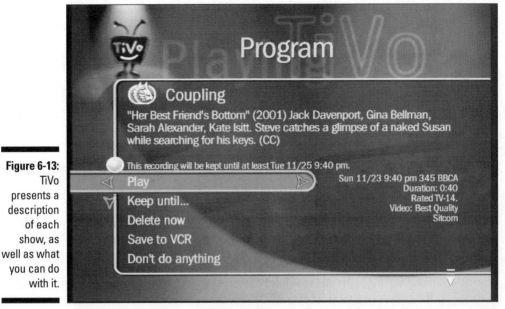

Figure 6-13:
TiVo
presents a
description
of each
show, as
well as what
you can do
with it.

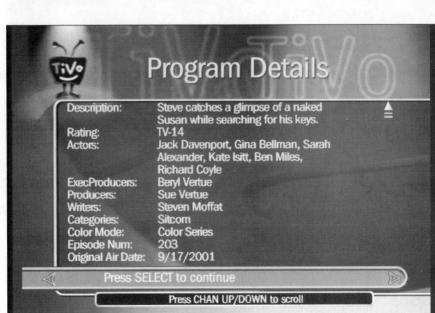

Figure 6-14:
The Now
Playing
screen lists
the details
of your
selected
show.

Choosing Keep Until lets you adjust how long TiVo saves the show: until you delete, until a specific day, or until TiVo needs space for incoming shows.

The Now Playing list normally lists shows in the order TiVo recorded them. For different views, press Enter to see them displayed alphabetically or in groups: all of your "Friends" episodes appearing under a single listing for "Friends," for example. (This comes in especially handy for TiVos with large hard drives.)

Understanding the Now Playing list's green, yellow, and exclamation point icons

Notice the icons to the left of some shows on the Now Playing list in Figure 6-12? The icon's shape and color helps you identify TiVo's deletion plans, should upcoming shows require the space.

You can change a show's deletion rank by selecting it from the Now Playing list and changing the Keep Until option.

Here's the rundown:

No icon: This show is less than a day old. TiVo won't touch it.

Green icon: This program will be saved until you personally delete it, no matter how long it hangs around.

Yellow icon: In less than one day, TiVo might delete this program to make room for other shows you've requested — but only if it needs the space.

Yellow with exclamation point: TiVo has flagged this show for deletion, but only if TiVo needs the space. The key word is *if* TiVo needs the space. TiVo only requires space after it has deleted all its Suggested items, and if you've requested more recordings than TiVo has room for. When faced with that situation, TiVo deletes your oldest shows to make room for the new.

Red: This show is currently being recorded. (You can still watch it, though, either from the beginning or live.)

TiVo: TiVo recorded this Suggestion in case you might be interested. If TiVo needs space for your programs, it deletes these first.

It's not uncommon for shows to hang around for weeks — or months — depending on how often you record new shows and how quickly you watch new shows (and whether you delete them after you've watched them). But if you *definitely* want to save a show, choose the "Save Until I Delete" option.

Using the Status Bar in recorded shows

Chapter 5 explains TiVo's Status Bar — that green bar running across the screen's bottom — and how it shows your current viewing position when watching live TV. The Status bar works the same way when watching recorded TV, but with a few key differences.

When you watch a recorded show, for instance, the Status Bar represents the show's entire length, from beginning to end. (When seen during live TV, by contrast, the Status Bar simply represents a one-hour time block.)

As with live TV, pressing Play or Pause brings up the Status Bar, shown in Figure 6-15. A glance at the Status Bar shows how much of the show you've watched and how much is left. (This comes in particularly handy during three-hour movies.)

Figure 6-15:
The green Status Bar places a visual perspective on your location within a recorded TV show.

0:00   0:07   0:31

techtv

In Figure 6-15, the numbers straddling the Status Bar reveal you're viewing a 31-minute show. The number seven above the little white bar means you're seven minutes into the show.

✔ Press Play to see the Status Bar; press Play again to clear it.

✔ The little triangle in Figure 6-15 means that the show's currently playing. A currently paused show replaces the triangle with two little white parallel lines, just like the ones on the Pause key. Each press of the Fast-Forward or Rewind key adds another triangle and increases the speed. (The triangles always point in the direction you're moving.)

✔ To jump ahead 15 minutes, press the Advance button. (You'll see little "ticks" that mark every 15 minutes on the show.) Pressing the Advance button four times, for instance, jumps ahead one hour.

Saving recorded shows to a VCR

If you connected your VCR and TiVo in Chapter 3, TiVo's happy to send over shows to create videotapes. Surprisingly few TiVo owners still touch their VCRs once TiVo enters the home, but if you're still a VCR user, here's what to do:

1. **Select your show from the Now Playing menu.**

2. **Choose Save to VCR from TiVo's list of options.**

3. **Turn on your VCR, and put in a tape.**

4. **Choose Start Saving from the Beginning on the TiVo.**

   To only record part of a show, stop watching TiVo's recording just *before* the part you want to record. That places another option on this menu, Save from the Paused Location. Select that option, instead.

5. **Quickly press the VCR's Record button.**

   TiVo begins playing its recorded show, sending it to the VCR, which records it onto tape. Just before playing an entire show, TiVo tacks on a nice informational screen, as shown in Figure 6-16. (Partial recordings don't get the info screen.)

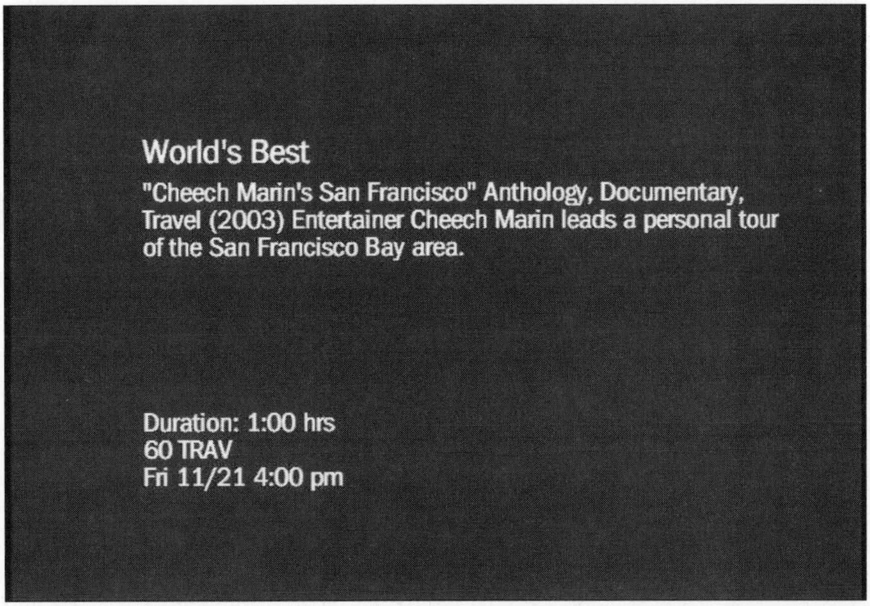

World's Best

"Cheech Marin's San Francisco" Anthology, Documentary, Travel (2003) Entertainer Cheech Marin leads a personal tour of the San Francisco Bay area.

Duration: 1:00 hrs
60 TRAV
Fri 11/21 4:00 pm

Figure 6-16:
TiVo adds a helpful informational screen to the beginning of any recorded shows you save to VCR.

✔ No, TiVo won't edit out the commercials from your recording. But if you stand next to your VCR, hitting its Pause button with your thumb at the right times, you can edit them out manually.

✔ To cancel a recording, press the TiVo button, and select Cancel this Recording at the next menu.

✔ Own a DVD recorder? Connect it just as if it were a VCR and use Save to VCR to record your show. TiVo doesn't know the difference, and you can record the show to DVD instead of videotape.

✔ Owners of Sony TiVos and Sony VCRs receive special, automated treatment: Attach an IR blaster between the Sony TiVo's i-Link port (IR jack) and the Sony VCR's infrared receiver. When you choose the Save to VCR option in Step 2, the Sony TiVo automatically turns on your Sony VCR, records the show to tape, and conveniently turns off the VCR when done. Sony ecstasy!

TiVo's Suggestions and Your Thumbs Up and Thumbs Down Buttons

Because TiVo never stops recording live TV, it temporarily fills empty space with shows, called Suggestions, that it thinks you may enjoy. TiVo's Suggestions don't rob you of any storage space; TiVo mercilessly deletes them when your own incoming shows need room.

How does TiVo know what to suggest? Partially through your remote's Thumbs Up and Thumbs Down keys. When you see a show you enjoy, either live or recorded, press your Thumbs Up button. Press it twice if you *really* loved it. (You can't press it more than three times.) TiVo automatically grants a single Thumbs Up to *every show you record*.

Hated something? Press the Thumbs Down button accordingly.

Even users who don't watch TiVo's Suggestions enjoy them as a gauge of "free space." Plenty of Suggestions means TiVo has plenty of free space. Don't see any Suggestions? That means TiVo's running low on space and may need to delete one of your oldest shows to make room for your next recording.

✔ To turn off TiVo's Suggestions, select Messages and Setup from TiVo Central. Head to Settings and then Preferences. Finally, choose TiVo Suggestions.

✔ A show's Thumbs rating appears next to the show's title on description screens.

✔ TiVo normally doesn't begin recording Suggestions until you've ignored it for 30 minutes. (You left TiVo sitting at a menu for half an hour, for instance.) That's when it enters "Standby" mode.

✔ If you delete a recorded Suggestion without watching it, TiVo usually takes the hint and is less likely to record it in the future.

✔ In general, one Thumbs Up means you liked that particular *show*. Two Thumbs Up means you liked that show *and* other shows like it. Three thumbs up means you loved that show, all the actors, the type of show, the director, your date, and the bottle of wine you shared.

✔ Stay away from the three Thumbs Down unless you *really* mean it. If overused, it can kill off not only that single show, but all its actors, and any shows like it. (Don't use it on a really awful "Seinfeld" episode, for instance, if you normally love the series.)

When does TiVo record Suggestions?

TiVo often records Suggestions in the background while you watch a recorded show. Or, after you've watched live TV for a long time without pressing the remote, TiVo assumes you may have wandered off. If so, it asks permission to change the channel and record a Suggestion. No reply? Then TiVo changes the channel to record the Suggestion.

DirecTV TiVos, unlike Standalone TiVos, come with two built-in tuners. The extra tuner lets TiVo record Suggestions in the background, so it doesn't ask permission to change channels except under one condition: If you've used

"Trick Play" functions on your DirecTV's background tuner recently, TiVo asks permission to change channels on the background tuner.

Although TiVo tries to sneak in a Suggestion or two when it can, it never forces you to wait until it's finished recording one. For instance, if you switch to live TV while TiVo happens to be recording a Suggestion, TiVo immediately stops recording the Suggestion, erases the remnant from your hard drive, and lets you watch live TV. (You'll probably never notice all this taking place in the background.

Recorded TV Remote Shortcuts

Here are the most common things you'll do with the remote when watching recorded TV. Some tricks involve pressing a single button several times or pressing several buttons in sequence.

Info Press Info (called Display on DirecTV TiVos) to see the full-sized Channel Banner; press again to remove. When the banner *isn't* visible, press the Right Arrow to bring up the banner in your favorite size; press the Left Arrow to remove it.

Pressing the Right Arrow while the banner is displayed presents a small, medium, and large version of the banner. Press the Left Arrow at the size you prefer.

Clear Remove any TiVo menus from the screen so you can see what you're trying to watch. (Works great when examining paused scenes in detail.)

Press when watching lists of show descriptions to jump from one description to the next.

Jump to the show's end or, for long shows, jump ahead 15 minutes.

Pause the action.

Jump back 8 seconds and begin playing again.

Fast-forward more quickly with each key press. When pressed while the screen is paused or in slow motion, TiVo moves forward, frame by frame.

Rewind more quickly with each key press. When pressed while the screen is paused or in slow motion, TiVo moves backward, frame by frame.

Some people swear by this "bonus" tip; others quickly outgrow its novelty. Pressing the following sequence of remote keys transforms the Advance button into a 30-second "skip ahead" button to jump past commercials: Press **Select**, **Play**, **Select**, **3**, **0**, **Select** *while watching a recorded show*. Your Advance button should now skip ahead 30 seconds with each press. Repeat the sequence to bring back your *old* Advance button.

Chapter 7

Fine-Tuning Your TiVo

● ●

In This Chapter

▶ Locating TiVo's Settings and Preferences menu

▶ Turning off the remote's beeps

▶ Weeding out unwanted channels and creating a Favorites list

▶ Reading TiVo's messages

▶ Changing TiVo's dial-out number and dialing options

▶ Adjusting for Daylight Savings Time

▶ Blocking certain programming with Parental Controls

▶ Setting a default video recording quality

▶ Turning on Secondary Audio Programming

▶ Turning off TiVo's Suggestions

● ●

*I*t's fun to ask children what they want to be when they grow up, but it rarely predicts their future. Today's budding veterinarians could just as well grow into happy podiatrists, typographers, thermodynamics engineers, or any other of the thousands of careers they've yet to explore.

Similarly, when TiVo's Guided Setup quizzes new users about their viewing habits and patterns, the TiVo novices don't grasp TiVo's subtleties until they've gained a bit of experience, pushing buttons and navigating real-world menus. Only then do new TiVo owners grasp the full picture.

Once you've matured as a TiVo user, this chapter explains how to fine-tune your TiVo to your lifestyle. A quick adjustment in its Settings and Preferences area turns off the remote's annoying beeps, for instance. (Or turns them back on, for those few who miss them.)

This chapter also explains how to add channels to your Favorites list, block inappropriate programs and channels from certain family members, and perform other adjustments that mold TiVo to your needs.

Finding TiVo's Settings and Preferences Menu

Friendly electronic gadgets stash their buttons behind convenient flip-down panels along the front. Find the panel, push the right button, and you're through. More insidious gadgets hide their buttons in the back, where they can't be reached without the help of long arms, mirrors, and bits of foul language.

Although TiVo hides its cables along the back, its settings live conveniently on its opening menu, TiVo Central. From there, it's fairly easy to tweak a setting or two.

To access TiVo's settings area, choose TiVo Messages & Setup from TiVo Central. Then choose the Settings area.

In this chapter, I explain the adjustments TiVo allows, how to change them, and how they each affect your TiVo's personality.

Turning Off the Remote's Beeps

Some people wish TiVo would contain its excitement at being unpackaged from its box. Specifically, the little guy beeps loudly in delight every time you press a key on your remote. It also beeps to get your attention, like when it asks if you'd like to delete a show after watching a recorded show. Here's how to quiet him down to a more comfortable level or shut him up completely.

1. **From TiVo Central, choose TiVo Messages & Setup.**

   Call up TiVo Central any time by pressing the TiVo button.

2. **Choose Settings and then Preferences.**

3. **Choose Audio Options.**

4. **Choose Sound Effects Volume.**

5. **Select Off, or choose a lower volume level.**

As shown in Figure 7-1, TiVo allows four different volume levels: Off, Low, Medium, and Loud. To merely muffle TiVo, try some of the lower volumes before stuffing the sock in his mouth with the Off option.

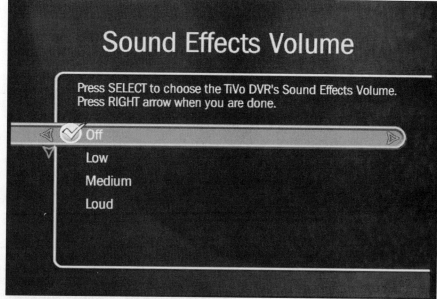

Sound Effects Volume

Press SELECT to choose the TiVo DVR's Sound Effects Volume.
Press RIGHT arrow when you are done.

✓ Off

Low

Medium

Loud

Figure 7-1:
Choose Off
to stop TiVo
from
beeping
when you
press a key
on the
remote.

Turning on TiVo's Secondary Audio Program

TiVo, like most stereo TVs and VCRs manufactured after 1995, supports *Secondary Audio Programming*, known as SAP. SAP lets broadcasters transmit two soundtracks for one show. A station could simultaneously broadcast a Spanish translation along with their English newscast, for instance, letting users turn on SAP to hear the Spanish translation.

Other stations help visually impaired users by using SAP to broadcast verbal descriptions of a show's onscreen action.

To hear a show's SAP in TiVo, follow Steps 1 through 3 in the "Turning Off the Remote's Beeps" section; then select TiVo's "Secondary Audio Program (SAP), if available" option. (The SAP takes effect the next time you change a channel.) TiVo will subsequently play back the currently viewed show's SAP — if an SAP is available.

Unfortunately, some cable or satellite boxes filter out SAP unless told otherwise, usually by pressing some buttons on the box's remote. If you've turned on TiVo's SAP — and you know that a show has a SAP — check with your cable or satellite company to see how to activate their box's SAP option.

SAP isn't included with every TV show, but it's slowly become more popular.

Finally, if your TiVo suddenly stops sending sound, check to make sure you haven't accidentally turned on SAP. If you turn on SAP to hear a show that *doesn't* broadcast in SAP, you won't hear anything.

Weeding Out Unwanted Channels and Adding the Favorites

Ever spotted a fantastic movie listed on TiVo's Guide, but then discovered you don't receive that channel? Or have you changed channels and stumbled upon a channel transmitting in a language you don't understand?

By removing those unwanted channels from TiVo's lineup, you can avoid future disappointments and distractions.

1. **From TiVo Central, choose TiVo Messages & Setup.**
2. **Choose Settings and then Preferences.**
3. **Choose Customized Channels.**
4. **Choose Channels You Receive.**

   TiVo lists all the channels available from your provider's channel lineup, as shown in Figure 7-2. TiVo assumes you watch any channels with checkmarks.

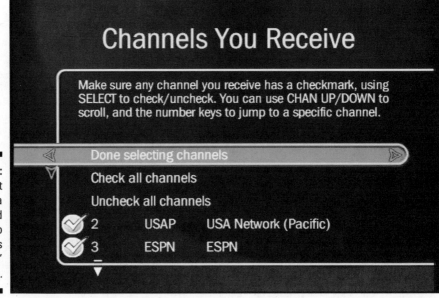

Figure 7-2: Press Select on a highlighted channel to toggle its "received" checkmark.

5. **Locate the unwanted channel.**

   If you remember the channel's number, enter it with the remote; TiVo jumps directly to the channel. Otherwise, push the Channel Down button to scroll down the list of channels, page by page. You'll probably recognize the channel's call letters or description.

6. **Press Select on the highlighted channel.**

   That removes the channel's checkmark, effectively wiping it from TiVo's consciousness (and its menus).

   Done? Press either your Left or Right Arrow key to save your options and move on.

7. **Make sure your Favorite channels are current.**

   While you're at the menu, check to make sure TiVo's Favorites list is up to date. Favorites, quite simply, are the handful of channels you find yourself watching repeatedly, usually because they carry a favorite show or two.

   To view your current set of Favorites — and change them, if needed — choose Favorite Channels in Step 4. Place a checkmark by every channel to include on TiVo's Favorites list. (Reducing the list to a dozen or so keeps it manageable.)

   ✔ Whenever TiVo presents a long list of channels, check the menu for an option called "Favorites." Choosing that option whittles the list from all channels to your smaller, Favorites list. Over time, you'll add new Favorites or remove ones that let you down.

   ✔ If your TV provider's anything like mine, they'll constantly add, remove, or change channel numbers. TiVo notifies you of these changes with a message, described later in this chapter, and it tracks these changes automatically. Still, it's a good idea to visit here and make sure your channels and Favorites are up-to-date.

   ✔ TiVo occasionally lists channels you don't receive in its TiVolution Magazine area. There's no way to remove those, unfortunately.

Reading TiVo's Messages

TiVo occasionally needs to tell you something. Your cable or satellite company may have added or deleted a channel, for instance. Or maybe TiVo received an update that added a new feature or two.

TiVo keeps you informed by sending a message. To herald its arrival, the message places a little "envelope" icon next to TiVo Messages & Setup on TiVo Central, as shown in Figure 7-3.

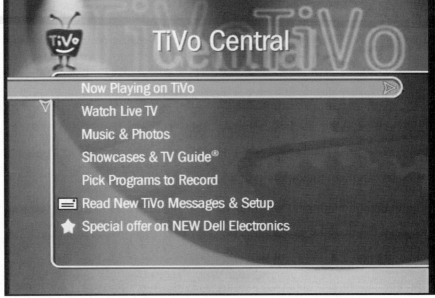

Figure 7-3:
An envelope
icon
appears
next to TiVo
Messages
& Setup
when TiVo
sends you a
message.

Follow these steps to read the message and delete it, if you want:

1. **From the TiVo Central menu, select Read New TiVo Messages & Setup.**

2. **Choose Read New TiVo Messages.**

3. **Read TiVo's latest message.**

   TiVo's latest message sits atop the list. Press Select to read it; you may need to press the Down Arrow several times to read all of the long ones.

   ✔ TiVo's messages rarely require any action on your part. Simply read them, nod your head and, if you're confident that you understand them, delete them.

   ✔ I never delete old messages, preferring to let them pile up. That leaves me a "log" of TiVo's activities, which might prove handy during a call to Tech Support.

   ✔ If TiVo mentions that your provider has changed your channel lineup, feel free to make sure your Currently Received Channels and your Favorites are up to date, as described in the previous section.

Changing TiVo's Phone Number and Dialing Options

If you've moved to a new house or apartment — but still use the same TV service provider — you may need to change TiVo's dial-up number to make sure it's not a long-distance call.

Or, if your TiVo somehow *does* dial a long-distance number to make its calls — often discovered from curious daily long distance phone charges on your phone bill — you can change to a different number. Here's how to check TiVo's current list of available dial-in numbers, and select a different one, if needed:

1. **From TiVo Central, choose TiVo Messages & Setup.**

2. **Choose Settings.**

3. **Choose Phone & Network Setup.**

   TiVo displays menus letting you change phone options, make test calls, and perform other troubleshooting tasks.

   Home Media Option users also see an informational screen explaining how TiVo currently connects with their home network, piggy-backing on their Internet connection to make its calls.

4. **Choose Edit phone or network settings.**

5. **Choose Phone Dialing Options.**

   TiVo lists your currently dialed number, as shown in Figure 7-4, as well as any special dialing circumstances: dialing "9" to reach an outside line, for instance, or turning off a call-waiting beep. (I explain these options in Chapter 3.)

6. **Select Set Dial-In Number.**

   Type your area code at the next screen (or verify that it's correct).

7. **Press Select to fetch the latest batch of phone numbers.**

   TiVo uses its current phone number to call TiVo's headquarters and grab a list of available phone numbers in your area.

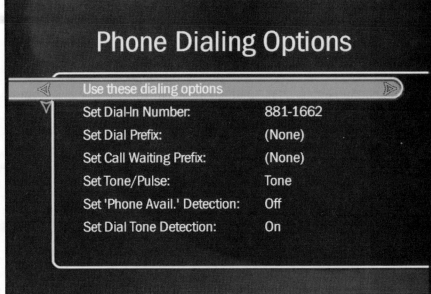

Phone Dialing Options

Use these dialing options

Set Dial-In Number: 881-1662

Set Dial Prefix: (None)

Set Call Waiting Prefix: (None)

Set Tone/Pulse: Tone

Set 'Phone Avail.' Detection: Off

Set Dial Tone Detection: On

Figure 7-4:
TiVo lets you select a different dial-up phone number and change your dialing options.

8. **Press the Up or Down Arrow to select a phone number.**

   TiVo presents a list of nearby numbers. Highlight one for TiVo to call, and press Select to choose it. (You may need to call your phone company to see which numbers are *really* local.)

I explain more solutions to phone problems, including avoiding long-distance charges, in Chapter 11. (In that same chapter, I explain how to set up TiVo should you move to new living quarters.)

Blocking Content with Parental Controls

When television entered the house in the late 1940s, networks wouldn't consider running a show unless it was appropriate for the entire family. In today's world of cable and satellite programming, that's no longer true.

TiVo provides several ways to control your TV's content, from blocking out individual channels to filtering individual shows based on their content. TiVo can even require a password to watch *any* channel, keeping the kids at bay until they've finished their last math problem.

To turn on TiVo's Parental Controls, follow these steps:

1. **From TiVo Central, choose TiVo Messages & Setup.**

   Call up TiVo Central any time by pressing the TiVo button.

2. **Choose Settings.**

3. **Choose Preferences and then Parental Controls.**

   TiVo's Parental Controls menu appears, as shown in Figure 7-5.

4. **Select Turn on Parental Controls.**

   TiVo asks you to punch in a four-digit password and then immediately asks you to punch it in again, just to make sure you've typed it in correctly. You'll now need to enter that password to watch blocked channels.

   Write down your four-digit password and hide it under the mattress. (If you forget the password *and* lose the mattress, this section explains the retrieval process.)

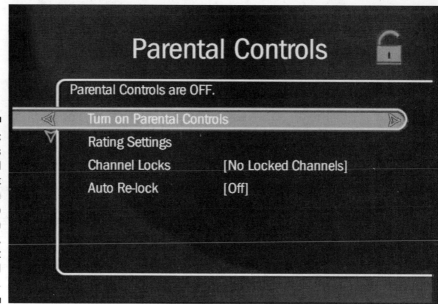

Figure 7-5: TiVo's Parental Controls let you set a password to certain channels, blocking out children and visitors.

Parental Controls

Parental Controls are OFF.

Turn on Parental Controls

Rating Settings

Channel Locks   [No Locked Channels]

Auto Re-lock   [Off]

5. Adjust the Parental Control Ratings Settings, if desired.

To simply block individual channels, jump ahead to Step 6; you don't need this step.

This area lets you block shows based solely on their audience maturity level, regardless of their channel. Many shows include a voluntary ratings system in their show description. Table 7-1 explains the rating system and how it sorts shows based on appropriate audience, type of content, and (for movies) their theatrical rating.

TiVo reads each show's rating, and chooses whether to block it based on the settings you choose here, as shown in Figure 7-6.

TV Rating Limit: This lets you block TV programs based on their maturity level. Each press of the Up Arrow blocks more types of content, eventually blocking *all* shows. Each press of the Down Arrow reduces the number of blocked shows, eventually allowing all shows.

The maturity ratings for TV, as shown in Table 7-1, are voluntary, and they cover only content created expressly for television.

Movie Rating Limit: Designed for theatrical releases, this blocks movies by their theatrical ratings: G, PG, PG-13, R, NC-17, and AO (adults only).

Block by TV Content: TiVo can also filter shows by their *type* of content: Suggestive dialogue, Language, Sexual Content, Violence, and Fantasy Violence. TiVo lets you mix and match from any or all of these categories, using the same six ranges found in the TV Rating Limit.

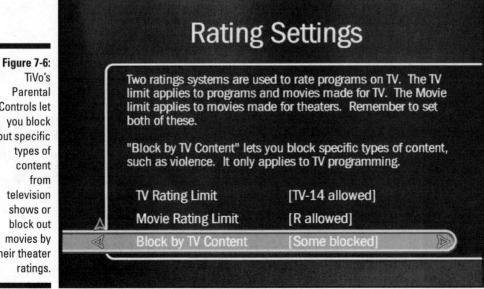

Figure 7-6: TiVo's Parental Controls let you block out specific types of content from television shows or block out movies by their theater ratings.

6. **Lock out specific channels, if desired.**

   Turn on any Channel Locks: This simple solution lets you block any or all channels, regardless of their content.

7. **Turn off Auto Relock, if desired.**

   After entering your password and watching a blocked show, will you remember to turn it back on at the show's end? TiVo's Auto Relock helps forgetful parents by automatically reinstating Parental Controls after nobody's touched the remote for four hours.

   Don't turn off the Auto Relock setting unless you can *always* remember to turn the controls back on yourself.

8. **Change Password, if desired.**

   If the kids figure out the password, head here to change it.

✔ To turn off Parental Controls and watch a blocked show, enter your password when TiVo asks. (TiVo's Auto Relock, if you haven't turned it off in Step 7, turns the lock back on for you four hours after you put down the remote.)

✔ If you stumble across a channel that you'd like to block, press Info to bring up the large Channel Banner. Press the Down Arrow to highlight the Parental Controls setting. Finally, press Select to jump quickly to the Parental Controls and add the channel to your "blocked" list.

✔ TiVo can't block out a specific show based solely on its title. Instead, block out the entire channel (Step 6), or block out all shows matching that show's maturity rating (Step 5).

✔ Curious about a show's maturity rating? Select the show from the Now Playing list, and press Enter when the show's description appears. The show's rating appears near the top of the list.

✔ Forgot your password already? Call TiVo's Customer Support at (877) 367-8486, Monday through Sunday, 8 a.m. to 8 p.m. Pacific Time. They'll ask for proof that you're TiVo's owner.

✔ Sometimes programs lack a rating in their show description. When TiVo encounters an unrated movie, TiVo gives the movie the highest rating (AO). When TiVo finds no ratings on shows that *aren't* movies, it gives them the lowest rating (TV-Y).

✔ A little "locked" icon next to menus and show descriptions means TiVo's Parental Controls are turned on. An "unlocked" icon means they're turned off.

Table 7-1	The FCC's TV Rating System
Rating	*Meaning*
TV-Y	**All Children — This program is designed to be appropriate for all children.** Whether animated or live-action, the themes and elements in this program are specifically designed for a very young audience, including children from ages 2 to 6. This program is not expected to frighten younger children.
TV-Y7	**Directed to Older Children — This program is designed for children age 7 and above.** Themes and elements in this program may include mild fantasy or comedic violence or may frighten children under the age of 7. Programs where fantasy violence may be more intense or more combative than other programs in this category will be designated TV-Y7-FV.
TV-G	**General Audience — Most parents would find this program suitable for all ages.** Although this rating does not signify a program designed specifically for children, most parents may let younger children watch this program unattended. It contains little or no violence, no strong language, and little or no sexual dialogue or situations.
TV-PG	**Parental Guidance Suggested — This program contains material that parents may find unsuitable for younger children.** Many parents may want to watch it with their younger children. The theme itself may call for parental guidance and/or the program contains one or more of the following: moderate violence (V), some sexual situations (S), infrequent coarse language (L), or some suggestive dialogue (D).
TV-14	**Parents Strongly Cautioned — This program contains some material that many parents would find unsuitable for children under 14 years of age.** Parents are strongly urged to exercise greater care in monitoring this program and are cautioned against letting children under the age of 14 watch unattended. This program contains one or more of the following: intense violence (V), intense sexual situations (S), strong coarse language (L), or intensely suggestive dialogue (D).
TV-MA	**Mature Audience Only — This program is specifically designed to be viewed by adults, and therefore may be unsuitable for children under 17.** This program contains one or more of the following: graphic violence (V), explicit sexual activity (S), or crude, indecent language (L).

Adjusting for Daylight Savings Time

TiVo resets its internal clock every time it calls in to grab updated show listings (usually every day). TiVo even adjusts automatically for Daylight Savings Time, so you don't have to worry about it.

However, TiVo's Daylight Savings Time adjustment is based on information you entered during its Guided Setup, covered in Chapter 3. If you ever move to a location that observes Daylight Savings Time differently, change TiVo's Daylight Savings Time setting by re-running TiVo's Guided Setup, described in Chapter 11.

Customizing the Channel Banner Display

Although TiVo's informational Channel Banner is helpful, it obscures most of your TV screen for about six seconds before vanishing.

TiVo lets you reduce that lengthy delay to just a few seconds, letting you return to the action more quickly. (People who prefer seeing the channel banner displayed by their cable or satellite provider often want to reduce the delay.)

1. **From TiVo Central, choose TiVo Messages & Setup.**

   Call up TiVo Central any time by pressing the TiVo button.

2. **Choose Settings.**

3. **Choose Preferences and then Channel Banner.**

4. **Choose Clear banner quickly.**

   To return to TiVo's regular banner, repeat these steps by selecting "Display banner normally" in Step 4.

You can cycle through the Channel Banner's three sizes by pressing the Right Arrow.

Changing the Default Video Recording Quality

When first set up, TiVo automatically chooses Best for your default recording quality.

You're free to change the recording quality when scheduling any new recording. But if you'd prefer that TiVo always use a different default quality — High, for instance, or Medium, to save recording space — TiVo lets you change it.

1. **From TiVo Central, choose TiVo messages and Setup.**

   Call up TiVo Central any time by pressing the TiVo button.

2. **Choose Settings.**

3. **Choose Preferences and then Video Recording Quality.**

   TiVo displays the screen shown in Figure 7-7, showing your currently selected default option and the approximate number of hours you'll be able to record at that quality.

Figure 7-7:
TiVo
highlights
your default
recording
quality and
lists other
qualities
and the
number of
hours TiVo
can record
at that
setting.

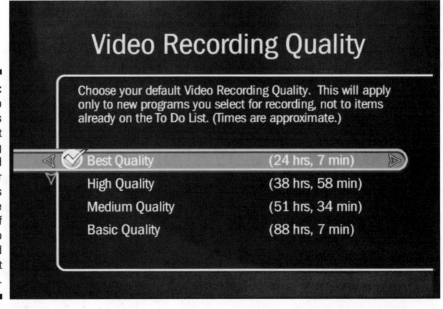

Video Recording Quality

Choose your default Video Recording Quality. This will apply only to new programs you select for recording, not to items already on the To Do List. (Times are approximate.)

✓ Best Quality	(24 hrs, 7 min)
High Quality	(38 hrs, 58 min)
Medium Quality	(51 hrs, 34 min)
Basic Quality	(88 hrs, 7 min)

4. Select a new default programming quality.

TiVo subsequently records all upcoming shows at that quality. (You'll still be able to change the quality when scheduling a recording, but TiVo defaults to your new quality setting first.)

✔ TiVo always displays live TV at Best Quality, no matter what quality you choose here. And if you press Record while watching live TV, TiVo will always save it in Best Quality. Suggestions, however, will be recorded at the quality you choose here.

✔ DirecTV TiVos always use Best recording quality because they simply record the incoming satellite data. The data arrives in a pre-compressed format, saving as much space as possible.

Making TiVo Stop Recording Suggestions

I like TiVo's Suggestions — shows it records based on my viewing habits. I don't watch many of them, but they let me know the amount of recording space left on my TiVo. When I see lots of Suggestions, I know TiVo has plenty of room for my upcoming recordings.

Plus, TiVo records Suggestions only when it has free space, and it automatically deletes them to make room for any incoming shows. Finally, TiVo's Suggestions definitely improve over time, as it learns your viewing habits.

But if you *don't* like Suggestions, here's how to stop TiVo from recording them:

1. From TiVo Central, choose TiVo messages and Setup.

Call up TiVo Central any time by pressing the TiVo button.

2. Choose Settings.

3. Choose Preferences and then TiVo Suggestions.

4. Select No, don't record TiVo Suggestions.

TiVo shows the screen in Figure 7-8, and it no longer records Suggestions.

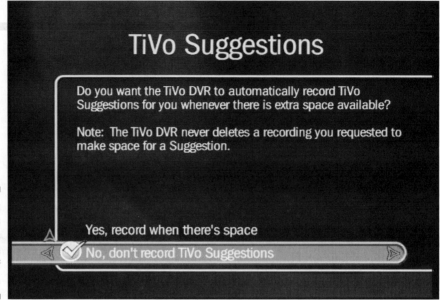

TiVo Suggestions

Do you want the TiVo DVR to automatically record TiVo Suggestions for you whenever there is extra space available?

Note: The TiVo DVR never deletes a recording you requested to make space for a Suggestion.

Yes, record when there's space

No, don't record TiVo Suggestions

Figure 7-8:
TiVo's
Suggestions
can be
turned off
easily.

You can still view a list of upcoming shows TiVo thinks you may enjoy, however, by choosing the list of Suggestions from TiVo's Pick Programs to Record menu. Feel free to record individual shows, if you want. But TiVo will no longer record all of the listed shows automatically.

Part III
The Home Media Option

The 5th Wave   By Rich Tennant

The 500 channel multimedia future

The Dental Network is starting a 10-hour, 3-day, 16-part miniseries on gum disease. Wanna watch?

In this part . . .

TiVo's lack of a keyboard and mouse disguises the fact that it's actually a *computer* — a close relative of the computer in your home or office. As you've no doubt noticed on the Internet, computers love to talk to each other. So it's no big secret that TiVo and your computer can talk, too.

TiVo charges admission for this family reunion, known as the *Home Media Option,* a handy toolbox that connects TiVo with its long lost relative, your computer. This part of the book explains how to get tickets and set up the party so nobody spills the punch.

One chapter explains how to set up a *network* that allows TiVo and your computer to talk comfortably. Another explains how TiVo can pour over your computer's digital photos, displaying them on the TV where all the visitors can see them. (TiVo can access your MP3 collection of digital music files as well.)

The last chapter in this part of the book explains how to push the Home Media Option to its limits through add-on software designed specifically for TiVo users. If you're a computer nut, this part of the book will keep you going for hours.

Chapter 8

Setting Up the Home Media Option

· ·

· ·

*Y*ou may not have spotted the scoundrels yet, but the entertainment, broadcast, and computer industries are battling over your TV — over your entire entertainment center, for that matter.

Computers started the feud by strolling onto TV's turf. Today's PCs store music, digital photos, and even movies. Unfortunately, all those things look dreadful on a PC. They're made for big TVs, loud stereos, and comfortable couches.

When the computer and entertainment center eventually merge, who will have control? Will an ugly PC sit next to your TV and stereo, feeding them digital pictures and music? Or will your TV and stereo become more like computers, storing your digital photos and managing your collection of music files?

Instead of joining the battle, TiVo offers its Home Media Option as a mediator, shuffling your songs and digital photos from your computer to your TV and stereo. In this chapter, I show how to introduce the Home Media Option to the warring parties and make peace between them.

Understanding the Home Media Option

TiVo doesn't come with the Home Media Option (HMO) built-in. Considered a premium option, HMO costs an additional $99. Soon after you've paid, TiVo headquarters shoots the HMO update software into your TiVo during its next phone call. You complete the process by downloading and installing some TiVo-supplied software onto your PC.

Finally, you link your TiVo to your PC, either through a cable or inexpensive "wireless" technology. When the two begin talking, HMO teaches TiVo four new tricks:

Digital Music: TiVo lists your computer's music files onscreen, letting you play any or all of them. TiVo plays *MP3* files — the same type of music people download from the Internet — as well as *playlists*: music arranged in a certain playing order. TiVo can even play some Internet radio stations, as I describe in Chapter 10.

Digital Photos: Elbow jostling in front of the computer monitor is no longer required when displaying family photos; the HMO option allows TiVo to display .JPG photos, the format supported by nearly all digital cameras.

Remote Scheduling: Ever wished you could phone your TiVo from work and tell it to record a particular show? HMO lets you log onto the Internet and schedule recordings up to two hours before they air. (Perhaps we've been lucky, but our TiVo schedules them just 15 minutes after we've sent the request.)

Multi-room Viewing: A perk for two-TiVo households, this lets you shuffle shows from one TiVo to the other on the same network. You must be the registered owner of each TiVo, ruling out sharing shows with a friend's or roommate's TiVo.

Tech talk about HMO

TiVo's Home Media Option supports music files stored in the MP3 format alone, as well as playlists stored in M3U, PLS, and ASX formats. TiVo will play an individual song, an entire folder of music, and even "nested folders," for people who want to hear the contents of a folder and every folder inside it.

TiVo understands Windows shortcuts, as well as MP3 tag information, displaying the song's title, artist, album, duration, year, and genre. By reading MP3 tag information, TiVo can list songs either alphabetically or by type of music. TiVo also plays most Internet radio stations when their broadcast address is saved in M3U playlist format.

TiVo's Digital Photos feature displays .JPG, .GIF, .BMP, .DIB, and .PNG file formats, and it plays slideshows of both folders and nested folders.

It displays up to 12 photo thumbnails onscreen; select a picture's thumbnail to view, rotate, or include it in a slideshow.

All your songs and photos remain stored on your computer; they don't consume any space on TiVo or limit your amount of television recordings.

TiVo can't combine your music with your slideshows, but that's excusable, considering that TiVo's constantly scheduling and recording your TV shows in the background. (If you still own any CDs, slip one into your stereo to supply the music.)

Knowing What Home Media Option Requires

Although it is ecstasy for computer nuts, TiVo's Home Media Option (HMO) places a few demands on the rest of us. Here's what HMO requires to bring its four features into your home:

1. **Money:** At the time of this writing, TiVo's HMO costs an additional $99. Own a second TiVo? HMO costs only $49 for the second one. (And $49 for your third TiVo, and fourth, and so on.) HMO comes only as a four-feature package; you can't pick and choose among its features for a reduced price.

2. **Series 2 TiVo with subscription:** HMO works exclusively on Series 2 TiVos — and only once you've activated their TiVo subscription. It won't run on the older, Series 1 TiVos. (Chapter 2 explains TiVo's different models and their various disguises.) At the time of this writing, DirecTV TiVos did *not* offer any portion of the Home Media Option.

3. **Internet connection:** HMO works best with *broadband*, the generic term for speedy, "always on" Internet connections found with cable or DSL connections. Dial-up connections still work, but add lengthy delays to recording requests sent through the Internet.

4. **PC or Macintosh:** Both PCs and Macs can run TiVo's software, "TiVo Desktop," to send music or photos to a TiVo. The computer needn't be a powerhouse, thank goodness; most of today's models meet the following requirements:

   • **PC:** PCs need Microsoft Windows 98, ME, 2000, or XP; a 233 MHz Pentium II processor or better; at least 64 MB of RAM; and at least 24MB of free disk space.

   • **Macintosh:** Macs need OS X v10.2 or later; a 400 MHz G3 processor or better; and at least 256MB RAM. They also need iTunes 3 or later for music and iPhoto 2 for photos.

5. **Network:** This simply means a way to connect several computers — or perhaps just TiVo and one computer — so they can share information. You can connect them with wires if they're nearby or connect them wirelessly if they're in separate rooms. (You can even network two TiVos *without* having a PC in the house.) Networking can be a tad technical, as you'll discover in the rest of this chapter.

6. **Network Adapter:** Just as telephones need phone jacks to make calls, everything on a network, including TiVo, needs a "network adapter" to plug into the network.

If your computer's already hooked up to a wireless network, plugging a wireless network adapter into your TiVo might be all you need to bring it into the loop.

Although HMO comes as a package of four separate features, not all features require an Internet connection, PC, computer network, or network adapter. Table 8-1 breaks it all down, feature by feature.

Table 8-1	Requirements for Each Feature of HMO			
HMO Feature	*Internet connection*	*Computer*	*Network*	*Network adapter*
Digital Photos	No	Yes	Yes	Yes
Digital Music	No	Yes	Yes	Yes
Remote Scheduling	Yes	Yes, at the location from where you want to schedule shows remotely	No, but scheduling requires one to two days' notice	No
Multi-room Viewing	No	No	Yes; however, two directly connected TiVos can share shows without a computer	Yes, one for each TiVo

Setting Up a Home Network and Connecting TiVo

Before opening the wallet for the Home Media Option, set up and test your network to make sure TiVo embraces your PC and its Internet connection. There's no sense paying for HMO if TiVo snubs your computer for some odd reason.

Connecting TiVo to your home network rewards you with a bonus, even if you don't want HMO: Once networked with a broadband Internet connection, TiVo no longer uses your phone line. TiVo piggybacks on your computer's broadband connection, downloading show schedules much more quickly.

Networks aren't always difficult to set up, especially with Windows XP or a Mac. TiVo will connect with your computers using *wire*, *wireless*, or a combination of both. In the rest of this section, I guide you through setting up a network that includes TiVo. I help you choose the right networking method that lets everything share messages (and the Internet) with a little gadget called a *router*.

To wire or not to wire: Choosing between a wired or wireless network

A simple way to choose between wired or wireless networks is to look at the distance between your TiVo and your computer. Wired networks work best for connecting equipment in the same room. Perks of wired networks include their ability to send information quickly, reliability, immunity to interference, and they're the easiest to set up.

The hard part is stringing those darn cables, especially between two rooms. In the crawlspace? Tucked along the carpet edge? Through the central vacuuming tubing? Dropping a network wire into a basement? It's all been tried. The people who gave up moved to wireless, instead.

The big benefit for wireless networks is that they are invisible. Plug in the wireless adapters, turn everything on, and the chatter begins, sometimes reaching several hundred feet.

Drawbacks? If one wireless adapter's placed too far away from the others, it acts like a car radio traveling between stations, barely picking up a signal.

Because wireless networks share radio space with some cordless phones, they're sometimes susceptible to interference. Walls, floors, and ceilings slow down the signal, too. Still, nobody has ever tripped over a radio wave; sheer distance sometimes makes wireless the only realistic option.

Gauge distances between all the components, weigh in the time you'd spend stringing wires, and choose accordingly.

Buying and installing the right network adapters

Once you've decided between wired or wireless, buy the matching adapter at your local electronics store. TiVo's extremely conscious of the adapter's brand, model, *and* version number, so head to www.tivo.com/adapters for its latest list of approved wired and wireless adapters. Be sure to note the adapter's specific version number because TiVo doesn't work with all versions. (I bought our TiVo's wireless adapter, the Linksys WUSB11 ver. 2.6, seen in Figure 8-1, through Amazon.)

Figure 8-1: This wireless network adapter plugs into TiVo to connect it with your computer and the Internet, or with another TiVo.

Courtesy of Linksys.

TiVo's adapters are easy to install. Just push the adapter's plug into one of TiVo's USB ports around back. (Leave TiVo turned on.) Keep your wireless adapter's antenna or cable visible; you'll be pushing it around to get a stronger signal, just as early TV owners tweaked the TV's rabbit ears to get a better picture.

Unlike TiVo, PCs usually embrace the cheapest adapter available. They'll use a USB wired or wireless adapter, just like TiVo, or a cheaper, under-the-hood "PCI card" model. If you buy the PCI card to save money, you'll save enough to buy my other book, *Upgrading and Fixing PCs For Dummies,* 6th Edition, from Wiley Publishing, Inc., which explains networking in much more detail.

Mac owners will discover TiVo works fine with Apple Airport wireless equipment.

At the time of this writing, TiVo supports only 802.11b wireless adapters, not the 802.11g (Wireless G) or 802.11a adapters. This technology changes rapidly, so be sure to check TiVo's Web site (www.tivo.com/adapters) before buying an adapter.

Connecting two TiVos *without* a computer network

If you simply want to transfer recorded shows between two TiVos, you don't need a fancy home network *or* a computer; just buy HMO and a network adapter for each TiVo. Here's how to connect the two TiVos so they can share shows, either wired or wireless:

Wired: Plug an approved USB wired network adapter into each TiVo's USB port. Next, connect a special "crossover Ethernet cable" between the two adapters. (Make sure you emphasize the word *crossover* or *crossover patch* cable at the computer store; a regular network cable won't work. Crossover cables are often yellow.) The two TiVos should recognize each other.

Wireless: Plug an approved wireless USB network adapter, like the one shown in Figure 8-1, into each TiVo's USB port. Later, when setting up each TiVo's network settings, choose "Peer to Peer" and choose the same network name and channel for each TiVo. When both TiVos pick up the HMO update through the phone lines, you'll be ready to swap TV shows.

Just connecting two TiVos rules out music and slideshows, but it allows swapping and remote scheduling (when given about 24-hours notice). If you don't have a computer or Internet connection, this might be all you need.

Placing a router at the network's center

At this point, you've added network adapters to TiVo and your computer (or computers). Now, you need something that lets them all share messages and your Internet connection.

Divvying up your Internet connection and routing everything to the right place requires a *router*, naturally. And if you're setting up your first broadband network, there's no question: Buy a wireless router with a built-in switch, similar to the one shown in Figure 8-2. (Note the cool antennas.) Then plug in everything, as I describe in this section. (If you already own a router, jump ahead to the next section.)

Figure 8-2:
A wireless router with a built-in switch connects your computer, TiVo, and a broadband modem, either with or without wires.

Courtesy of Linksys.

Buy a *wireless* router even if you're using a wired network; you may want to add a wireless gadget later, like a second computer or laptop. To safeguard your network's security, turn off the router's wireless feature until you need it.

Routers are advertised by their number of "ports." Buy a model containing enough ports to plug in everything on your network. My router has four ports, for instance, allowing four wired connections in addition to the wireless ones.

Already own a router, but don't have a spare port for your TiVo? Your solution is to buy a "switch" with four or eight ports. Connect the switch's "uplink" port to any port on your router. Then plug the TiVo into one of the switch's ports.

1. **Connect your broadband modem to the wireless router.**

   Examine the router's lineup of numbered network jacks for connecting wired equipment. You'll spot one jack off to one side, usually labeled WAN.

   Unplug your modem's network cable from your computer's network adapter, and plug it into the router's WAN jack. (Cable modem owners usually have to call their ISP and tell them the newly installed router's "MAC address." Another solution that's trickier requires using your router's "clone MAC" feature to "clone" the MAC address of your PC. Check your router's manual for model-specific directions.)

2. **Connect any wired adapters to the router.**

   Using wired network adapters? Run a cable from every adapter to one of the router's numbered ports.

3. **Run the router's setup software on your computer.**

   As you run the router's software on your computer, you'll choose a "name" for your network. As you enter its Wired Equivalent Privacy (WEP) area, be sure to make up your own password.

   Don't use the standard password that came with the router. Be sure to make up your own password. Otherwise, strangers can break into your computer network. For extra safety, change your wireless network's "name" (its "SSID") to something that only you will know.

   As you set up the router, write down these three important things:

   • Your wireless network's "name" (also called SSID) and your encryption password. You should have made up your own SSID and encryption password when setting up the router.

   • Whether your password is "alphanumeric" or "hexadecimal."

   • Write down your password's "encryption level" number (usually either 40, 64, or 128).

You must tell TiVo these three things in the next step so it can connect. (Hide your encryption password under the mattress; you may need it later.)

4. **Run your computer's Internet Connection software on your computers.**

   If you're just adding TiVo to an existing network, ignore this step.

   But if you're setting up a network for the first time, you must tell the computers about your new router. Run Windows XP's "Network Setup Wizard," for instance, and tell it you connect to the Internet through a "residential gateway."

TiVo supports only 802.11b wireless adapters. Those adapters still work with an 802.11g router, but only at 802.11b speeds; the mismatch could slow down the rest of your 802.11g network. To avoid this, use a wired 802.11b adapter on TiVo, and plug that into a wireless 802.11g bridge. The bridge translates the speed difference, thrilling network engineers everywhere.

Connecting TiVo to the home network

Once you've plugged in the network adapters and introduced the new setup to your computer, tell TiVo the good news so it can connect, too. This takes two steps for wireless networks, but only one for wired, so I'll start with wired.

Connect a network cable between TiVo's wired network adapter and one of the router's ports or a port on a switch connected to the router. You're done. Jump ahead to the section on setting up TiVo's TCP/IP settings. Wireless users encounter an extra hurdle, described in the following section.

An encrypting conversation

Most people keep encryption turned off until the entire network talks happily with the router. Once everything works, they return to their router's software and turn on the encryption, known as the Wired Equivalent Privacy (WEP) key.

Why bother turning on wireless security? Because wireless signals travel about 300 feet, most likely reaching neighboring houses. Neighbors might accidentally or deliberately log onto your computer and rummage through your files.

Changing your password every month or so keeps out all but the most dedicated snoops.

Telling TiVo about its wireless connection

Wireless networks, being more complicated than their wired counterparts, require more setup work. To introduce TiVo's wireless adapter's antenna to your router's antenna, follow these steps:

1. **From TiVo Central, choose TiVo Messages & Setup.**

2. **Select Settings, and then select Phone & Network Setup.**

   TiVo displays what it currently knows about your network and adapter, as shown in Figure 8-3.

3. **Select Edit phone or network settings.**

4. **Select Wireless Settings, read the information, and choose Continue to next step.**

   TiVo reminds you that you need the three things you wrote down in the previous section: The network's name and password, password type, and encryption level.

5. **Select the name of the network to use.**

   TiVo displays the names of all the networks it detected. As shown in Figure 8-4, TiVo found two wireless networks — mine, named *Lars*, and a neighbor's, named *linksys*. Be sure to select the name *you* chose when setting up your router's software, or you might connect to a neighbor's network by accident.

Figure 8-3:
TiVo displays what it currently knows about your network and adapter.

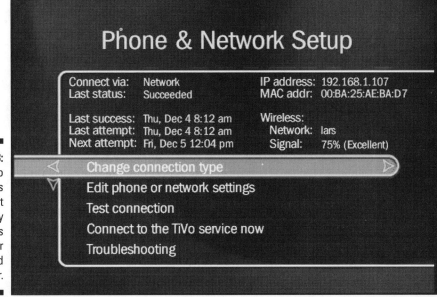

Phone & Network Setup

Connect via: Network	IP address: 192.168.1.107
Last status: Succeeded	MAC addr: 00:BA:25:AE:BA:D7
Last success: Thu, Dec 4 8:12 am	Wireless:
Last attempt: Thu, Dec 4 8:12 am	Network: lars
Next attempt: Fri, Dec 5 12:04 pm	Signal: 75% (Excellent)

◁ Change connection type ▷

Edit phone or network settings

Test connection

Connect to the TiVo service now

Troubleshooting

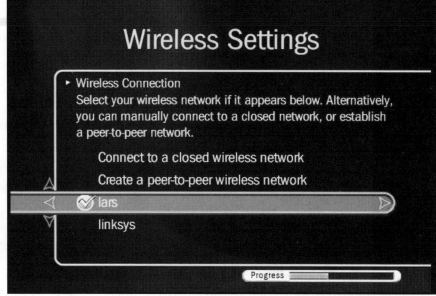

Figure 8-4:
TiVo
displays the
names of
nearby
wireless
networks.

If TiVo doesn't list your network's name, select Connect to a closed wireless network, and enter your network's name.

6. Choose Password Format or no Password.

Hopefully, you remember the wireless *WEP password* you used when setting up the router. TiVo needs to know your password, as well as the *type* of password.

7. Enter the password, and select Done entering text.

Enter the password's numbers and letters with TiVo's remote. (To make letters uppercase or lowercase, use the Thumbs Up/Down buttons.)

TiVo will say, "This network was successfully located" when you've entered the same password settings as you did on your router.

If TiVo can't find your network, don't worry yet. Head back to your router, and turn off its *encryption*. When TiVo is able to locate your network, turn on the router's encryption and return to this section, making sure you tell TiVo the correct password.

8. Choose Accept these settings.

TiVo should immediately locate your wireless network, although it may not work immediately until you set the TCP/IP settings, which I describe next.

Setting up TiVo's TCP/IP settings

Although the words "TCP/IP settings" sound dreadfully complicated, they're really one of the easiest parts of setting up any network, either wired or wireless. Follow these steps for both wired and wireless networks:

1. **From TiVo Central, Select TiVo Messages & Setup.**

2. **Select Settings, and then select Phone & Network Setup.**

   TiVo displays what it currently knows about your network and adapter, as shown earlier in Figure 8-3.

3. **Select Edit phone or network settings.**

4. **Select TCP/IP Settings.**

5. **Choose Obtain IP address automatically or Specify static IP address.**

   Nearly everybody sets up their router to assign the IP addresses automatically, so choose that. If you set up yours using a static IP address for some technical reason, then you're technical enough to choose the static IP address option and set up TiVo that way.

6. **Enter a DHCP Client ID, if you have one.**

   You probably don't have one, so move along by choosing I don't have a DHCP Client ID. (If your ISP required you to set one up, enter the one you set up on your router.)

7. **Make sure TiVo accepts the values.**

   When TiVo flashes a screen like the one shown in Figure 8-5, make sure it says, "These settings appear to be valid." If it doesn't, it's time to check the connections. If you're still stumped, head for the troubleshooting section at this chapter's end.

TIP

Telling TiVo to use your network instead of the phone

When you've completed the "Setting up a home network and connecting TiVo" section, TiVo's finally connected to your computer and the Internet. The Home Media Option should work fine.

But as an added bonus, TiVo can now use your broadband Internet connection to make its daily call to fetch updated show listings, eliminating the need for a phone line near your TV. Your hard work earns you this treat even if you *don't* purchase the Home Media Option.

(continued)

(continued)

To make TiVo start using the network for maintenance, follow these steps:

1. **From TiVo Central, select TiVo Messages & Setup.**

2. **Select Settings, and then select Phone & Network Setup.**

3. **Choose Change connection type and select Network.**

TiVo should stop using your phone, switching to your network, instead. There's one more thing:

If you ever need to repeat TiVo's Guided Setup, usually because you've moved or switched TV providers, stop at the menu where TiVo asks for your phone prefix and enter this:

    ,#401

That secret code overrides Guided Setup's need for a phone line, and tells it to use the Internet instead. Press the remote's Pause button to enter the comma; press the Enter button to enter a pound sign (#).

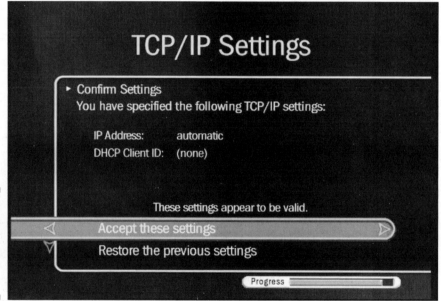

Figure 8-5:
TiVo tests your connection and reports the results.

Purchasing the Home Media Option

Once you've set up your network and seen TiVo flash a "These settings appear to be valid" message, described in the previous section, you know it's safe to buy TiVo's Home Media Option. After your network is set up, installing the Home Media Option is a breeze.

1. **Log onto the TiVo Web site's "Manage My Account" area.**

   TiVo's handy Manage My Account area (`www.tivo.com/manage`) lets you schedule recordings, view billing history, change to a different credit card, or, in this case, buy the Home Media Option.

   If you used TiVo's Web site to Activate your TiVo with a credit card, log on using your same name and password. First-time visitors must create an account.

2. **Buy the Home Media Option and name your TiVo (or TiVos).**

   The Web site asks a few questions, asks for your credit card number, and asks you to choose a name for your TiVo (or TiVos). You'll use those names when transferring shows between two or more TiVos.

   After running your credit card through its computer, the Web site authorizes a download of the Home Media Option software into your TiVo during its next call.

3. **Tell TiVo to download the Home Media Option.**

   Instead of waiting for TiVo to call, make it download the software *now*. Select TiVo Messages & Setup from TiVo Central, and choose Settings. Then select Phone & Network Setup.

   Finally, choose Connect to the TiVo Service now, as shown in Figure 8-6. TiVo connects with TiVo headquarters and automatically grabs and installs its newly sent HMO software. If the update doesn't immediately take place, repeat the process an hour or two later.

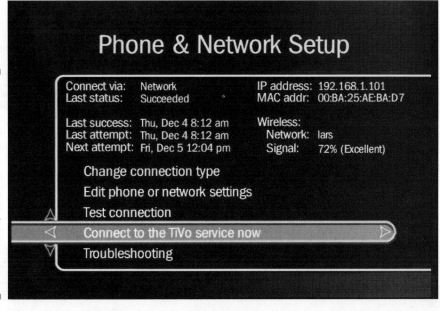

Figure 8-6: Choose Connect to the TiVo Service now; TiVo makes its daily call, picking up your newly purchased HMO software in the process.

TiVo Central offers the first clue to HMO's arrival; it sports a new "Music and Photos" option. But when you open that new menu, you'll only find a few promo songs and generic photos. Where's *your* stuff?

TiVo can't see it because you haven't visited your computer and specifically chosen any music or photos for TiVo to display. To do that, use TiVo Desktop software, covered in the next section.

Installing TiVo Desktop on Your Computer

You don't want TiVo to automatically root around in your computer and put all your photos and songs on display for the entire household. As a convenience and security measure, you must decide what to show and then "publish" it onto the TiVo's onscreen list.

Your publisher comes in the form of the TiVo Desktop software, free for the download at www.tivo.com/desktop. Once downloaded and installed on a PC or Mac, the software lets you pick and choose the folders you want "published" and available for TiVo to use.

While you're downloading the software from TiVo's Web site, download the latest copy of the Home Media Option manual, too. The manual's stored in Adobe PDF format, opened only with Adobe's free Acrobat Reader, available at www.adobe.com/reader.

Feel free to browse the manual while installing TiVo Desktop on your computer. It's full of troubleshooting tips and detailed explanations for more advanced setups.

Once you've installed TiVo Desktop, you've finished the hard work; your network's complete. In Chapter 9, I explain how to publish your music and photos with TiVo Desktop and play them on your TiVo.

Troubleshooting the Home Media Option

When a network's up and running, it doesn't require much work. But if it's not working yet, fixing it involves running through a series of steps to isolate and repair the problem.

Start by turning off the encryption and password on both your router and TiVo. Passwords are designed to keep things away from people, and right now, you're trying to get *in*.

Then run through the following steps, in order. Once your network's finally working, turn encryption back on. (And if the encryption breaks the network, you know you're entering your password wrong on the TiVo.)

1. **Check the wireless signal strength.**

   Because a wireless adapter relies on radio waves to pick up the signal, TiVo always displays the adapter's current signal strength. To see it, open TiVo Central and select Messages & Setup. Choose Settings and then Phone & Network Setup. See the strength percentage listed near the top of Figures 8-3 and 8-6?

   If TiVo doesn't show Excellent strength, try these things:

   - Slowly move the wireless adapter in different positions around the TiVo. TiVo updates the signal strength only every few seconds, so move slowly, stop to read the signal strength, and repeat until you've found the best spot. Most wireless adapters prefer a fully extended antenna that points straight up.

   - Wireless signals don't like walls, and they travel best when unobstructed. Can you line up the two at the ends of a long hallway? Can you move one closer to the other?

   - If the signal simply won't reach, buy a wireless signal booster to sit between the TiVo and the router. The booster serves as a telephone pole, keeping the signal connected.

2. **Check the network adapters and cables.**

   Make sure you're using an approved adapter listed on TiVo's Web site at www.tivo.com/adapters. If you have some leftover network cables, try swapping them to check for bad cables.

   Every network adapter comes with a secret number known as a MAC address that it sends to everything it connects with. (Short for *Media Access Control*, MAC has nothing to do with Macintosh computers.) If TiVo can't read its network adapter's MAC address, then it's not communicating with the adapter.

   To see if TiVo's reading its adapter's MAC address, choose TiVo Messages & Setup from TiVo Central. Select Settings, and choose Phone & Network Setup. No MAC address listed? That means TiVo can't recognize its adapter, and you've found your problem.

   Make sure all the network and USB cables are pushed in firmly.

3. **Restart TiVo.**

   TiVo's essentially a computer; sometimes a restart cures the strangest problems. Start at TiVo Central to restart TiVo. Select Messages & Setup, and then choose Restart or Reset System. Choose Restart the DVR, and, to show TiVo you mean it, press Thumbs Down three times, followed by the Enter key.

   Restarting TiVo doesn't erase your recordings; it simply turns off TiVo and starts it up again.

4. **Examine the network's parts, and restart them.**

   Is the router turned on? The computer? Make sure they're all plugged in, as well as any other network gadgetry. Are the lights blinking? (Blinking lights mean they're talking; no lights mean problems.)

   Unplug the router and cable modem, wait about 30 seconds, and plug them in again. Restart your computer, too, for good measure.

5. **Check the network's settings.**

   Now that you've ruled out the obvious things, start picking at details. Run through TiVo's network setup menus again. Make sure encryption's turned off. (Turn it back on when everything works correctly.)

6. **Check the more complicated settings used by wireless.**

   Wireless menus ask you to create a name (SSID) for your wireless network; others come set to a default name, like LINKSYS. Make sure all wireless equipment uses the same name, especially the router and the TiVo.

   Make sure you've told the TiVo and router to "Obtain an IP Address Automatically." Don't use a Static IP address on your network unless you know what you're doing.

7. **Grasp at straws.**

   As a last resort, visit the Web sites for your router and other networking equipment and check the version of their downloadable *firmware* — the internal software that makes them work. (The router's setup menu displays the current firmware version number.) Companies routinely post updated firmware versions that correct small problems; the newest firmware might fix yours.

   - Visit some of the Web sites listed in Chapter 13. Many TiVo users frequent these places, answering user questions. TiVo's customer support may be able to help, too.

   - If you simply don't like the Home Media Option, or can't make it work, TiVo will refund your money, as long as your TiVo subscription is still good. To arrange a refund, call TiVo Customer Support at 877-367-8486.

Chapter 9

Putting TiVo's Home Media Option to Work

*T*he Home Media Option lets TiVo make friends with your computer. When you tell your computer what items to share, TiVo dutifully places them on its handy menus.

Your PC can't share video with TiVo or vice versa, however; HMO isn't *that* cool yet. Still, TiVo expands the viewing potential of your digital photo library. Plus, if you're a digital music lover, you'll love turning TiVo into a digital jukebox, playing your computer's music through your home stereo.

HMO also hands TiVo an Internet portal, letting you schedule recordings from work, an airport's computer lounge, or an Internet café in Istanbul. Own two TiVos? The Home Media Option lets you send shows back and forth, effectively doubling your TiVo's storage capacity.

Whether you're interested in digital photos, digital music, remote scheduling, or TiVo transfers, this chapter explains how to make it all work.

Scheduling Recordings through the Web

After a few months of TiVo, you'll rarely worry about missing shows. You tell TiVo what you want, and TiVo automatically grabs them; case closed. But what happens if you hear about an exciting new show when you're away from home? How can you tell TiVo to record something when you're on vacation, visiting a friend, or at work?

TiVo's Remote Scheduling feature places your TiVo within earshot of any Internet connection. TiVo's Web site lets you search by show name, title, actor, or director. When you locate your show and select it, the Web site routes your request to your TiVo. TiVo records it — with as little as 15 minutes notice, if your TiVo connects through broadband.

Here's how to make Remote Scheduling work as promised:

1. **Purchase and install TiVo's Home Media Option.**

   I describe purchase and installation details in Chapter 8.

2. **Log on to "TiVo Central Online" at TiVo's Web site.**

   When the buzz of that "can't miss" new show vibrates your ears, head to "TiVo Central Online" (www.tivo.com/tco). Log on using the e-mail address/password combination you used when purchasing the Home Media Option. (Lost them already? The nearby sidebar explains your options.)

   TiVo Central Online appears, as shown in Figure 9-1. The site already knows a little about your TiVo — what you named it when signing up for HMO, for instance. (Names help identify individual TiVos in two-TiVo households.) Figure 9-1 reveals we've dubbed our TiVo "Upstairs."

3. **Search for and select your upcoming program.**

   TiVo Central Online allows the same searches as TiVo's menus: show title, keyword, actor, or director. Enter your search, click Go, and TiVo Central Online scans the next seven days of listings. For instance, Figure 9-2 shows the results for upcoming Audrey Hepburn movies.

   Choose the program you'd like to record. In this case, I chose the Saturday morning showing of "Breakfast at Tiffany's." (My wife's reading the book.)

   TiVo Central Online's Browse by Channel option lets you view a day's listings for any channel you receive, up to seven days in advance.

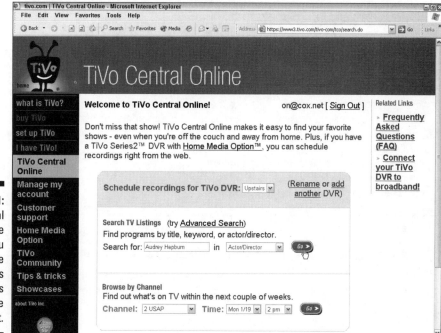

Figure 9-1:
TiVo Central
Online
lets you
schedule
your TiVo's
recordings
on the
Internet.

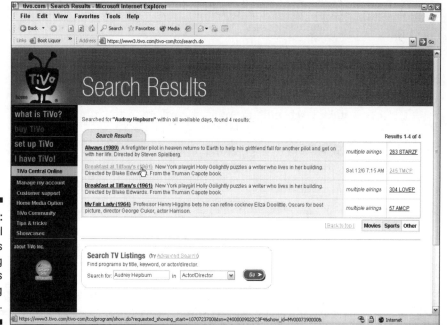

Figure 9-2:
TiVo Central
Online lists
upcoming
shows
matching
your search.

TiVo's Web site won't let me in!

Forgot your password? Never logged on before? In either case, visit the Web site's Manage My Account area (www.tivo.com/manage) to fix things. Click the Register button and enter the e-mail address you used when Activating TiVo; you'll receive a temporary password. Enter your new temporary password at the Manage My Account login screen, and you can choose a permanent password. Stash this one under the mattress with everything else.

E-mail address changed or perhaps forgotten? Head to TiVo's Manage My Account area (www.tivo.com/manage). By entering your TiVo's Service Number and other information, you can add your new e-mail address to the Web site.

Tired of dealing with machines? Call TiVo Customer Support at (877) 367-8486 between 8:00 AM and 8:00 PM PST.

4. **Verify your recording time, and choose Record this episode.**

   When you choose a show, TiVo lists its description and first upcoming airing, as shown in Figure 9-3. Any upcoming showings appear in a list below the description.

   Click the Record this episode button to tell TiVo to record that particular airing of the show.

   Because the selected show airs in only six hours, the top of the Web site warns, "May not record." If my TiVo used a dial-up modem, this recording request probably wouldn't arrive in time. But because our TiVo connects through a broadband connection, the request will arrive in plenty of time. (It did.)

5. **Set your recording options, and then click Schedule It.**

   TiVo's Remote Schedule has one basic flaw: It doesn't know if you've already scheduled another recording for that time slot. And it won't discover any conflicts until it talks to your TiVo.

   To deal with this potential problem, the Web site asks *you* what it should do, as shown in Figure 9-4:

   • Only record if nothing else conflicts.

   • Cancel other programs if necessary.

   Requests made over the Internet usually carry a sense of urgency, so if you absolutely *must* see this exciting show, choose Cancel other programs if necessary. (You can probably pick up anything cancelled, whatever it was, on a rerun.)

If you're reluctant about canceling a scheduled recording, check out any upcoming showings for that program. Send in a request for one that airs during the wee hours, when you're less likely to be recording something else.

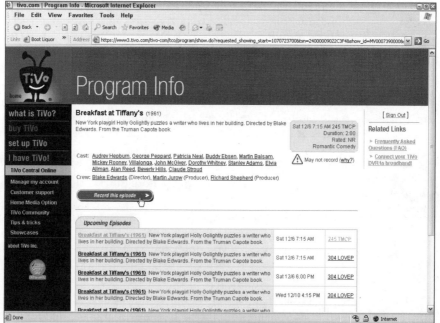

Figure 9-3:
To schedule the recording request, choose Record this episode.

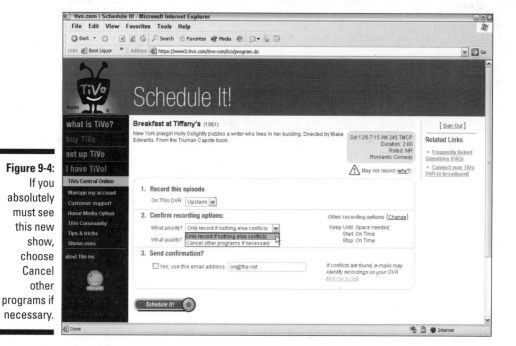

Figure 9-4:
If you absolutely must see this new show, choose Cancel other programs if necessary.

✔ If you have an hour or so, fix the dilemma by choosing "Send Confirmation" to receive your TiVo's response by e-mail. If TiVo says there's a conflict, you'll know which show is at risk, letting you tailor your next recording request. With a few e-mail exchanges, you can usually schedule what you want and minimize the damage.

✔ TiVo's Web site sends requests using your TiVo's default recording quality and options. Feel free to choose "Change" under "Other recording options" to change the recording quality, pad the show's start and stop times, or change its deletion date.

✔ Trapped in a boring conference call? Use that wireless laptop to browse upcoming show listings on TiVo Central Online. Your computer keyboard flips through show listings much more quickly than "thumbing" the letters with TiVo's remote.

✔ TiVo Central Online knows the channels your TiVo can receive, but it doesn't know whether you subscribe to them all. For instance, the Web site lists HBO even if you don't subscribe to HBO. If you accidentally choose a non-subscribed channel, TiVo's e-mail confirmation exposes your gaffe.

✔ With a broadband Internet connection, you can send in recordings quickly, catching shows that air in just 15 minutes. Without broadband, your Remote Scheduling request won't arrive until your TiVo makes its next phone call — up to 30 hours later.

✔ If you're using a cookie manager on your Internet browser, you must allow TiVo.com to use cookies.

Publishing Music and Photos to TiVo

TiVo Desktop software, described in Chapter 8, lets you *publish* — a fancy word for *list* — your computer's music and photo folders on TiVo, where they're as easy to reach as TV shows.

You'll find TiVo Desktop very easy to use, either from a single computer or from several computers on a network. Making a file accessible to TiVo is as simple as dragging and dropping it. It works like this:

1. **Open TiVo Desktop.**

    When installed as discussed in Chapter 8, TiVo Desktop appears as a little TiVo icon near your clock. Double-click the icon to bring TiVo Desktop within view.

If the icon's not in view, you'll find TiVo Desktop on the Start menu's All Programs area.

2. **Click the tab describing what you want to publish: Music or Photos.**

   TiVo Desktop separates song and photo files into their own areas, each accessible with their own tab. To publish music, for instance, click the Music tab, shown in Figure 9-5. (By itself, TiVo and the TiVo Desktop only publishes MP3 files; some third-party software covered in Chapter 10 uses special tricks to overcome this limitation.)

   The top of TiVo Desktop shows the music files on your computer; below, it shows the music files currently published on TiVo. (Click the Photo tab, and TiVo switches the view to your photo files.)

3. **To publish a file or folder, drag it from TiVo Desktop's top half to its bottom half.**

   Any music or photos you drop onto TiVo Desktop's bottom portion appear on your TiVo's menu. Feel free to drop individual files or entire folders. (Dropping a folder also publishes all the folders within it.)

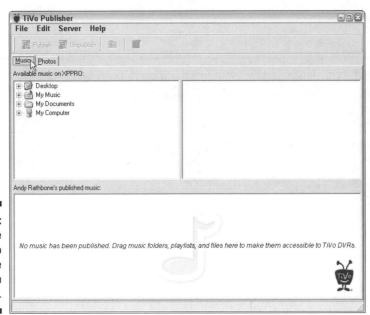

Figure 9-5:
Click the Music tab to list some music on your TiVo.

Figure 9-6, for instance, shows that I've given TiVo access to all the music from these folders: Phish, Robben Ford, St Germain, and the Allman Brothers. At the list's bottom sits one Jimi Hendrix song, "Hey Joe."

To publish all your music and photos in Windows XP, for instance, drag and drop your My Music and My Pictures folders onto their respective tab areas.

Anything you publish appears immediately on TiVo's "Music and Photos" menu, ready to be played or viewed.

4. **To remove a single file or folder, right-click it and choose Unpublish.**

To remove accidentally published material, right-click its name from the Published list and choose Unpublish. It immediately disappears from the published list, as well as from your TiVo.

To temporarily suspend publishing, don't unpublish everything. Instead, choose Pause from TiVo Desktop's Server menu. To put everything back in place, choose Start/Resume from the same menu.

Figure 9-6:
TiVo now has access to songs by Phish, Robben Ford, St Germain, and the Allman Brothers, as well as the song, "Hey Joe."

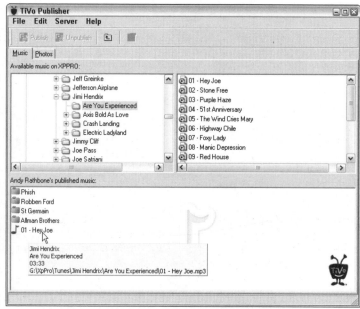

- Sitting at a network? TiVo Desktop lets you publish your own files, as well as shared files on networked computers. Or, if you wish, place a copy of TiVo Desktop on every computer on your network. My wife's computer publishes all our photos, for instance; I publish our music from my computer.

- To see or hear the file you're about to publish, double-click its name from within TiVo Publisher. The program quickly plays your song or displays your photo, helping you make your publishing decision.

- If you inadvertently leave TiVo paused on a song, your computer may not let you move or change that song or folder. To undo TiVo's "lock," press the TiVo button; TiVo jumps to TiVo Central, quickly releasing your file.

- TiVo Desktop won't list any "hidden" files or folders on your computer, effectively stopping you from publishing them. Click the Hide attribute on a song or picture you *don't* want to publish, and TiVo still lists the other items in that folder.

Publishing songs and photos on a Macintosh

Publishing songs and photos on a Macintosh works differently than on a PC.

1. **From the Apple menu, click System Preferences.**

2. **Under Other, click TiVo Desktop.**

3. **Click Start to begin publishing content.**

4. **To publish music, select Publish my music from the Music tab.**

   Select Publish my entire iTunes Library to list all your music on TiVo. Or, to publish a few playlists, select Publish only these playlists, selecting the playlists you want published. (TiVo can't list or play AAC files, even if they're published; TiVo handles only MP3 files.)

5. **To publish photos, select Publish my photos from the Photos tab.**

   Select Publish my entire iPhoto Library to publish your whole iPhoto library. To publish just a few photo albums, select Publish only these albums, and select each album you want published.

   Problems? Make sure you've installed iPhoto 2 and iTunes 3.0 or later. You'll also need iTunes or iPhoto to create or change your playlists and albums.

Fiddling with TiVo Desktop

Choose "TiVo Properties" from TiVo Desktop's Server menu for under-the-skin access to the program's inner workings. Several useful goodies await you.

✔ The IP address TiVo uses to access your network — a big help when troubleshooting.

✔ A toggle for automatically loading TiVo Desktop when you start your computer.

✔ Multi-TiVo households can keep one or several TiVos from accessing published material.

If you're having trouble with your network, check TiVo's IP address with your router logs to monitor the connection.

Viewing Digital Photos on TiVo

Once you've published your music and/or photo files with TiVo Desktop, TiVo dutifully lists them on the screen, just like your recorded TV shows. TiVo offers several tricks when displaying photos, including customized slideshows. Here's how to display your computerized shoebox of photos on your TV screen.

1. **Choose Music & Photos on TiVo Central.**

   A software update, received shortly after you purchased the Home Media Option, offers the first sign that HMO has arrived: TiVo Central sports a new "Music & Photos" item, shown in Figure 9-7.

   Choose the Music & Photos menu to see everything published by TiVo Desktop.

2. **Choose your computer from the list.**

   TiVo lists each networked computer that offers published music or photos. As shown in Figure 9-8, my wife's computer, CLEMENTINE, published some photos; my computer, XPPRO, published both music and photos. Every month or so, the TiVo company dumps some music and photo promos in the "TiVo Online" area.

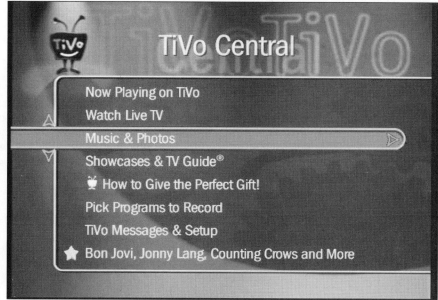

Figure 9-7:
Visit TiVo
Central's
"Music &
Photos"
item to
begin
playing
music and
viewing
photos
from your
computer.

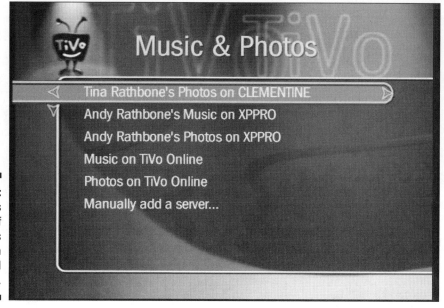

Figure 9-8:
TiVo lists
names of
computers
with
published
material.

TiVo lists your computer by its network name; your name reflects your computer's user name. (You can't change the names from within TiVo or TiVo Desktop; you must change them from your computer's menus.)

Select a computer's name to see the goodies it offers.

3. **Navigate to the appropriate folder.**

When you select a computer's name, TiVo lists the computer's published files and folders. For instance, Figure 9-9 shows that Tina has published her entire "My Pictures" folder, granting TiVo access to every folder inside it. (Sharp-eyed readers looking along the screen's bottom will notice that TiVo's currently displaying the folders by their date, rather than in alphabetical order.)

To see a folder's contents, select it with the remote. TiVo displays pictures as thumbnails, as shown in Figure 9-10.

4. **Highlight a photo and press Play to view it.**

Highlighting a photo and pressing Play fills the TV screen with that photo, as shown in Figure 9-11.

Should you find yourself viewing a photo taken sideways, press TiVo's Instant Replay button. TiVo quickly rotates the photo 90 degrees. Repeat as necessary.

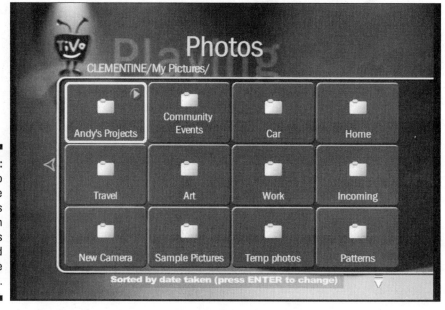

Figure 9-9: TiVo displays the computer's folders, with a folder's path listed along the top.

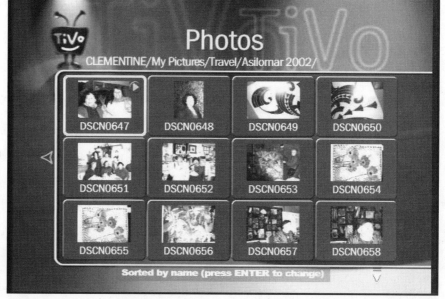

Figure 9-10:
TiVo
displays
thumbnails
of each
photo in a
selected
folder.

Figure 9-11:
Highlight a
photo and
press Play
to view it.

5. **Press Play on a currently viewed picture to start a slideshow.**

   Pressing Play on a currently viewed picture or slideshow starts a slideshow of that picture's folder.

   ✔ Press Enter any time to change your slideshow options. You can control each picture's viewing time, as well as whether photos should repeat endlessly, include subfolders, display alphabetically, or display at random.

   ✔ To see different display options for a particular thumbnailed photo, press Select instead of Play. TiVo lets you view, rotate, or start a slideshow with that picture.

   ✔ Rotating a photo only rotates it on the TV screen; it doesn't rotate the original file that's stored on your computer. In fact, your TiVo can't delete or change any files on your computer.

    ✔ Stuck at the top of a long list of files? Press the Jump to End (Advance) button, and TiVo jumps straight to your vacation photo folder from Zambia.

Playing MP3s on TiVo

Before TiVo, MP3s only rocked from your computer or your MP3 player. Neither one boasted great sound. And neither hooked up easily with the stereo. HMO turns TiVo into your personal jukebox, making it easy to find the right tunes at the right times. I love finding just the right album for dinner.

TiVo sounds best, of course, when hooked up to your home stereo, covered in Chapter 3. TiVo lets you play songs the same way you display photos.

1. **Choose Music & Photos.**

   Select Music & Photos from TiVo Central.

2. **Choose your computer from the list.**

   Single-computer households see only one computer; on networks, choose the computer that published the music you want.

3. **Navigate to the appropriate folder.**

   Push the Arrow buttons to move between folders; press Select to open a folder.

4. **Play the song or folder.**

   Press Play on a folder to play *everything* inside. Press Play on a single song to play that song, followed by the rest of the folder's songs.

   Organizing a large MP3 or photo collection takes some work, as I discuss in the next chapter. Hopefully you've kept the songs for each artist or album in their own folder. (TiVo may tucker out if you've stuffed a few thousand folders into a single folder.)

5. **Press Enter for options.**

   While playing a song, TiVo offers the same options as with slide shows: repeat playing the folder's songs, shuffle the songs when playing, and whether or not to include subfolders.

   ✔ Stuck in the middle of a drum solo? To find out when a jam session will end, press Play. Up pops the familiar green Status Bar, pointing out the song's beginning, end, and your current location.

   ✔ The remote's Volume controls the loudness; you can't turn it up or down from your computer.

   ✔ Stuck at the top of a long list of files? Press the Jump to End (Advance) button, and TiVo jumps right to Zappa.

Sharing Shows between Two TiVos

Copying shows from one TiVo to another is pretty simple; the problem is the amount of time a transfer needs. Transfers usually happen in *real-time*, a fancy way of saying that a two-hour show takes two hours (or even longer) to transfer.

Luckily, you can begin watching a show on one TiVo as soon as you begin sending it on the other.

To begin a transfer, head for the TiVo that needs to receive the show.

1. **From the "receiving" TiVo, locate the show on the "sending" TiVo.**

   You'll see your other TiVo's name at the bottom of the Now Playing list. Select that TiVo's name to see its list of recorded shows.

2. **Select the show you want to watch and choose Watch on this TV.**

   Spot the show you want? Select it, and choose Watch on this TV; TiVo begins sending the show.

   You can begin watching immediately, but a slow transfer may force you to pause, waiting for more of the show to arrive before watching again.

- Shows recorded at lower visual quality transfer more quickly than shows recorded at the high-quality setting. Also, a wired network transfers faster than wireless. (I explain in Chapter 8 how to set up both wired and wireless networks.)

- If a TiVo's already transferring one or more shows, it places the new transfer request on its To Do list and sends the show when it has time.

- When transferring shows, you're *copying* them, not moving them. Once you've transferred the entire movie, feel free to delete the original from the other TiVo machine, if you want.

- Never delete a show before it's completely transferred to the other TiVo, or you'll cut off the end of the show.

- Sure, your friends can bring their TiVos to your place. They can even hook them up to your network. But they can't siphon off your latest "Sopranos" episodes. TiVos must be registered in *your* name before they'll share. You can't even share shows with a roommate's TiVo. Specifically, TiVos must both be on the same account and the same network subnet to share shows.

- Feel free to rename your TiVo or TiVos by heading to Manage My Account (www.tivo.com/manage) on TiVo's Web site and choosing "DVR Preferences."

Tips and Shortcuts for Music and Photos

Dog-ear this page and keep the book handy for when you're playing music (Table 9-1) or viewing digital photos (Table 9-2). You'll find yourself using these keys over and over, even if you can't remember them.

Table 9-1	Remote Shortcuts for Playing Music
Press This . . .	*To Do This . . .*
Play	Play a song or all songs inside a folder.
Channel Up	Press once to go to the beginning of a song. Press twice to go to the previous song.
Channel Down	Jump to the next song.
Select	Open a folder or display song options.
Fast-Forward/Rewind	Fast-forward or rewind the current song.

Press This . . .	To Do This . . .
Instant Replay	Quickly rewind a song by eight seconds.
Right Arrow	Display information about the currently playing song.
Clear	Clear the screen of everything.

Table 9-2	Remote Shortcuts for Viewing Photos
Remote Key	**Function**
Enter	Select different options for browsing and slide show displays.
Play	Display current photo.
	Press twice on a highlighted folder to play a slide show of that folder's photos.
Channel Up	Jump to previous photo.
Channel Down	Jump to next photo.
Select	Open folder or display options for a photo.
Fast-Forward/Rewind	Play slide show faster or slower.
Instant Replay	Rotate displayed photo 90 degrees.
Right Arrow	Display banner during slide show.
Clear	Clear screen of extra menus.

Chapter 10

Fancy Home Media Option Tricks

· ·

In This Chapter

▶ Organizing music and photo files for easy TiVo access

▶ Playing Internet radio stations on TiVo

▶ Making playlists for special events

▶ Finding other software to expand the Home Media Option

· ·

*T*he TiVo Desktop software included with TiVo's Home Media Option (HMO) simply dumps your computer's files and folders onto TiVo's menus, with nary a thought to organization. If you're accustomed to "mousing around" to find the digital camera photos you've tossed into your "My Pictures" folder, you'll do the same on TiVo, only while holding an awkward remote.

The same holds true for all the music files in your MP3 collection. TiVo's only as organized as what your computer throws at it.

You have two options to make your files easier to retrieve from TiVo: Organize your photo and music files yourself, sorting everything into proper folders. Or, you can bring in the hired help by installing one of a number of programs designed to organize your awkward bundle of information and present it to TiVo in a thoughtful way that only requires a few thumb pokes to access.

Some of these programs whip out music playlists to match any mood; others publish certain sets of photos on the fly: everything shot during last summer's trip to Budapest, for instance.

This chapter explains both approaches. It shows how to organize your own files, and it presents the resumes of the hired help, letting you know what to expect, should you let them in the door.

Organizing Your Computer's Files for TiVo

When it comes to TiVo, Apple users have it easy. Apple computers include built-in music and photo organizers — iTunes and iPhoto. Better yet, Apple and TiVo joined heads to integrate TiVo technology into both programs. Apple users can publish music playlists and photo albums at the push of a button, as seen in Figure 10-1.

Microsoft, by contrast, snubbed TiVo as a competitor to its own media-related software offerings. Windows Media Player doesn't integrate with TiVo, forcing users to scramble for alternatives.

The next few sections explain how to manually organize your computer's music and photo files on Windows so they're fairly easy to fetch from TiVo and its remote. If spending the afternoon organizing computer files doesn't excite you, don't bother. Just jump ahead to this chapter's section on third-party programs that automatically organize your information and serve it up to TiVo.

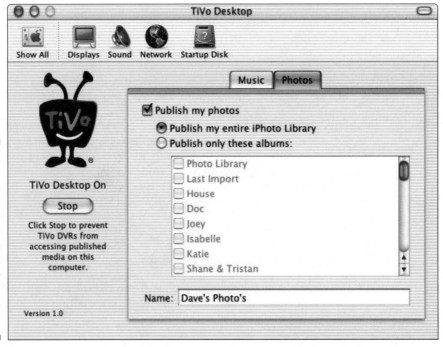

Figure 10-1:
TiVo and Apple worked together to integrate TiVo access into the popular iTunes and iPhoto programs.

Grab the HMO manual!

Believe it or not, TiVo's Home Media Option comes with a manual — and you don't even have to buy HMO to take a peek at HMO's details. To grab the manual, head for TiVo's Guides area (www.tivo.com/guides) and look for the Home Media Option Premium Features Guide. The 70-page, indexed guide spells out the Home Media Option features in detail. It's well worth the download.

The manual's stored in Adobe Acrobat "PDF" format. If necessary, you can download Adobe Acrobat's free reader at Adobe's Web site (www.adobe.com/acrobat).

While visiting TiVo's Guides area, feel free to download a copy of your TiVo's manual. (The electronic version comes in handy when the paper manual disappears behind the couch.)

Organizing your own music files

Just as there's no perfect breakfast, there's no perfect way to organize music files. Instead of aiming for perfection, I'll describe the method that works well on both my computer and TiVo.

I create a new folder for every artist's name, sorted by their entire name: "Count Basie" warrants his own folder, for instance, not "Basie, Count." Inside each artist's folder, I create a folder for each of their releases. My folder for Stevie Ray Vaughan and Double Trouble, for example, looks like Figure 10-2.

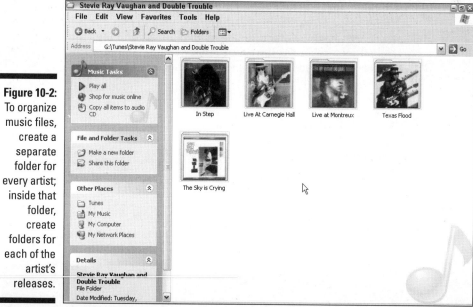

Figure 10-2: To organize music files, create a separate folder for every artist; inside that folder, create folders for each of the artist's releases.

Create "Various" folders as needed to handle CDs where two or more artists team up. If Bob Dylan and Britney Spears team up for a funk CD called "Jive," store the songs in a "Jive" folder in your "Various Funk" folder. To make the CD easy to find, place a shortcut to the "Jive" folder in both Bob's and Britney's folders.

The TiVo remote's Play button subsequently becomes a powerful way to play *everything* by an artist. Highlight Bob Dylan's folder, for instance, press Play, and TiVo plays every CD inside Bob Dylan's folder. (The shortcut even tells TiVo to play Bob and Britney's CD.)

- ✔ I name all my song files by track number, a hyphen, and song name. Stevie Ray Vaughan's song "Crossfire," for instance, appears as `02 – Crossfire`. Since TiVo plays songs in alphabetical order, pressing Play on a CD's folder plays the songs in the order they appeared on the CD. (TiVo places numbers before letters when sorting alphabetically, so TiVo starts by playing the song with the numbers "01.")

- ✔ To place a picture of the CD's cover on the folder, as seen in Figure 10-2, find a picture of the cover online — Amazon (`www.amazon.com`) shows covers for most releases, for instance. Right-click the picture, choose Copy, and Paste the album cover's image file into your folder. Finally, rename the file with the simple name `folder`. Windows XP subsequently displays that picture on the CD's folder when in Thumbnail view.

- ✔ Even with the Home Media Option, TiVo can't display photos while playing music. So it can't show your CD's cover while playing that CD's songs, for instance.

- ✔ TiVo supports *only* MP3 files. People with music stored in WMA (Windows Media Player's preferred format) will need a third-party program, discussed later in this chapter. (When you play the WMA file, those programs quickly convert the file to MP3 format and feed the results to TiVo without delay.) At the time of this writing, TiVo does not support the AAC format offered by the Apple iTunes Music Store and iPod.

Tagging your files

When TiVo plays a song from your computer, it displays the artist's name, song title, length, album, and other information, as seen in Figure 10-3. But sometimes TiVo doesn't display that information for every song; occasionally, it even displays the *wrong* information. Why?

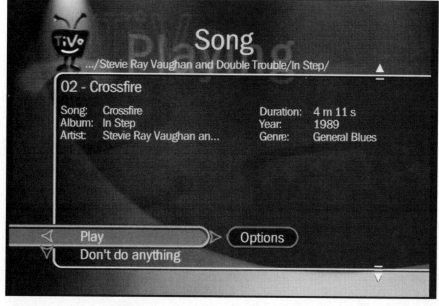

Figure 10-3:
TiVo uses
a music
file's _tag_
information
to display its
information.

TiVo only reads the information buried _inside_ the music file, in a storage area known as a "tag" or "ID3 tag." When filled out properly, the tag lists everything seen in Figure 10-3. Sometimes the tag contains even _more_ information — comments, for instance, or the song's genre and track number.

Nothing beats a music collection with complete "tag" information. Just about every song organizer — including TiVo — relies on accurate tags to recognize and sort your songs.

Windows XP recognizes tags; Windows XP's Media Player 9 even identifies songs and fills out the tag for you automatically, if you want. Sometimes, however, even Media Player won't fill out a tag properly. In that case, here's a quick way to fill out a tag manually in Windows XP.

1. **Right-click the music file's name and choose Properties.**

   Windows XP brings up the file's Properties window, but doesn't yet display the tag information.

2. **Click the Summary tab along the top.**

   Windows XP displays the file's tag information, seen in Figure 10-4. (If you don't see the tag information, click the window's Advanced button to display it.)

Figure 10-4:
Windows
XP places a
built-in MP3
tag editor in
each music
file's
Properties
area.

3. **Click the tag line that needs changing, and fill it out properly.**

   Change any lines within the Music and Description areas. You can correct or add a song's title, for instance, or enter information about a
   track, artist, genre, and several other items.

4. **Click OK to save your changes and close the window.**

   Done? Click OK to save your changes, and repeat with other files lacking
   proper ID.

   ✔ Don't try to edit a song's tag while TiVo's currently playing or displaying
     it. Your computer and TiVo will bicker, keeping you from editing the tag.

   ✔ You'll occasionally want to apply the same change to many files —
     giving them all the same artist's name or genre, for instance. To do that
     quickly, highlight all the files that need changes, right click one and
     choose Properties. Any change you make will be applied to all the high-
     lighted files.

   ✔ Windows XP Media Player 9 includes a more full-featured tag editor.
     Right-click the file to change and select Advanced Tag Editor from the
     menu. Media Player doesn't stick to recognized standards, unfortu-
     nately, so other tag editors probably won't recognize the additional
     information.

✔ The Internet's stuffed with hundreds of tag editing programs. ID3-TagIT (`www.id3-tagit.de`) boasts plenty of power, but everybody has his own favorite. I like MP3 Tag Tools (`http://massid3lib.sourceforge.net`). Winamp (`www.winamp.com`) plays MP3 files, fill out tags automatically, lets you edit tags yourself, and plays Internet Radio stations from Shoutcast (`www.shoutcast.com`).

✔ MP3 tags come in several versions. The Web site "ID3v2" (`www.id3.org`) contains lots of information about ID tags, their history, their use, and ways developers can use them.

Creating your own playlists

When you want to hear certain songs in a certain order, you need a *playlist* — a file listing each song's location and order, along with enough code to keep computers happy. When TiVo reads the playlist, it finds the songs and plays them back the way you asked.

Windows Media Player creates playlists and can save them in the format TiVo understands — but only when you ask it to. (It can convert old playlists to a TiVo-compatible format, too.) Here's how to ask the right way:

1. **Open Windows Media Player and choose Media Library.**

   Media Player immediately displays all songs, video, and other goodies.

2. **Choose New Playlist from the File menu, and create a new playlist.**

   When the window pops up, click on songs in the order you'd like to play them. Double-click an artist's name to see their CDs; double-click a CD's name to see its songs, as seen in Figure 10-5.

Figure 10-5:
Click a file's name to add it to the playlist; name the playlist to save it.

Delete highlighted songs by clicking the red X; click either the Up or Down Arrow to change a highlighted song's playing order.

3. Name the playlist and click OK.

Done setting the order? Enter a name in the "Playlist Name" box and click the OK button for Windows to save your file.

4. Save the file as an M3U playlist and publish it.

Highlight your newly created Playlist file, choose Save As from the File menu, and save it as an M3U Playlist (*.m3u). Media Player normally saves files in WPL format, and makes TiVo choke and refuse to list them.

✔ Playlists take a little time to create, but they're fun to whip up for parties or special events. Be sure to store them in their own published Playlists folder so they're easy to grab on the fly.

✔ To avoid repeats, don't store playlists in folders with songs. If you store Neil Young's "Harvest" playlist in the same folder as the Harvest CD's songs, for example, TiVo will play that CD *twice* — once for the folder's songs and again when it reaches the playlist.

✔ If you move any song in a playlist, edit the playlist to show the song's new location. When TiVo discovers a missing song in a playlist, it ignores your faux pas, moving quickly to the next song.

✔ TiVo handles playlists stored in the M3U (most players), PLS (Winamp), ASX (Microsoft), and B4S (Winamp) formats. It doesn't like Media Player 9's new WPL format, unfortunately.

Playing Internet radio stations on TiVo

Even for people without huge MP3 file stashes, the Home Media Option can bring a *huge* variety of music into your living room through Internet radio. The secret is simply hiding the station's broadcast location — *its IP address and port* — within an M3U standard playlist.

It's easy for Mac users to publish an Internet radio station on TiVo; they simply drag the radio station link over to a published playlist, then see if TiVo can handle the station. Windows users have it a little rougher. They must save the station's IP address in an M3U file. For example, here's a playlist that makes TiVo play an Internet radio station called "Secret Agent Radio" (www.somafm.com):

```
#EXTm3U
    #EXTINF:,Secret Agent Radio
    http://205.188.245.130:8010
```

To create your own Internet Radio station playlist, replace the boldfaced words and numbers with your own favorite station's name and IP address and port. The easiest way to locate this information for stations is with Shoutcast (www.shoutcast.com) and the program Winamp (www.winamp.com).

To find a station's IP broadcast address, head to Shoutcast and begin playing it in Winamp, Shoutcast's recommended media player software. Right-click the station's name as it plays, and choose File Info. Winamp lists the address at the very top. Save that address as an M3U file using the format above, publish it, and you're ready to listen.

One caveat: TiVo's finicky about its broadcast streams. Lengthy broadcast streams like `http://205.188.245.130/stream/1015` won't work, as TiVo can't handle the word `stream` in the address. If your station broadcasts in a different format, you might want to consider some of the third-party Home Media Option enhancers I cover in this chapter.

Organizing photos

Since pictures are worth a thousand words, how can anybody possibly create a descriptive filing system? Photos are *much* more difficult to categorize than music. Most feature groups of people, for instance, ruling out the "separate folder for each person" method.

Most photos revolve around four main areas — People, Places, Events, and Home — so I've created those four folders as a starting point, splitting them into subfolders when needed. People, for instance, is divvied up between Friends and Relatives. Home is split into Inside and Outside. Events is split up into Holidays, Parties, Travel and Other.

Keeping photos sorted by these main categories gives me a place to begin when searching for that long-lost photo; it usually only takes a few clicks or remote pokes to find what I'm after.

✔ Many digital cameras "stamp" a digital photo's file with information about the camera's settings, including date and time you took the picture. To keep that stamp accurate, be sure to set your digital camera's clock every time you change its battery. TiVo can sort your photos by date taken (or alphabetically), making them much easier to find.

✔ When you tell TiVo to "Rotate" a photo, it doesn't alter your original photo on your computer. TiVo just rotates the photo on the TV screen.

Enhancing TiVo Publisher with Other Programs

TiVo's Home Media Option simply connects TiVo and your computer. Several third-party programs build on that connection, turning the most scattered music and photo collections into organized lists on your TiVo.

Here's a look at software that adds extra power to TiVo Publisher, or even replaces it altogether.

MoodLogic for TiVo

MoodLogic (www.moodlogic.com) brings two tricks to TiVo and your computer: On your computer, MoodLogic cleans up and organizes a messy MP3 collection, automatically stuffing artists into their own folders, correcting ID tags and renaming song files consistently. MoodLogic also organizes TiVo's menus, seen in Figure 10-6.

After MoodLogic finishes that boring maintenance work, it becomes your personal on-call disc jockey, whipping up quick playlists to match your current mood. The company's breezy PR banter goes like this:

"Imagine the day that you walk into your living room and say aloud 'I want to hear some good jazz. Something like Breezin' by George Benson.' As soon as the words are out of your mouth, your stereo lights up and a smooth jazz mix starts to play a mix based on Breezin'."

Figure 10-6:
MoodLogic
organizes
your MP3
files and
whips up
quick
playlists to
match your
mood.

MoodLogic won't add voice recognition to TiVo, but a quick press on your remote will indeed start up your new Breezin' mix. Actually, MoodLogic lets you churn out on-the-fly playlists based on nearly *anything* you toss at it: romantic songs from the forties, for instance, fast '70s dance music, aggressive jazz songs, and more. To do this wonderwork, MoodLogic compares your song collection with its computerized algorithms and spits out a quick match for your mood.

MoodLogic cranked out some great on-the-fly mixes based on specific songs, genres, decades, tempos, and of course, moods. I enjoyed the way it tossed in favorites I hadn't heard for awhile. People who constantly craft their life's soundtrack will love serving up on-the-fly mixes through their TiVo.

✔ In order to create its mood mixes, MoodLogic must become intimately acquainted with your MP3 collection. I found its "Activation" process a little creepy, as it spent several hours perusing my collection, comparing my songs with its mammoth mood database.

✔ The program's raw edges occasionally interrupt the mood. MoodLogic won't weed out duplicate files from your hard drive, for instance, and it's a little awkward to move the program from one computer to another. And unlike other CD databases, MoodLogic only fills out the artist and title, ignoring the track number.

✔ MoodLogic is only as strong as your MP3 collection. It can't create moods if you don't have the songs. It's not a song-sharing service; it only creates playlists based on your existing song files.

✔ People with carefully filled out ID tags needn't worry; MoodLogic won't change tags or names without your permission.

✔ MoodLogic's biggest downer comes from its price: currently $29 for a year of Activation, then a yearly renewal fee. If you stop paying, the pouting MoodLogic immediately stops talking to your TiVo.

J. River Media Center

Unlike MoodLogic, J. River Media Center (www.musicex.com/mediacenter/) handles both music and photos. Perhaps most important to TiVo, it takes items that TiVo normally can't handle — WMA files, for instance — and converts them on the fly to MP3, streaming the results to TiVo.

It rips CDs and DVDs on your computer, if your computer has the appropriate burners, providing a convenient "all-in-one" package for handling computerized media.

The program's more of an organizer than anything else, grouping your songs and photos by their tag information rather than physical location. (You can still view songs by folder, if you want, just as with TiVo.)

J. River Media Center, like MoodLogic, spits out on-the-fly playlists, as seen in Figure 10-7, based on files you've heard or viewed recently.

J. River Media Center isn't as easy to figure out or navigate as MoodLogic, however. Although powerful on the desktop, the program's TiVo capabilities seem more like a throw-in with little thought to ease-of-navigation with a remote. But if your computer's stuffed with unorganized digital photos and a mixed bag of music files, it might be what you need.

Java Home Media Option (JavaHMO)

Programmed by a team of TiVo fans (who happen to be programmers), JavaHMO (http://javahmo.sourceforge.net) replaces TiVo Publisher, adding several new features for Windows, Apple and Linux computers. TiVo owners may never leave their TV again, as JavaHMO displays local weather reports (including forecasts and radar images), local movie theater listings (seen in Figure 10-8), and WebCam photos, as well as the standard songs and photos.

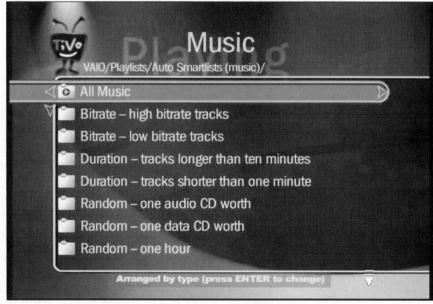

Figure 10-7: J. River Media Center creates automatic "Smart" playlists based on your listening habits.

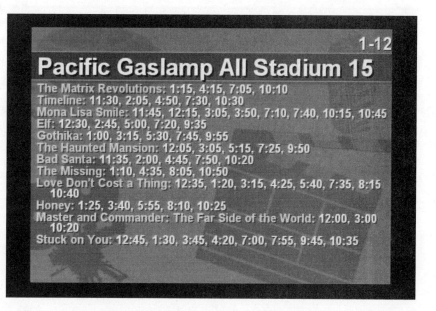

1-12

Pacific Gaslamp All Stadium 15

The Matrix Revolutions: 1:15, 4:15, 7:05, 10:10
Timeline: 11:30, 2:05, 4:50, 7:30, 10:30
Mona Lisa Smile: 11:45, 12:15, 3:05, 3:50, 7:10, 7:40, 10:15, 10:45
Elf: 12:30, 2:45, 5:00, 7:20, 9:35
Gothika: 1:00, 3:15, 5:30, 7:45, 9:55
The Haunted Mansion: 12:05, 3:05, 5:15, 7:25, 9:50
Bad Santa: 11:35, 2:00, 4:45, 7:50, 10:20
The Missing: 1:10, 4:35, 8:05, 10:50
Love Don't Cost a Thing: 12:35, 1:20, 3:15, 4:25, 5:40, 7:35, 8:15
     10:40
Honey: 1:25, 3:40, 5:55, 8:10, 10:25
Master and Commander: The Far Side of the World: 12:00, 3:00
     10:20
Stuck on You: 12:45, 1:30, 3:45, 4:20, 7:00, 7:55, 9:45, 10:35

The price? The software's free — although it costs more in computer know-
how than MoodLogic or J. River Media Center. If you're fairly well-versed in
computers, download a copy and begin customizing it to meet your needs. For
instance, adding your own Zip code lets you view local weather information,
as seen in Figure 10-9.

TiVo's SDK for advanced hacks

TiVo's Software Developer's Kit (`www.tivo.com/developer/`) not only offers tricks for programmers, but hope for the future. It ensures more programs will take advantage of TiVo's window into your entertainment center.

In particularly, look for *plug-ins* written specifically to enhance TiVo Publisher. For instance, one plug-in brings Windows Media Player 9 support to TiVo, letting you view files on your TiVo just as they appear in Media Player: sorted by artist, album, or genre. The plug-in also lets you play Media Player's playlists that are created automatically based on when and how often you play certain files. You'll find the plug-in at `http://jemfiles.home.comcast.net/TiVoPlugin/`.

Whereas some programs toss in support for TiVo as an afterthought, the programmers of JavaHMO built the program *specifically* to address TiVo's HMO shortcomings, adding and fine-tuning features as they continue to work. Even as it stands, though, JavaHMO already outdoes the commercial offerings in scope.

✔ JavaHMO displays photos in BMP, GIF, FlashPix, JPEG, PNG, PNM, TIF, and WBMP format. It also plays MP3 files and Shoutcast Internet radio stations, playlists in M3U and PLS formats, images from the Internet, and other goodies.

✔ The JavaHMO programmers hope to add support for more games (it already supports Tic-Tac-Toe), as well as e-mail, Internet searches, weather alert information, daily comic strips, horoscopes, stock charts, and other information. Through the use of clever programming tricks, JavaHMO can pluck virtually any image or data from the Internet and display it through TiVo.

Adobe Photoshop Album 2.0 and Picasa

MoodLogic works only with music; J. River Media Center and JavaHMO can handle both music and photos. Adobe Photoshop Album 2.0 (`www.adobe.com`) and Picasa (`www.picasa.net`) work only with photos. Both programs let you organize your digital photos into categories and publish photo collections to TiVo. After you create a slideshow, for instance, pushing a Publish to TiVo button sends the pictures to your TiVo as well as your computer monitor.

Photoshop Album lets you retrieve photos by the date you snapped them (provided you set the clock on your digital camera). Once you've found your proper vacation photos, publish them on your TiVo for the enjoyment of your impatient relatives. (Plying them with eggnog often helps ease the short delay.)

Part IV
Upgrading and Fixing Your TiVo

The 5th Wave By Rich Tennant

"It's amazing how they always fall asleep during 'The Crocodile Hunter', but are able to watch three hours of TiVo'd pasta machine infomercials."

In this part . . .

How do you reconfigure TiVo once you move to a new place? What happens if TiVo lists the wrong shows for one of your channels? How do you set up an old TiVo bought from a friend? What can you do about TiVo's misguided Suggestions?

This part of the book answers these questions and more, tossing in a fix for a TiVo that never seems to have enough storage space for all your shows.

Chapter 11

When Things Go Wrong . . .

*W*hen TiVo's on track, it's a dream machine, automatically trimming away television's nightmares, leaving only the pleasant and enjoyable. Underneath its magic, however, TiVo is, quite simply, a computer. And, like all computers, it occasionally wakes up from its dream world and faces real-life problems.

This chapter tackles some of the problems most frequently experienced by TiVo users. You probably won't experience more than one or two of them during your TiVo's lifetime. But when you do, this chapter holds the quick fixes that return you and your TiVo back to TV DreamLand.

Fixing Wrong Channel Lineups

To catch a requested show, TiVo examines your channel lineup, matches your channels with their show schedules, and records the right channel at the precise moment your show airs. But if TiVo doesn't know exactly what channels you receive, or those stations haven't reported their schedules correctly, TiVo can act up, with some pretty depressing consequences.

In this section, I explain what can go wrong with channel lineups, why these things happen, and how to keep them from happening again.

TiVo doesn't list my channels correctly

Today's cable or satellite providers offer several hundred channels, and they routinely tailor their offerings by adding or subtracting channels. Whenever a provider changes your channel lineup, TiVo usually notices and explains the results through a prominent Message icon on the opening TiVo Central screen. Your vigilant TiVo even examines your scheduled recordings and adjusts them, if possible, to match the new lineup so you won't miss any shows.

But if TiVo *doesn't* list some of the channels you receive — or if TiVo lists channels you *don't* receive, here's how to make TiVo's channel lineup match your own.

1. **Head to TiVo Messages & Setup from TiVo Central.**
2. **Choose Settings, then select Preferences.**
3. **Choose Customize Channels.**

Examine the lineup carefully to make sure TiVo lists your correct subscription package, and that you've placed checkmarks next to the channels you receive, as seen in Figure 11-1.

I give more extensive information about tweaking TiVo's channel lineup in Chapter 4.

Examine a copy of your latest cable or satellite bill when adjusting TiVo's channel lineup. It helps you understand your subscription package, as well as the channels not included in your subscription.

Instead of simply placing checkmarks next to all your received channels, feel free to *uncheck* channels you receive but never watch. Most people uncheck shopping channels, for instance, just to keep them off TiVo's menus.

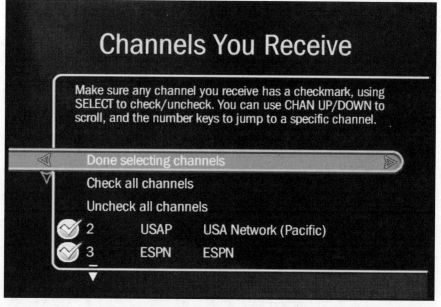

Figure 11-1:
Make sure
TiVo lists
your correct
subscription
package,
and that
you've
placed
checkmarks
by the
channels
you actually
receive.

TiVo doesn't list the right show descriptions for my channel

Most channels release their upcoming schedules weeks in advance. When a schedule's late or incorrect, poor TiVo doesn't know what show it's monitoring — or sometimes it lists the wrong shows or descriptions. To fix TiVo's natural confusion, try these three things:

1. **Notify TiVo of the problem.**

   Head to the Customer Service area of TiVo's Web site (www.tivo.com). You'll find a form to fill out and send to their Lineup Specialists. (Can't find the form? Try heading directly to http://customersupport. tivo.com/caseSubmitLineup.asp.)

2. **Notify the station of the problem.**

   Our cable company listed a local university's TV station, for instance, but didn't list descriptions for any of its shows. I found the station's e-mail address on its Web site, told them of the problem, and sent them links to TiVo. They sent the information to TiVo, and their show descriptions appeared on TiVo's lists in about two weeks.

3. **Follow up in two weeks.**

> Sometimes you simply must be persistent. If the show descriptions haven't appeared after two weeks, fill out the form again. Contact the station to make sure they know of the problem.

✔ Make sure your TiVo knows the channels you receive, as described in the previous section. The descriptions may be wrong because TiVo thinks you subscribe to a different service or subscription package.

✔ TiVo receives its show description information from Tribune Media Services, which lists the same show descriptions online at Zap2It (www.zap2it.com). Visit Zap2It, enter your Zip code, and choose your TV provider to browse your show listings. If that Web site doesn't list the correct information for a channel or show, your TiVo won't, either. (That helps confirm that the problem lies with the station, not your TiVo.)

TiVo records the wrong show

A Reuter's news article probably summed it up best: "Only TiVo fans know the radical disappointment of settling in to watch a recording of, say, a biography of actor Johnny Depp, and discovering that TiVo has captured a kitchen knife infomercial instead."

This problem can't really be blamed on TiVo, though. TiVo turned to the correct channel at the correct time and recorded for the correct duration. But the station pulled a "bait and switch": While claiming to run the bio, the station snuck in a last-minute infomercial, zapping Depp's biography in the process.

Short of squirming uncomfortably, nothing helps this situation. If TiVo missed the show because it tuned to the wrong *channel*, however, TiVo's "IR Blaster" probably needs some tweaking. I describe that process in this chapter's "Channel Changing Problems" section.

✔ If TiVo records a show in the wrong language, your Secondary Audio Programming could need adjusting. I explain how to do so in Chapter 7's sidebar, "Turning on TiVo's Secondary Audio Program."

✔ Sometimes TiVo records a Suggestion that's broadcast in a foreign language. This usually happens because you've left a foreign-language channel "checked" in your Channels Received list. I explain how to remove it — along with any unwanted shopping channels — earlier in this chapter, in "TiVo doesn't list my channels correctly."

Buying or selling a used TiVo

You're free to buy or sell a used TiVo; you'll find plenty for sale on eBay (www.ebay.com), for instance. They require a little extra work, mainly to make sure the account is transferred correctly to the new owner.

If you're selling a TiVo with a monthly service account, cancel your contract by calling TiVo Customer Support at 877-367-8486 between 8 a.m. and 8 p.m., PST. Wait until the last minute, as Customer Support pulls your account immediately. The new owner will immediately face the "Activation" nag screens until they Activate their TiVo at TiVo's Web site (www.tivo.com/activate).

If you're selling a TiVo with Lifetime Service, remember that the Lifetime Service is tied to your *TiVo*, not to you. If you buy a replacement TiVo, you must buy new service, either monthly or lifetime. And when you sell, either you or the TiVo's new owner must call TiVo Customer Support to transfer the lifetime ownership to the new owner.

Be very careful when buying a used TiVo with Lifetime Service, especially through the mail. There's no way of knowing whether that TiVo *really* has Lifetime Service until you plug it in, read its Service Number, and tell that number to TiVo's Customer Support staff. Be forewarned: There's no such thing as a DirecTV TiVo with "Lifetime Service," as DirecTV doesn't offer that option. Somebody may be trying to rip you off.

Controlling Your TV's (And/Or Stereo's) Power and Volume with TiVo's Remote

Juggling a handful of remotes during a movie makes it difficult to manage the popcorn. To fix the problem, set up TiVo's remote to control your TiVo and your TV. If you route your sound through your home stereo, set the remote to control that, instead.

To teach these tasks to TiVo's remote, head to Messages and Setup from TiVo Central; then into Recorder (or Receiver) and Phone Setup. There, you'll find Remote Control Setup, along with instructions on how to program TiVo's remote to work with your TV or home stereo.

I describe the process in detail in Chapter 4.

Fine-Tuning TiVo's Suggestions

TiVo records Suggestions based on the shows you've watched in the past, as well as how you've rated shows with your Thumbs Up and Thumbs Down buttons.

But sometimes TiVo just doesn't "get it," and its Suggestions don't capture the "real you." To get an idea of who TiVo thinks you are, choose Pick Programs to Record from TiVo Central and choose TiVo Suggestions. After a quick calculation, TiVo reveals its list of upcoming Suggestions, seen in Figure 11-2.

If TiVo's Suggestions seem wildly off-base, start from scratch: Choose TiVo Messages & Setup from TiVo Central, and select Restart or Reset System. Choose Reset Thumb Ratings & Suggestions, and press Select. TiVo saves your recorded shows, WishLists and Season Passes, but "forgets" what shows you've watched previously, as well as how you've used the Thumbs Up/Down buttons.

Then, to teach TiVo your idea of a good time, try to balance your use of the Thumbs Up and Thumbs Down buttons: Vote for something you like as often for something you dislike. Most importantly, reserve your three Thumbs Up and Down ratings for shows that *really* affected you in some way. Sticking to the more modest two presses keeps TiVo a little more balanced.

Anything with a three Thumbs Up often becomes an automatic Suggestion. TiVo records it frequently (but not always) when there's available space.

Figure 11-2:
Visit
the TiVo
Suggestions
area to
see what
Suggestions
TiVo plans
to record.

TiVo Suggestions

The Duke	Tue	12/16
South Park	Mon	12/15
Zelig	Thu	12/18
NYPD Blue	Mon	12/15
Seinfeld	Mon	12/15
Spin City	Tue	12/16
3rd Rock From the Sun	Wed	12/17
Friends	Thu	12/18

Some people like TiVo's Suggestions merely as an indicator of free space on their hard drive: Lots of Suggestions mean lots of empty space. You can turn them off if you want, however. Select Messages & Setup from TiVo Central, and choose Settings. Select Preferences, then choose TiVo Suggestions to turn them off or back on.

Troubleshooting Video Problems

This section explains how to troubleshoot problems your TiVo may have when displaying video, from a completely black screen to low-quality video.

If you're only missing some channels from TiVo's Channel Guide, check to see if the Guide's "filter" is turned on. (I cover the Guide and its filters in Chapter 5.) Press Enter and remove the filter; TiVo should display all the channels listed in its Channel Preferences area, covered earlier in this chapter.

TiVo doesn't display any video

We're talking no video at all here: a completely blank screen. Zilch. Nada.

1. **Check the power.**

   Rule out the easy stuff first. Have you turned on your TV (or VCR/stereo, if the TiVo connects through those)? Press your remote's TiVo button to make sure TiVo hasn't dropped into "Standby" mode.

2. **Check the cables and Line Input settings.**

   Chapter 3 describes how to connect your TiVo to your TV and other equipment. Are all the correct cables plugged in tightly?

   Many TVs, VCRs and stereos accept more than one video source. Look for the Line Input button, and make sure you've selected the TiVo as the source.

3. **Turn TiVo on and off again.**

   Unplug TiVo from its wall outlet and wait fifteen seconds before plugging it in again. Look for TiVo's reassuring startup screens announcing that it's woken back up.

4. **Isolate the problem.**

   Remove anything you've connected between TiVo and the TV, bypassing your VCR, home stereo, or other items. See if TiVo works when plugged directly into your TV. If it works, start connecting other items to see which one causes the problem. When you find it, adjust its settings until TiVo appears.

To make sure the problem isn't starting at the source, connect your cable or satellite box straight to your TV. Our TiVo's biggest problems start when our cable box freezes or sleeps. I unplug the cable box from the power outlet, wait a few seconds, and plug it back in to solve the problem. (One time I called the cable company; they flipped some switches on their end, and it began working again.)

- To make sure you don't accidentally turn off your cable box, hide its remote. If you accidentally turn it off, TiVo won't be able to record anything. Also, your cable or satellite company sometimes turns off the box after sending it a software update, leaving TiVo unable to record shows. Make sure the box's power light is always on.

- Did TiVo record a black screen instead of a TV show? If other recently recorded shows also contain a black screen, TiVo's not receiving the video signal. Check your cable connections, and try unplugging your cable or satellite box, waiting fifteen seconds and plugging it in again. If other recently recorded shows are okay, the station probably experienced a blackout when the show aired. (Particularly ugly storms occasionally black out video for satellite users.)

The video looks grainy

TiVo lets you record shows in several different video qualities. Without a doubt, Best Quality looks the best. If you use lower qualities, you'll probably notice slight video discrepancies, usually during rapid movements. Action movies, sporting events, and other fast-moving shows bring out the worst quality problems. The bigger your TV, the more noticeable the quality level.

Not all people notice these problems. (In fact, they don't affect DirecTV TiVos, as they always record in Best Quality.) But if you do, choose Options when choosing to record a problem and record the show in Best Quality. (Chapter 12 describes a simple way to increase your TiVo's storage space, allowing you to record everything at Best Quality.)

- Use TiVo's S-Video output, if your TV or stereo equipment allows the connection, described in Chapter 3. S-Video consistently provides a sharper picture than other methods. The better your picture, the better TiVo's picture will be.

- If you're watching Live TV and suddenly the picture starts to look grainy, it's probably because TiVo began recording the show at less than Best Quality. Either stop the recording and watch the show live or change the show's recording quality to Best. (You can usually do this through TiVo's Season Pass Manager, covered in Chapter 6.)

Using TiVo's Troubleshooting menus

TiVo includes several built-in Troubleshooting menus. You'll find them on the TiVo Messages & Setup menu, accessible through TiVo Central. The Troubleshooting menus offer help in five areas:

✔ Parental Controls

✔ Phone

✔ Channel Changing

✔ Network

✔ Transfer (for Home Media Option users)

The Troubleshooting menus are more of a helpful memory jogger than anything else, summing up information buried in the manual. However, sometimes that's all you need to understand why TiVo's not acting the way you expected.

Troubleshooting Sound Problems

When you don't hear any sound coming from your TiVo — but you see the video — start from the top of this list and work your way down, ruling out possible causes along the way.

1. **Check your power, mute and volume controls.**

   Make sure your TiVo's plugged in, as well as your TV, cable/satellite box (and stereo, if used). Is the mute turned off and the volume turned up?

2. **Check the cable connections.**

   Are TiVo's sound cables connected correctly? (Chapter 3 gives the whole rundown.) Yellow cables connect the video; the red and white cables connect the sound. Using an S-Video cable? You still need to connect the red and white cables for sound. (S-Video only carries video.)

   Try connecting the TiVo straight to the TV, removing anything in between (VCRs and stereos, for instance.) Still nothing? Try connecting the TV straight to your cable or satellite box to see if TiVo's the problem.

   Before blaming TiVo, try using different types of cables. (Your TiVo came boxed with quite a few, if you recall.) For instance, use the coaxial connector instead of the yellow, red and white ones or vice versa. I describe cables and connectors in Chapter 3.

3. **Restart TiVo.**

   If you can see the video, choose Messages & Setup from TiVo Central. Select Restart and System Reset, and choose Restart the DVR. TiVo will turn itself off, then on again. Can't see the video? Then unplug TiVo, wait 15 seconds, and plug it back in.

4. **Check your TV (and stereo, if used).**

   Make sure you've turned off your TV's SAP (Secondary Audio Programming), and the TV is set to the correct Line Input. (You may need to pull out your TV's manual to find these switches; they vary among TV models.) Check your stereo's Line Input switches, too. The stereo might still be trying to play your DVD player, for instance, instead of TiVo.

5. **Connect the TiVo directly to your TV.**

   Remove anything that's connected between the TV and your TiVo, including VCRs or stereos. Also, try connecting your cable or satellite box directly to your TV. This helps you decide if the problem stems from TiVo, the TV, or perhaps the TV signal itself.

   ✔ If your sound and video appear out of sync, press the Pause button, then start playing again. If the problem continues, make sure you're playing both the video *and* sound through TiVo. I once tried routing the sound through my 5.1 Surround Sound stereo; the video was about a half-second delayed from the sound.

   ✔ Use your home stereo or boom box to play the sound directly from your cable/satellite box. That helps determine if the sound's coming from your cable/satellite box or not.

Channel Changing Problems

TiVo almost always changes channels correct with simple setups — where the TiVo connects directly to an antenna or a cable dangling from the wall. Channel changing problems using happen when TiVo connects through a cable or satellite box. Here are some of the major problems, and their solutions.

If possible, connect TiVo to your cable or satellite box through the box's *serial port*. This almost eliminates channel changing problems. (Unfortunately, many boxes don't come with serial ports that support channel changing.)

Keeping TiVo from changing channels during live TV

Instead of watching TV, some people listen to the radio stations that come in through their cable box. Suddenly, TiVo bumps Sinatra and begins recording SpongeBob Squarepants. What gives?

Similar problems plague people who watch lots of live TV (although this can sometimes be fixed by setting up TiVo in a slightly different way, described in Chapter 3). TiVo suddenly switches to a different channel.

The problem breaks down to this: TiVo always needs full control of your cable box. When TiVo needs to record a scheduled show, it needs to change the channel and begin recording. (Sometimes TiVo changes the channel simply to record a Suggestion.)

The easiest solution is to call the cable company and rent a second cable box. Connect that cable box directly to TiVo, being careful to place a shield or "tent" around the front of the box where TiVo's IR blaster connects.

Then use the other box for watching "live TV" or listening to cable radio, uninterrupted.

- ✔ Some people tell TiVo to record their favorite cable radio channel for three hours during the late-night, when nothing else is being recorded. When they want to hear cable radio, they simply play back their TiVo recording. (Record the "Seasonal" channel to provide uninterrupted music for your holiday parties.)

- ✔ If you've recorded your music to MP3s, check out TiVo's Home Media Option. It lets you listen to MP3s through your TiVo, bypassing the need for the cable radio station.

- ✔ Chapter 3 explores different ways to connect TiVo to a single box so you can still watch live uninterrupted TV.

Sometimes TiVo won't change channels on my cable box!

When first setting up your TiVo, described in Chapter 3, you place a little black "IR Blaster" over the front of the cable box. The IR Blaster mimics the remote for your cable box. To change a channel, TiVo sends the cable box's remote signals through the IR Blaster, which in turn tells the remote to change channels.

But if the IR Blaster isn't positioned correctly, the cable box never gets the signal to change the channel, and TiVo ends up recording whatever channel the box happens to be delivering.

One of these things should fix the problem:

1. **Double-check the link between TiVo and your cable box.**

   First, make sure one end of the TiVo's "IR blaster" cable is plugged into TiVo's IR port. The other end should be taped to your cable box, with the IR Blaster pointing into the cable box's IR receiver. (You'll find complete instructions in Chapter 3.)

   While pressing the TiVo's Channel Up or Down button, try moving the IR Blaster to different locations around the cable box. It may not be close enough, or sometimes too close.

2. **Check the speed of the signal.**

   Adjust the speed of your IR Blaster's signals. In Chapter 4, I explain how to change the codes TiVo uses, as well as the speed it sends them.

3. **Place a "tent" around your cable box with the IR Blaster inside.**

   I've taped the IR Blaster in front of our cable box, then bent some aluminum foil over the cable box's front, being careful not to block any air vents. The foil keeps the IR Blaster's signals close to the cable box, and keeps other remotes from interfering.

Many digital cameras and camcorders can "see" the light from a remote. Watch the remote through the camera's viewfinder, and push the Channel Up button to see whether you spot a light. (Don't confuse the Infrared light with the red light that lights up on most remotes. The Infrared light is a second light, and it often appears white.) This trick sometimes helps diagnose a faulty remote. TiVo sells replacement remotes online (https://store.tivo.com).

Examining the Recording History

When TiVo doesn't record something it should — or deletes something it shouldn't have, find out why by probing TiVo's most detailed records: its Recording History. To see TiVo's Recording History, choose Pick Programs to Record from TiVo Central, and choose the To Do List. Finally, choose View Recording History at the list's top.

TiVo displays a list of its current actives, highlighting the current date, as seen in Figure 11-3. From there, you can scroll forward or backward two weeks in either direction to see TiVo's explanations of events.

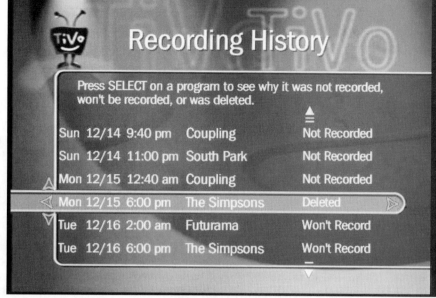

Figure 11-3:
Highlight an entry in TiVo's Recording History and press Select to see TiVo's explanation.

Press the Right Arrow or Select to read that event's description. In Figure 11-4, for instance, TiVo explains that TiVo deleted "The Twisted World of Marge" episode of "The Simpsons" because the "Keep at Most" limit had been reached.

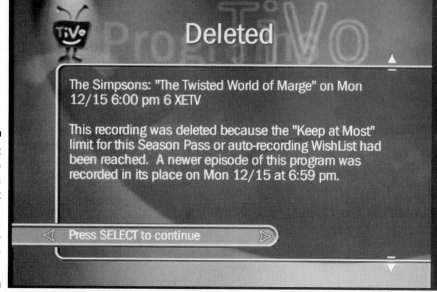

Figure 11-4:
TiVo explains that it replaced that episode with a new one, as per instructions.

I'd set that limit when setting up my Season Pass for The Simpsons. So, TiVo simply obeyed my instructions by deleting that episode and replacing it with a newer one.

- ✔ To flip quickly through the Recording History page by page, press the Channel Up or Channel Down buttons.

- ✔ You won't get away with deleting a roommate's show and blaming it on TiVo. When your roommate examines TiVo's Recording History, TiVo will list the deleted show along with the message, "This program was deleted because someone in your household removed it from Now Playing on 4/15 at 9:36 am." The date and time will differ, of course, according to the time of your evil deed.

Solving Phone Problems

Standalone TiVos need to phone TiVo headquarters every day or so to download the latest show listings. That's the only way it can keep almost two weeks of show listings on call. Here are some tricks to figure out phone problems. (DirecTV TiVos receive their guide data through the satellite, not the phone, so this section probably doesn't apply to them.)

Forcing TiVo to make a phone call

If you currently leave a phone cord strung across your living room floor, put it away. Just plug TiVo into the phone jack once a week — on weekends, for instance, if that helps you remember — and then tell TiVo to make its call:

1. **Choose TiVo Messages & Setup from TiVo Central.**
2. **Select Settings and choose Phone & Network Setup.**
3. **Select Connect to the TiVo Service Now.**

TiVo makes its call, downloads any listings or updates it needs, and hangs up. When TiVo's finished, roll up the phone cord until next week.

To test whether TiVo's connecting with the phone correctly, make a test call by choosing Test Connection from the same menu, seen in Figure 11-5. TiVo calls in, sets its clock, and hangs up, constantly displaying its progress onscreen. If it doesn't finish, something's wrong.

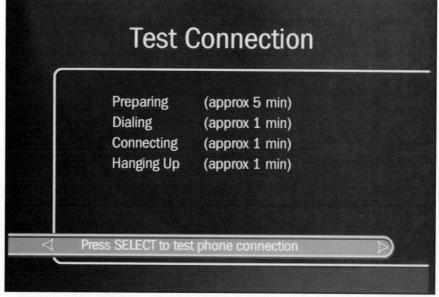

Figure 11-5:
Tell TiVo to make a quick test call to see whether it's connecting.

✔ If something's wrong with your TiVo's phone dialer (its *modem*), call TiVo's Customer Support number, as described near the end of this chapter. Be sure to have your information ready, and don't call during lunch hour — that's when you'll have the longest wait time.

✔ If your TiVo's modem dies, you can ship it off to TiVo or the manufacturer for repair (free, if it's within warranty, although you pay for shipping). Chapter 13 also lists several places that repair TiVos and sell replacement parts to do-it-yourselfers.

Keeping TiVo from calling long-distance numbers

TiVo needs to contact its headquarters to fetch your latest channel listings. If your TiVo's currently dialing a long-distance number, you might be able to find a local one.

1. **Choose TiVo Messages & Setup from TiVo Central.**

2. **Choose Settings, then Phone & Network Setup.**

3. **Choose Edit phone or network settings, then Phone Dialing Options.**

4. **Choose Set Dial-In Number.**

5. **Enter your area code using the remote control, and press Select.**

   TiVo dials a toll-free number to fetch its latest list of phone numbers in your area.

6. **Select the number closest to you.**

   If in doubt, look in your phone book or call the operator to find a number that doesn't charge a toll.

7. **Tell TiVo how to dial the number and confirm the results.**

   To accommodate different phone setups, TiVo needs to know whether you dial the number only, the prefix followed by the number, or add a 1 before the prefix and the number. Choose the format your phone prefers. When TiVo lists your correct setup, press Select.

TiVo uses MCI's dial-up access numbers for its daily call. If you're having trouble finding a free number, check online for the most recent list at `http://www3.tivo.com/tivo-misc/popfinder.do`.

If you're handy with computers, TiVo can leave its phone fixation behind and connect through your computer's broadband Internet connection, as I describe in Chapter 10.

✔ With all the area code splits taking place these days, numbers in different area codes are sometimes local calls. Try a neighboring area code to see if any of those numbers may be free.

✔ If you're stuck with long-distance, check your phone calling plan. Strangely enough, some plans offer out-of-state calling rates that are lower than your own state's rates. Check with your phone company, explain your situation, and ask if they have a different plan that might reduce your charges. You might even find lower rates by using a calling card.

I Need More Storage Space!

If you're constantly running out of room to hold your recorded shows, slip in a larger hard drive, described in Chapter 12. WeaKnees.com (`www.weaknees.com`) ships some of the simplest TiVo upgrade kits around. Seen in Figure 11-6, the company's Web site leads you through the purchase of the right kit for your particular TiVo model. The company then sends you the hard drive, the printed instructions, and all the tools you need to finish the job.

It's so simple, my mom could do it. (I might have to help her remove TiVo's case, though, as that's the hardest part.)

Figure 11-6:
The
WeaKnees
Web site
sells
customized,
do-it-
yourself
upgrade kits
that add
hours to
your TiVo.

If adding storage space isn't an option, your only alternative is use a lower recording quality or TiVo's "Save to VCR" feature, covered in Chapter 6, which lets you save shows to videotape for later viewing.

Gathering Information about Your TiVo

Should you give up all hope and visit TiVo's Web site or phone their customer service department, you'll need to give them specific information about your TiVo model. You'll find much of this information on TiVo's System Information screen:

1. **Choose Messages & Setup from TiVo Central.**

2. **Choose System Information.**

   The System Information screen, seen in Figure 11-7, shows your TiVo's most important information. Write them down below for reference. (Use pencil for the software version, as it changes occasionally.) Press the Channel Down button to see even *more* information, including the date of its last successful connection to TiVo headquarters, and its current operating temperature.

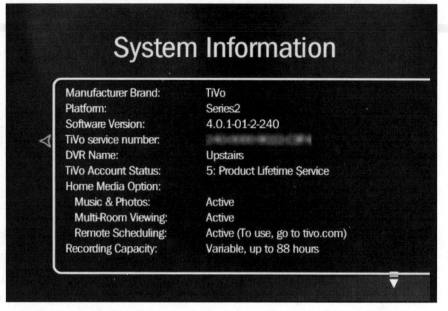

System Information

Manufacturer Brand:	TiVo
Platform:	Series2
Software Version:	4.0.1-01-2-240
TiVo service number:	▓▓▓▓▓▓▓▓▓
DVR Name:	Upstairs
TiVo Account Status:	5: Product Lifetime Service
Home Media Option:	
Music & Photos:	Active
Multi-Room Viewing:	Active
Remote Scheduling:	Active (To use, go to tivo.com)
Recording Capacity:	Variable, up to 88 hours

Figure 11-7: Press the Channel Down button to read even more boring information about your TiVo.

My TiVo's Vital Statistics:

Manufacturer:_____

Software Version:_____

Platform:_____

TiVo Service Number:_____

TiVo Account Status:_____

Temperature:_____

Model Number (listed on back of TiVo):

_____

TiVo's network IP address and signal strength

This information, only applicable to Home Media Option users, lives on TiVo's Phone & Network Setup page, seen in Figure 11-8. (I cover TiVo's Home Media Option in Chapter 10.)

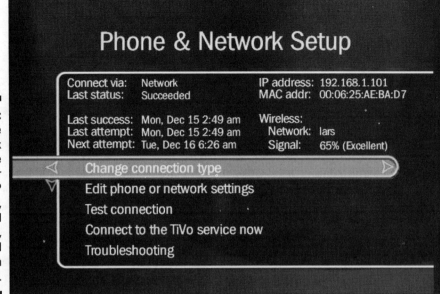

Phone & Network Setup

Connect via:	Network	IP address:	192.168.1.101
Last status:	Succeeded	MAC addr:	00:06:25:AE:BA:D7
Last success:	Mon, Dec 15 2:49 am	Wireless:	
Last attempt:	Mon, Dec 15 2:49 am	Network:	lars
Next attempt:	Tue, Dec 16 6:26 am	Signal:	65% (Excellent)

◁ Change connection type ▷

▽ Edit phone or network settings

Test connection

Connect to the TiVo service now

Troubleshooting

Figure 11-8:
TiVo's Phone
& Network
Setup page
lists your
network's IP
address,
signal
strength,
and
connection
information.

Checking TiVo's recording history

To see a record of why your TiVo decided to record, skip, or delete certain shows, head for its Recording History. Choose Pick Programs to Record from TiVo Central, and choose the To Do List. Finally, choose View Recording History at the list's top.

I discuss TiVo's Recording History earlier in this chapter.

Checking TiVo's available storage space

TiVo consumes more storage space the higher you set its video qualities. To see how many hours of shows your TiVo can record, choose TiVo Messages & Setup from TiVo Central, and select Settings. Choose Preferences and select Video Recording Quality. As seen in Figure 11-9, TiVo lists the approximate number of hours of recording time you receive at each quality level.

TiVo lists your total storage area on this page — not just the amount of hours you have left. You can increase the amount of total storage by replacing or adding a hard drive, covered in Chapter 12.

Figure 11-9:
TiVo lists the
approximate
number of
hours you
can record
at each
video
quality.

TiVo doesn't provide a way to see how much free space is left, as that number changes constantly depending on how many shows you've currently recorded, when you've recorded them, your upcoming recordings, and your quality settings. Look at the number of recorded Suggestions to gauge your available free space.

Setting Up TiVo When You Move

Once you've unpacked your TiVo at its new home (hopefully you saved its old cables), begin connecting it to your TV, as I describe in Chapter 3. When you're through, you need to run through a few menus, introducing TiVo to its new environment. Here are the hoops to jump through:

1. **Check TiVo's phone number and dialing options.**

   From TiVo Central, select TiVo Messages & Setup, then Settings. The phone menus lead you to the area for changing the dialing options. Even if you don't have to change the dialing options (prefixes that turn off Call Waiting, for instance, or dial long-distance numbers), change TiVo's Dial-Up phone number to one in your new area code.

2. **Select your new television providers.**

   Chances are, you'll be receiving new channels, either through a new cable or satellite service or by moving within range of a different broadcast antenna. To select your new channel lineup, repeat the Guided Setup I describe in Chapter 4. While there, check your Time Zone and Daylight Savings Time information.

3. **Update your contact information.**

   Visit TiVo's Web site (www.tivo.com), select Manage My Account, and update your contact information. Make sure TiVo has your correct address, phone number, and e-mail address.

When TiVo makes its first call from its new location, it may take longer than usual to come to its senses, particularly if it's been turned off for more a week or two. (It needs to index lots of new information.)

Restarting or Resetting TiVo, or Starting from Scratch

When TiVo seems to be acting up, it's time to call in the big guns. Choose TiVo Messages & Setup from TiVo Central, and select Restart or Reset System. TiVo offers several options, seen in Figure 11-10, and they all sound scary. Here's the damage control assessment for each one.

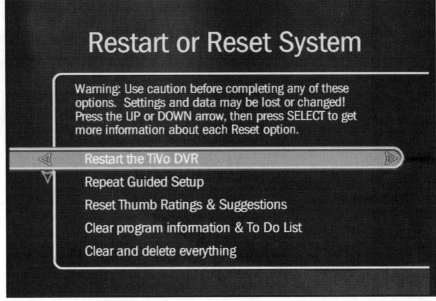

Figure 11-10: When trouble arises, head to this screen to choose an option for Restarting or Resetting your TiVo.

Restart or Reset System

Warning: Use caution before completing any of these options. Settings and data may be lost or changed! Press the UP or DOWN arrow, then press SELECT to get more information about each Reset option.

Restart the TiVo DVR

Repeat Guided Setup

Reset Thumb Ratings & Suggestions

Clear program information & To Do List

Clear and delete everything

Restart the TiVo DVR: This simply turns off TiVo, then starts it up again — sort of a safe way unplugging it and plugging it back in. You won't lose any recorded shows, Season Passes, WishLists, or Suggestions. Like flipping a computer's power switch, this little kick in the butt sometimes fixes odd problems.

Repeat Guided Setup: Use this mostly if you move or change your TV provider. It resets the list of Channels You Receive and Favorite channels, but your recorded programs, Season Passes, WishLists, and Suggestions remain untouched.

Reset Thumb Ratings & Suggestions: If TiVo's Suggestions seem way out of whack with your interests — or if the kids start playing haphazardly with the Thumbs Up/Thumbs Down buttons — use this clear things up. TiVo clears its memory of your Thumbs ratings and recorded Suggestions. Your recorded shows, Season Passes, WishLists and Suggestions stay safe.

Clear Program Information & To Do List: A potentially dangerous move, this clears all scheduled recordings, cancels Season Passes, wipes out the To Do list, and removes all Thumbs ratings. Your recorded shows stay safe, however. During its next call, TiVo receives fresh program information, which could take about an hour of processing. Don't try to schedule any recordings until it's through.

Clear and Delete Everything: This is the most biggest gun, and it's plenty powerful: TiVo returns to the state it was *when first taken out of the box*. You lose *everything*. Use only as a last resort, or perhaps when selling your TiVo.

Calling Tech Support

Before calling TiVo's Customer Support, try solving the problem yourself with the steps in this chapter. Check out TiVo's Web site (www.tivo.com), too. Once you finally get through to a live person at TiVo, they'll run you through the same steps outlined here and on the Web site — and you'll probably be paying for the long-distance call. If you try these fixes yourself, you'll spend a little less time with the customer service person.

DirecTV TiVo owners must contact DirecTV for support; TiVo's only responsible for the TiVo Service on those units, not the box itself.

Still ready to call? It works like this: TiVo Incorporated offers two types of customer service. When you call their toll-free number, a robotic voice guides you through a touch-tone question/answer session. You'll find most of the robot's answers available either in TiVo's manual or on its Web site.

When you give up on the robot, the creature hands you TiVo's *real* Tech Support phone number in California. This number is sometimes toll free, but most-likely long distance, and it has wait times of anywhere from a few minutes to more than a half-hour. I found the staff to be knowledgeable, communicative, and friendly during my call. After about a half-hour of running through some of the tests described here, they announced my new TiVo as Dead On Arrival. (They sent me a new one.)

Before calling Customer Support, spend some time on TiVo's Web site. It's quite impressive, especially since there's no such thing as "a" TiVo. Several manufacturers build TiVo, and many use slightly different software versions and setup combinations. The Web site remembers which brand and model of TiVo you own, and screens out material pertaining to other models, making it easier to find answers that pertain to your own TiVo, not your neighbor's.

If you can't find your answer through the Web site's guided menus, click "Browse All Articles" to dig through the wealth of information. TiVo offers e-mail support, as well. You may wait twenty-four hours for a response, but it sure beats waiting on hold.

Finally, I list several Web sites devoted to TiVo in Chapter 13; give them a look before calling TiVo's Customer Support lines. I've found the people at the TiVo Community Forum (www.tivocommunity.com) to be especially helpful and informative.

Chapter 12

Adding More Storage Space to Your TiVo

. . . .

In This Chapter

▶ Understanding your upgrade options

▶ Buying a larger hard drive

▶ Removing TiVo's case

▶ Removing the old drive

▶ Adding the new drive

▶ Replacing TiVo's case

. . . .

*H*undreds of unwatched TV shows flow past us every hour, but that doesn't ease the pain when a recorded show scrolls off your TiVo for lack of room. The best way to ease that pain is to increase TiVo's storage space — its *hard drive*, just like the one in your computer. And, just as with a computer, TiVo's old hard drive can be upgraded with a new, higher-capacity drive fairly easily.

Adding a new hard drive to TiVo once fell exclusively to techies who understood words like "Torx" and "Linux." Now that TiVo's been enthusiastically greeted by a more mainstream crowd, several companies sell ready-to-go upgrade kits designed specifically for ease of installation. An upgrade kit makes it easy to double or even triple the number of television hours you can hoard in your TiVo's storage space.

This chapter describes the step-by-step process of upgrading your TiVo, from buying a new hard drive to viewing the menu that displays your newly increased storage capacity. Budget yourself about a half hour for this one, and don't hesitate. You'll *love* the extra storage space.

Understanding Your Upgrade Options and Risks

Tinkering with any consumer electronics product involves some risks. Take these risks into consideration before upgrading your TiVo:

🗸 Removing TiVo's case voids its warranty. If you break something while tinkering, don't expect TiVo to repair it for free. (TiVo's warranty for most models covers 90 days of free labor and one year of free parts exchange; the warranty for your model may differ.)

🗸 Like other consumer electronics devices, TiVo's power supply can store a powerful jolt of electricity — even when TiVo's not plugged in. Don't touch parts unnecessarily, and give TiVo some settling time before opening its case.

That said, upgrading TiVo is fairly easy. Replacing its hard drive is nearly identical to replacing a computer's hard drive. And since an upgrade kit's hard drive comes pre-loaded with TiVo's software, everything works as soon as you plug TiVo back in.

Buying a Hard Drive Upgrade Kit

You can upgrade your TiVo's storage space several ways. I've ranked them here from easiest to most difficult.

Buy an already upgraded new TiVo. Some companies sell new TiVos prestocked with larger hard drives. Whereas many of today's TiVos come with either a 40MB or 80MB hard drive, companies like WeaKnees and PTVupgrade (both covered in Chapter 13) sell new, ready-to-go TiVos with more than 300 hours of storage capacity.

Send in your TiVo for upgrades. Both WeaKnees and PTVupgrade will upgrade your TiVo for a fee. You merely pack it up and mail it to them. (PTVupgrade can even send you a customized packing box, complete with return shipping label.)

Replace TiVo's existing hard drive yourself. The easiest method for do-it-yourselfers (and the method I explain in this chapter), this entails opening

TiVo's case, removing TiVo's existing hard drive, plugging in the replacement drive upgrade kit, and replacing TiVo's case.

> **Pros:** A replacement hard drive upgrade kit comes pre-loaded with TiVo software. When plugged in, TiVo wakes up in like-new condition — but with much more storage capacity. You can save your old drive as a backup against problems down the road. Being factory new, the replacement drive is less prone to failure than TiVo's existing drive, especially for older TiVos.

> **Cons:** Replacing your drive will wipe out your existing recordings, settings, Season Passes and WishLists. You'll have to run TiVo's Guided Setup again to tell TiVo your connection settings, channels, and other information.

Add a second drive to TiVo. Pop open TiVo's case, add a second drive upgrade kit, and close TiVo's case. That gives TiVo *two* drives for show storage.

> **Pros:** Your recorded shows and settings stay intact, and TiVo immediately begins filling the second drive with shows, more than doubling your current storage.

> **Cons:** Adding a second drive requires more work and skill. Depending on your TiVo model, you'll be adding extra cables, brackets, and perhaps even an extra fan for cooling. TiVo keeps using your older drive, leaving a higher chance of failure down the road. Experienced computer users can handle these things, but first-time do-it-yourselfers may find them overly demanding.

Several companies sell TiVo upgrade kits through the Internet. I list them and their Web sites in Chapter 13. The replacement hard drive upgrade kit I purchased for this chapter came from WeaKnees (www.weaknees.com). Like all the kits, it arrived with the tools necessary for installation and a detailed, step-by-step instruction sheet customized for my particular TiVo model. The new drive arrived a few days after I ordered it, and it installed without a hitch.

The rest of this chapter describes the rough steps necessary for replacing TiVo's existing hard drive with a new, larger one using an upgrade kit similar to the ones sold by WeaKnees (seen in Figure 12-1). Use this chapter only as a *general guide* to how upgrade kits work. Your own replacement kit will contain instructions written specifically to cover *your own* TiVo model, and you should follow those.

Figure 12-1:
The TiVo
Upgrade
Wizard on
WeaKnees'
Web site
walks you
through the
process of
ordering the
right hard
drive
upgrade kit
for your
particular
TiVo model.

Opening Your TiVo

Before upgrading your TiVo, examine your upgrade kit and its instructions to make sure you've received all the necessary parts and tools. Make sure the upgrade kit and its instructions are written for your particular TiVo model. If something is missing, phone or e-mail the store, and ask for the missing part or tool.

When this chapter's instructions differ from your kit's instructions, *follow your kit's instructions.* They're customized to your exact TiVo model; these are not.

The hard drives in upgrade kits come with TiVo's software pre-installed. If you simply buy and install a hard drive from the computer store, your TiVo won't work. The drive must first be properly configured for your TiVo model.

1. **Write down your TiVo's old settings.**

   Replacing TiVo's hard drive returns TiVo to a "like new" condition. If you've spent a lot of time creating WishLists and Season Passes, write them down on paper so you can re-enter them later.

2. **Prepare your work area.**

   Clean off a table large enough to hold TiVo, your upgrade kit, and its bundled tools. Don't place TiVo on carpet, especially if you live in a dry, static-prone area.

3. Unplug TiVo's power cord and cables.

TiVo doesn't use an "On/Off" switch. To turn it off, just unplug it from the wall. Unplug all its attached cables, and place it on your work area's table. If you like to plan ahead, label the cables with some sticky notes so you know where to plug them back in.

Wait five minutes before removing TiVo's cover; this gives the power supply a little time to discharge.

4. Unscrew the screws on TiVo's cover with a Torx wrench.

Depending on your TiVo model, your upgrade kit came with one or two Torx wrenches. (A Torx wrench's end looks like a "star" that fits perfectly in the screw's indentations. Regular screwdrivers won't work.) Use the Torx wrench to remove the screws holding TiVo's cover to its chassis, seen in Figure 12-2. Be sure to remove *only* the screws on the cover itself; avoid removing screws that hold other parts to the chassis.

Put the screws in a safe place so you don't lose them. I use an empty egg carton, placing each set of removed screws into a different egg's compartment.

5. Remove TiVo's cover from its chassis.

Slide TiVo's cover from its front toward the back. (You may have to push rather hard, sometimes with your palms along the top's side edges.) As the cover slides back, lift it up and off TiVo.

Once you're inside, be careful of static electricity. If you live in a static-prone area, use an anti-static wrist strap (available at Radio Shack and other places) to avoid harming TiVo's sensitive internal organs. No anti-static strap around? Then you can always touch the metal chassis with your hand before touching any electronic components.

Figure 12-2:
Remove only the screws holding TiVo's cover to its chassis, being careful not to remove any other screws.

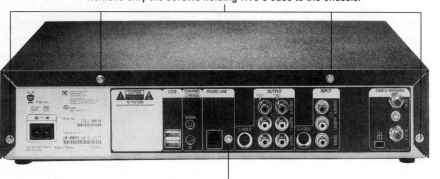

Remove only the screws holding TiVo's case to the chassis.

Don't remove screws from the chassis itself.

Removing the Old Drive

Once you've removed TiVo's cover, exposing its internal organs, identify the parts inside. You need to detach everything from the old hard drive so you can replace it with the new one.

1. **Locate and identify TiVo's hard drive and cables.**

   Your TiVo will look somewhat like the one in Figure 12-3. Take some time to locate its hard drive, drive bay or bracket, IDE cable, power cable, and anything else listed in your kit's instructions.

   The IDE cable is flat and wide, often with a black or blue connector. The power cable consists of four cables that attach to the hard drive with a white connector.

   TiVo's hard drive — the silver rectangular thing — is screwed into its drive bay or bracket.

IDE cable   Power cable   Hard drive

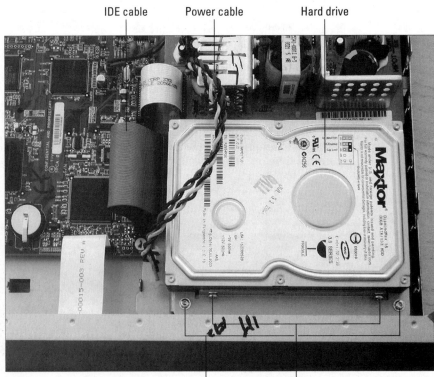

Figure 12-3:
Examine
TiVo to
locate its
hard drive,
drive bay,
IDE cable,
power
cable, and
anything
else listed in
your kit's
instructions.

Screws holding drive to bracket

Screws holding mounting bracket to chassis

2. **Remove the hard drive from its bracket and unplug the drive's IDE cable and power cable.**

   Depending on your kit's instructions, you may first need to remove your hard drive's bracket from the chassis in order to remove the hard drive from TiVo. If so, use the Torx wrench to remove the screws holding the bracket to TiVo's chassis. Save the bracket and its screws to attach to the new drive.

   Next, remove the drive from its bracket, usually with the same Torx wrenches. Drives usually attach with four screws.

   Finally, unplug the IDE and power cables from the hard drive, leaving their other ends firmly attached to TiVo's internal organs. Pull on the cables' *connectors* — not on the wires themselves — when detaching them from the drive. Figure 12-4 shows the connectors; the power cable's white connector is above the IDE cable's black connector. You may need to rock the connectors back and forth slightly to unplug them.

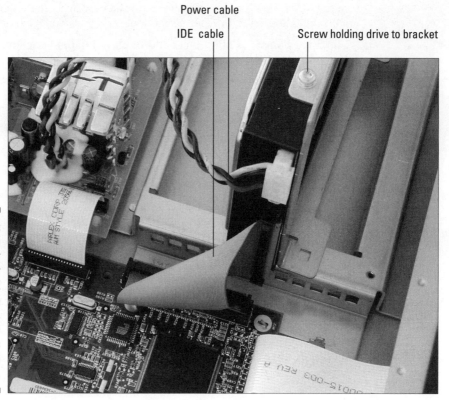

Power cable

IDE cable

Screw holding drive to bracket

Figure 12-4: Unplug the power connector and IDE cable from the drive, but leave both cables attached to TiVo.

3. **Place your old drive in a safe place.**

You probably won't need it again, but keep your old hard drive in a safe place, inside the new drive's protective bag, as a backup. If something ever goes wrong with your new drive, pop in the old drive while you wait for a replacement to arrive.

Drives are sensitive. Don't drop them.

Adding the New Drive

Your new hard drive may bear a different brand name, but it should look very similar to the one you removed. Follow these instructions to place it inside TiVo, connect the cables, and fasten it down.

1. **Attach the new drive to the old drive's bracket.**

Use the Torx wrench and the old drive's screws to fasten the new drive to the old drive's bracket. The holes on the new drive match perfectly with the holes in the bracket. Whoopee!

The drive's Master, Cable Select and/or Slave jumpers are already set to the proper positions for each upgrade kit. Don't try to second guess anybody by switching the jumpers.

2. **Plug in all the cables.**

Carefully reattach the drive's IDE cable; it only fits one way. (The little notch on the cable's connector lines up with the hole on the drive's connector.)

Push the power cable's connector back into the drive, as well. (Like the IDE cable's connector, the power cable's connector only fits one way.) It sometimes requires a healthy push.

3. **Reattach the drive bracket to TiVo.**

If you removed the drive's bracket from TiVo, use the Torx wrenches to fasten its screws back onto TiVo's chassis.

Reattach any other items you removed according to your kit's instructions.

If your TiVo has a fan, be sure to push the cables away from the fan so they don't get stuck.

Replacing TiVo's Case

Before screwing down TiVo's case, make sure you haven't left any stray screws inside TiVo. Give it a shake or two to see if you hear anything rattling around. Are all the cables tight? If you accidentally knocked any other connectors askew, carefully push them back in place.

Everything look good? Then go ahead and reattach TiVo's cover. It slides on easier than it came off, thankfully.

1. **Slide TiVo's case back over the chassis.**

   The case slides on just the way you slid it off, but usually without as much pushing. Make sure the cover's lip sits flush against the chassis, with the holes lining up.

2. **Reattach the screws.**

   Using the Torx wrench, reattach the cover using the screws you removed earlier. Tighten them firmly, but don't bear down on them. They usually stay put.

Making Sure TiVo Works

Now comes the moment of truth — to see if the darn thing still works. Feel free to head to Chapter 3 if you have trouble remembering which cable connected to which port.

1. **Reattach TiVo's cables.**

   Always route the cables from one gadget's Out port to another one's In port. Never connect them from In to In or Out to Out.

2. **Plug in TiVo's power cord and turn on your TV.**

   Plugging in the power turns on TiVo automatically. You'll see the "Powering Up" screen, followed by the "Almost There . . . " screen. Eventually TiVo's familiar menu will reappear on your TV screen.

3. **Run TiVo's Guided Setup and enter your settings.**

   I cover Guided Setup in Chapter 4. If you wrote down all your Season Passes and WishLists before replacing your hard drive, now's the time to enter them all back in.

   4. **View TiVo's upgraded storage capacity.**

   To see the results of your handiwork, head to TiVo's Video Recording Quality settings:

   1. **From TiVo Central, choose TiVo messages and Setup.**

   2. **Choose Settings.**

   3. **Choose Preferences, then Video Recording Quality.**

   TiVo displays the screen shown in Figure 12-5 showing the approximate number of hours your newly expanded TiVo will be able to record.

   If something seems wrong or TiVo won't load properly, fire off an e-mail to the upgrade kit vendor. Describe your problems in minute detail, including any error messages you see, so they'll be able to identify the problem and its solution.

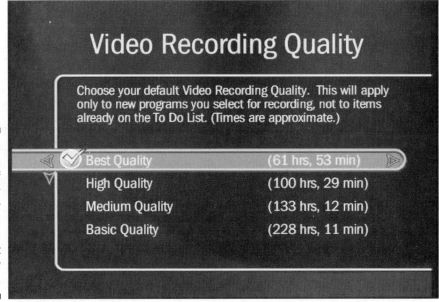

Figure 12-5:
TiVo lists the amount of hours your newly expanded TiVo can record at each quality level.

Video Recording Quality

Choose your default Video Recording Quality. This will apply only to new programs you select for recording, not to items already on the To Do List. (Times are approximate.)

✓ Best Quality	(61 hrs, 53 min)
High Quality	(100 hrs, 29 min)
Medium Quality	(133 hrs, 12 min)
Basic Quality	(228 hrs, 11 min)

Chapter 13

Finding More TiVo Information on the Web

*B*eneath all its magic, TiVo is simply a computer. With such a heritage, it's only natural that the Internet brims with Web sites devoted to TiVo. This chapter describes some of the most popular sites available, as well as the information they offer.

Once you've visited one or two sites, you'll quickly spot links to other sites offering similar fare.

Because Web sites change location often, you'll find a complete list of updated links at my Web site (www.andyrathbone.com).

TiVo's Own Web Site

TiVo's own Web site (www.tivo.com) contains a remarkable amount of information. Here's the rundown on what information TiVo offers at its site, seen in Figure 13-1, as well as shortcuts that take you directly to the page you need.

Figure 13-1:
TiVo's own
Web site
contains
a wide
range of
information
about using,
trouble-
shooting,
and
optimizing
a TiVo.

`www.tivo.com`: When friends ask what TiVo's all about, point them to TiVo's Web site for an animated explanation of the TiVo lifestyle they're currently missing. (Even better, invite them over and hand them your remote for a few minutes.)

`www.tivo.com/manage`: Head here to Activate your newly purchased TiVo (if you didn't Activate through the TiVo itself). You'll need to enter a user name and password, or set up a new account.

You'll also visit here to purchase TiVo's Home Media Option (HMO), name your TiVo (important when swapping shows between two or more TiVos with HMO), or update your TiVo account information.

When you move or change e-mail addresses, be sure to keep TiVo up-to-date on your whereabouts — especially if you're paying for monthly service.

`www.tivo.com/support`: If TiVo ever leaves you scratching your head, this site offers extensive customer support, tailored for your particular TiVo model. You'll also find troubleshooting tips, an e-mail address to ask questions, and a handy list of answers to the most frequently asked questions about TiVo.

`www.tivo.com/desktop`: When you sign up for TiVo's Home Media Option (HMO), head here to download the TiVo Desktop application for your PC or Macintosh. You need that software to send your digital photos and/or MP3 music files from your computer to TiVo. (I describe other programs that control TiVo through HMO in Chapter 10.)

`www.tivo.com/tco`: Once you've signed up for TiVo's Home Media Option, visit here to schedule recordings on your TiVo from any Internet connection. If you've set up TiVo through a broadband connection, you can schedule a recording with only half an hour's advance notice.

`www.tivo.com/adapters`: TiVo's happy to connect with your computer through the Home Media Option, but it's quite picky about the network adapters that make the connection possible. This site lists the USB network adapters proven to work with TiVo. (Although other brands of adapters may work, the ones listed here provide the best chance of success.)

`www.tivo.com/guides`: This area contains downloadable manuals for every TiVo manufacturer and model. You'll also find a downloadable manual for TiVo's Home Media Option.

`https://store.tivo.com`: This site lets you purchase nearly anything TiVo offers: new TiVos, professional installations, TiVo antenna balls, stuffed TiVo toys, and other items.

`www.tivo.com/mediapartners`: Several companies sell products and services that work with TiVo's Home Media Option. You'll find many of them listed here, as well as discussed in Chapter 10.

`www.tivo.com/privacy`: TiVo spells out its privacy policies in complete detail here, as well as its terms of service. The downloadable documents come in Adobe Acrobat format; if you have difficulty opening them, head to `www.adobe.com/reader` to download free "Adobe Acrobat Reader" software.

`www.zap2it.com`: TiVo receives its program information from a company called *Tribune Media Services*. If anything is wrong with the schedule data, the TiVo company must make Tribune correct their listings. This Web site

shows you what Tribune currently lists for your area's channels and offerings. If it's wrong, your TiVo will be wrong, too. Head to `www.tivo.com/
support` to alert them of the error.

`www.linksys.com/support`: Although not a link to TiVo, this site contains
detailed information about setting up a home network, as well as information
on some network adapters (wired and wireless) that work with TiVo.

`www.uk.tivo.com`: TiVo sells units and provides service only in the United
States and United Kingdom. United Kingdom customers find TiVo support at
this site.

`www.directv.com/dvr`: DirecTV customers use TiVos from DirecTV
designed specifically to record satellite streams. DirecTV offers customer
support through its Web site, e-mail , or by phone at 1-800-DIRECTV
(1-800-347-3288).

Web Links to TiVo Fan Sites

Many of TiVo's more than one-million users lean toward the fanatical. Some
set up Web sites devoted to discussing TiVo, its use, or even its implications
for the world. Some sites remain tightly focused around TiVo specifics; others
border on standard water cooler chatter. Either way, you'll find plenty of TiVo
information at the sites listed here.

TiVo Community Forum

Partially supported by the TiVo company and other TiVo-related companies,
the TiVo Community Forum (`www.tivocommunity.com`) easily ranks as the
largest TiVo "fan" site. Seen in Figure 13-2, the site encompasses a wide variety of issues, from tips on removing bird poop from new car paint to last-
minute alerts on networks that change their program lineups.

New users ask questions about their TiVo in the "TiVo Help Center" forum;
TiVo tinkerers hang out in the "Underground" forum, exploring ways to push
TiVo to its limits.

The only thing you *won't* find here is talk about the "forbidden" subjects: any
type of service theft, video extraction, or hacks to remove ads from TiVo software. (Don't talk about TiVo's stock, either.) It's a moderated, family forum,
so any posts deemed inappropriate for family viewing may be removed without notice.

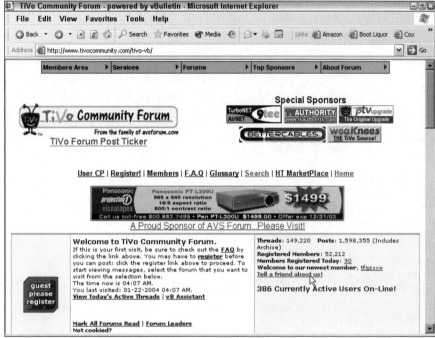

Figure 13-2:
By far the biggest TiVo site, the TiVo Community Forum attracts a wide variety of TiVo users, from hardcore to novice.

TiVo FAQ (www.tivofaq.com)

Still have a question about your TiVo or its service? The TiVo Frequently Asked Questions site (www.tivofaq.com) should answer many of them. Members of the TiVo Community Forum collect newcomers' most frequently asked questions, and answer them here in one lump sum.

Although a bit out of date, it's chock-full of basic information and a valuable time-saver both for yourself and the poor folks at the TiVo Community Forum who constantly hear the same questions asked over and over again.

PVR Blog (www.pvrblog.com)

Dutifully run by Matt Haughey, the PVR Blog (www.pvrblog.com) comments on anything related to TiVo and Digital Video Recorders (DVRs). Seen in Figure 13-3, the site specializes in announcements of new models, comments on the latest DVR news, information about new third-party TiVo programs, and observations on how DVRs affect society at large.

Figure 13-3:
The PVR
Blog covers
all aspects
of digital
video
recorders,
including
TiVo, and
their effect
on society
at large.

TiVo Hacking Sites

These sites deal with "white hat" hacking — ways to tinker with TiVo to add
features while staying within the law. Most of these modifications won't stay
within your TiVo's warranty, however. Although you probably won't care
much about these sites, feel free to pass them on to a curious friend as a
starting point. Once you visit one or two sites, you'll find links to other sites
with similar information.

The Unofficial TiVo Hackers site

Another site running under the wing of the TiVo Community Forum, the
Unofficial TiVo Hackers site (www.tivofaq.com/hack) offers a primer on
what sort of smarts you need to dig into your TiVo's guts, and why you'd
want to in the first place.

TiVo Web Project

The software behind the TiVo Web Project (http://tivo.lightn.org) offers a way to add different features to your TiVo. You'll need to know *a lot* about computers in order to start, however. But if you've outgrown TiVo's own Home Media Option features (and the various enhancement programs I describe in Chapter 10), you might want to peek here.

Jeff Keegan's "Hacking TiVo" support site

Jeff Keegan, TiVo hacking superstar and author of *Hacking TiVo* for Wiley Publishing, Inc., supports his mammoth book at his own site (http://keegan.org/hackingtivo/). With its intricate explanations of TiVo's inner workings and how to tinker with them, Keegan's book quickly became *the* book to own by the TiVo hacking community. On his site, seen in Figure 13-4, Keegan offers updated links, ordering information, and corrections to the published text.

Figure 13-4: Jeff Keegan supports his *Hacking TiVo* book with tips on modifying TiVo's inner workings.

Links to Upgrade Kit Vendors

Several sites offer upgrades to TiVo — parts replacements, hard drive upgrades, and similar goods. Visit all three companies and choose the one that matches your needs most closely.

WeaKnees

I've installed two hard drive upgrade kits from WeaKnees (www.weaknees.com), including the one described in Chapter 12; both went off without a hitch. The company includes detailed directions and tools with each kit. And if you spill coffee on the directions, simply download another copy from its Web site, seen in Figure 13-5.

A "TiVo Wizard" on the site guides you to the correct kit or parts you'll need for your TiVo. The site sells new TiVos online, as well.

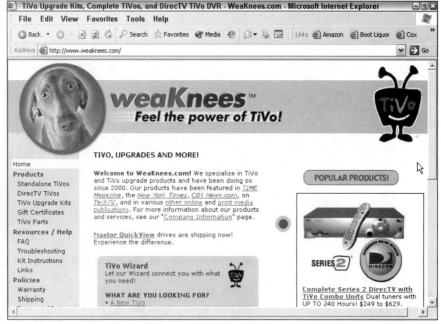

Figure 13-5: WeaKnees sells TiVo hard drive upgrade kits like the one described in Chapter 12.

9th Tee Enterprises

Another site with upgrade kits and parts, 9th Tee Enterprises (www.9thtee.com) sells items similar to WeaKnees, as well as some computer parts, tiny remote control cars, and other items with geek appeal.

PTVupgrade

Seen in Figure 13-6, PTVupgrade (www.ptvupgrade.com) sells items similar to those found at WeaKnees and 9th Tee Enterprises: upgrade kits, TiVo parts, and items designed for TiVo hackers. Based in Chicago, the company's been in business for three years. If you're willing to pack up your TiVo, PTVupgrade even offers to upgrade your TiVo's hard drive for you and ship it back.

Figure 13-6:
PTVupgrade not only sells TiVo hard drive upgrade kits, but also will upgrade your TiVo if you send it in.

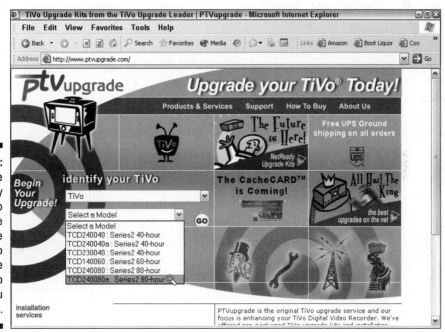

Part V
The Part of Tens

In this part . . .

A tradition in *For Dummies* books for more than a
decade, the "Part of Tens" provides a perfect place for
helpful morsels that don't fit anywhere else on the plate.
This is the place where you'll find titillating TiVo tips and
tidbits.

You'll find tips for watching *live* TV, tips for watching
recorded TV, and even more tips for scheduling recordings
that catch the right target. When a warning screen pops up,
you'll find its solution. You'll find out the big differences
between TiVo and the DVRs (Digital Video Recorders) the
cable companies toss around these days.

Oh, and you'll find tips for sharing a TiVo equitably between
roommates, spouses, and/or children. (Yes, one of the tips
involves getting another TiVo.)

Chapter 14

Tips for Watching Live TV

By now, you're probably familiar with TiVo's standard bag of live TV tricks. Pause, Rewind, Instant Replay, and Slow Motion place a powerful arsenal at your fingertips.

This chapter presents a few lesser-known tricks that apply mostly when watching live TV. Some take advantage of TiVo's handy recording *buffer* (covered in Chapter 5). The first and most important tip, however, helps keep you from watching live TV at all. Only when you give up live TV will you experience TiVo in its purest form.

Keeping Away from Live TV

Although TiVo enhances live TV in several ways, TiVo's not meant for watching live TV.

After growing accustomed to commercial skipping and a diet of shows you've specifically requested, live TV will make you feel oddly uncomfortable, both at home and away. Live TV robs you of control, leaving you stuck with whatever the TV currently offers.

If you're having trouble weaning yourself from live TV, try these three tips:

1. **Before turning on your TV, press the TiVo button twice.**

   When you turn on your TV, TiVo's Now Playing list replaces the live TV screen. That stops you from being sucked into a live TV show, and it lets you grow accustomed to TiVo and its offerings.

2. **Take some time to teach TiVo what you like.**

   Make WishLists for your favorite actors, directors, and subjects, and put your absolute favorites on autorecord. Additional tips for filling TiVo with shows tailored to your tastes await you in Chapter 16, as well.

3. **If you find yourself enjoying a live TV show, tell TiVo about it.**

   Don't just press the Thumbs Up button; press the Pause button. Then create a Season Pass or autorecording WishList for that show. TiVo will automatically grab the show when it airs, and you'll never have to watch it live again. Lather, rinse, and repeat when necessary for other shows.

Recording Live Shows On-the-Fly

 Spotted something irresistible when you first turned on the TV? Push the Record button: TiVo quickly saves the show's past 30 minutes, then records the rest of the show to its completion.

How can TiVo retrieve 30 minutes of a show's previously aired footage? It's possible because TiVo constantly records whatever channel it happens to be tuned to, usually something on the last channel it recorded. TiVo places its constant recordings into a *buffer* — a temporary holding tank that's 30 minutes long.

So, when you press Record, TiVo reaches into its buffer, grabs up to 30 minutes of the current show, and tacks that portion to the beginning of your recording. (If TiVo finds part of an earlier show in the 30 minute buffer, it discards that earlier show, saving only the current one.)

There's one catch, however. If you change channels, TiVo erases its buffer and begins recording anew. If you press the Record button while channel surfing, TiVo's buffer probably won't have much of the show's recently aired fare to dish out.

Recording a Short Portion of a Live Show

Sometimes you'll be watching a live show and only want to record part of it — the musical guest's appearance on David Letterman, for instance.

When you press the Record button, TiVo normally scoops up to 30 minutes of the show from its buffer and tacks it onto the beginning of the recording. While this is generally a good thing, TiVo's buffer dipping can turn a quick three-minute recording of Outkast's performance into a 33-minute recording stuffed with a monologue.

To avoid this, flush TiVo's buffer by quickly changing channels at the right time: Just before the musical guests appear, press the Channel Up button followed by the Channel Down button. When TiVo returns to your show, press the Record button.

With its buffer cleared, TiVo begins recording from that point onward. Press the Record button again to stop the recording, and your intentionally brief recording will remain brief.

Cutting Commercials from Live TV

Sometimes you'll set up TiVo to record a show, but you still want to watch the show live. For instance, to watch an 8 p.m. show "live" and still be able to fast-forward through the commercials, wait until 8:20 p.m. *Then* start watching TiVo's recording of the show from the beginning.

That lets you fast-forward through the show's commercials, usually catching up to the recording's end at the same time as the show's "real" ending.

By fast-forwarding through the commercials, TiVo gives you twenty minutes of your life back!

Returning to a Paused Show

TiVo takes the Pause button to a new dimension with its ability to keep on recording while the screen freezes. But when you return to a paused show — either live or recorded — it's easy to forget where you left off.

To refresh your memory, press Instant Replay to hear the last line or two. Press the Instant Replay button several times if you're returning after a lengthy delay; each press jumps back another eight seconds.

Recording Digital Cable Music Stations

Some cable and satellite services broadcast commercial-free digital music channels. But if you're listening to a music channel when TiVo suddenly needs to record a program, TiVo flips the channel, cutting off your tunes in the process. Sometimes TiVo cuts off the music simply to record a Suggestion — committing a real party foul in the process.

You can fix this any one of five ways:

- ✔ Subscribe to DirecTV satellite TV, because DirecTV lets you record one channel while watching another live. (A DirecTV TiVo comes with the deal for a small monthly fee.) Listen to your cable music station while recording TV in the background.

- ✔ If the music comes through a digital channel, buy a second cable/satellite box. Devote one box to TiVo, and use the second for live TV, including playing your music channels. (Place TiVo's dedicated box inside a "tent," described in Chapter 11.)

- ✔ If a second cable box isn't an option, use TiVo's manual recording option: Tell TiVo to record several hours of your favorite station once a week while you're asleep. To listen to your music, just play back your weekly recording. (DirecTV's TiVos won't let you record MusicChoice channels, unfortunately.)

- ✔ Buy TiVo's Home Media Option and listen to Internet Radio or your MP3 music files, instead. (I cover the Home Media Option in Part III.) TiVo flips its channels and records in the background while you listen to uninterrupted Internet Radio or MP3 files.

- ✔ You might also look into TiVo's partnership with XM Radio. Home Media Option users can tune in to their subscribed XM Satellite Radio stations through a Series 2 TiVo.

Toggling between Two Live Shows

 Can't decide which live show to watch? Tune in the first show you want to watch, and then enter the second channel with the remote's keypad.

Press the Enter/Last key to flip from one channel to the other, letting you keep up on the action of both.

If you're using a DirecTV TiVo, tune in the first show, then tune in the second show on the second tuner. Press the Down Arrow to move between tuners, flipping between the two shows.

Chapter 15

Tips for Watching Recorded TV

. . . .

In This Chapter

▶ Letting shows scroll off naturally

▶ Fast-forwarding in 30-second increments

▶ Turning on Closed Captioning for extra features

▶ Repeating missed dialogue

▶ Playing or deleting saved shows quickly

▶ Saving recorded shows to a VCR

. . . .

*O*nce TiVo has started recording your favorite shows, you'll spend much of your TV time watching TiVo, not your TV.

This collection of tips comes in handy when watching *recorded* shows, rather than live programming. Some help TiVo users deal with the guilt felt when they see shows scrolling off TiVo's Now Playing list, unwatched. If you don't want to lose *any* shows, another tip offers a refresher on how to save shows to a VCR.

You'll also find one of the most coveted tips of all: Activating TiVo's secret 30-second skip ahead feature for conveniently bypassing a commercial at the press of a button.

Letting Shows Scroll Off Naturally

Don't feel guilty when TiVo deletes older shows before you have a chance to watch them. They're *supposed* to scroll off. You're noticing their loss only because TiVo pointed them out.

Instead of juggling your recordings and constantly adjusting your save times, learn to let go. You missed plenty of shows before TiVo arrived, and you lived!

Besides, everything repeats, given enough time. Don't delete your WishList and that show will turn up again, perhaps when you have more time to watch it.

In the meantime, TiVo will continue to retrieve fresh, new shows to lessen your feeling of loss.

Fast-Forwarding 30 Seconds at a Time

Television networks are understandably squeamish about the way DVRs let users fast-forward through commercials. One of TiVo's competitors even unveiled a way to skip commercials completely *and* automatically. The networks panicked, sent in their lawyers, and the competitor removed the feature from its newer models.

The TiVo corporation took a much less combative stance; it doesn't advertise the fact that TiVo, too, allows users to skip commercials — not automatically but by skipping ahead in 30-second increments. Although the 30-second jump is neither officially supported by TiVo nor covered in its manuals, here's how to activate this hidden feature and begin using it:

✔ While watching a recorded show, press these keys in the following sequence:

If TiVo's sound effects are turned on, TiVo will make three "ding" sounds to show that you've activated the feature. (Unless you've turned off TiVo's sound effects, of course, in which case you won't hear anything.)

 When a commercial begins, quickly press the Skip-to-End (Advance) button to jump 30 seconds ahead; repeat until you've skipped past the commercials and your show begins.

✔ The feature disappears if TiVo loses power or resets itself. Reenter the code sequence to turn it back on.

✔ To turn off the 30-second skip and return normal function to your Skip-to-End button, reenter the key sequence.

✔ Personally, I prefer fast-forwarding through commercials, because it gives me more control over the timing. I don't use the 30-second skip feature, but you might want to give it a go.

 ✔ Toshiba's combo TiVo/DVD player (SD-H400) doesn't support the 30-second skip feature as of this writing. As a matter of fact, because TiVo doesn't officially support the 30-second skip feature, it could be discontinued at any time.

Repeating Missed Dialogue

The eight-second Rewind button comes in handy to catch up on the action when you return to a paused show. But I use it even more often to repeat missed lines of dialogue. It jumps back eight seconds each time you push it, letting you repeat entire conversations — quite handy when unraveling convoluted mysteries like Spielberg's *Minority Report*.

Creative Uses for Closed Captioning

The Fast-Forward button's a quick way to speed through boring segments of a show, whisking you past the opening monologue or through awful comedy segments of "Saturday Night Live." But your television's Closed Captioning feature adds another quick way to breeze through some shows.

Most TVs support Closed Captioning — usually turned on with a "CC" button on the TV's remote — that places a moving transcript of the show on the screen. Designed mainly for the hearing-impaired, Closed Captioning provides a way to understand the show without hearing the actual dialogue.

TiVo passes a show's Closed Captioning information through to your TV, and turning it on provides interesting features like these:

✔ To speed through talk shows or news programs, turn on your television's Closed Captioning and press TiVo's Fast-Forward button *once*. (Pressing more than once won't work.) TiVo plays back the show more quickly, yet you can still read the dialogue. By speeding up playback (and fast-forwarding through commercials), you can watch two talk shows in the space of one.

✔ If you can't figure out what somebody said during a pivotal point of a movie, turn on Closed Captioning and do an Instant Replay to read the mumbled lines. Turn it back off when through, if desired. This tip's essential for Californians trying to decipher mumbled *Sopranos* dialogue, for instance.

Playing or Deleting Saved Shows Quickly

TiVo lets you play or delete any show on your long list of saved shows fairly quickly. When you press Select, TiVo displays the show's description; you choose to delete or play the shows from there.

But to play a show directly from the Now Playing list, simply highlight its name and press Play instead of Select. TiVo immediately begins playing the show.

Similarly, highlight a show's name and press Clear instead of Select to delete it. (TiVo still tosses you an "Are you sure?" screen, to weed out the chance of the cat stepping on the remote's Clear button.)

Saving Recorded Shows to a VCR

Most folks ignore their VCR after TiVo, because it seems so awkward.

But if you absolutely must complete your *Dawson's Creek* library or tape a show for a friend, TiVo's "Save to VCR" option speeds things up a little. Chapter 6 covers it in full, but here are the steps for quick reference:

1. **Place a blank, rewound tape into your VCR.**
2. **From TiVo's Now Playing menu, select your show.**
3. **Select Save to VCR, and choose Start saving from the beginning.**
4. **Press the VCR's Record button, and take a break.**
5. **Press the VCR's Stop button when the show's through recording.**

Press the TiVo button twice to cancel, a tip that comes in handy for recording just part of a show. A little juggling of the TiVo's Play button and the VCR's Record button lets you perform crude edits, as well.

If your VCR has a "One Touch Record" button that records in 30-minute increments, use it so your VCR stops recording automatically.

Feel free to hook up a DVD recorder, instead of a VCR — TiVo doesn't know the difference.

Finally, check out "TiVoToGo," a new option for TiVo slated for late 2004 that lets you send shows to your PC for watching or recording. See TiVo's Web site (www.tivo.com) for details.

Chapter 16

Tips for Recording Shows

● ●

● ●

*W*hen TiVo records enjoyable shows, you find yourself enjoying TiVo. This collection of tips helps make sure your TiVo's stocked with shows that meet your current interests, no matter how eclectic they may be.

You'll find yourself using these tips over and over again when setting up recordings on TiVo.

Finding Interesting Shows to Record

Cut down on your movie rental tab by using TiVo as your customized movie grabber. Use these tips to fill TiVo with movies both you and your friends will enjoy:

   ✔ To find upcoming movies, press the TiVo button and the number 4 to jump to TiVo's Search by Title screen. Choose Search by name, highlight Movies, and select your favorite type of movie from the subcategory — Westerns, for instance. Instead of typing in a specific title, press 0 on the remote. TiVo lists all movies in that category airing in the next two weeks. Select and record the ones you like.

✔ Missed a movie during its theater run? Create an autorecording WishList with the movie's name to catch it during its TV run. (The movie arrives much more quickly if you subscribe to "premium" cable channels like HBO, Cinemax, or Starz.) TiVo can't order a "Pay Per View" movie, but a WishList will locate a title when it's finally available for purchase.

✔ Check out the Internet's lists of best movies, and enter some movie titles as autorecording WishLists. You'll find "Best Movies" lists online at Amazon (www.amazon.com), The Greatest Films (www.filmsite.org), and the Internet Movie Database (www.imdb.com), among others.

✔ Visit your WishList items once a week or so. Unless set for Autorecord, TiVo doesn't automatically record what you've entered. In fact, it doesn't even tell you when a match pops up. To see what items are available, head for the WishList area and choose View all upcoming WishList programs. TiVo displays all the current matches, letting you pick and choose what to record.

Making Sure TiVo Doesn't Miss the Very End (Or Beginning) of Your Shows

When recording shows, TiVo relies on the start and stop times supplied by the networks. Unfortunately, even the networks sometimes take a wild stab at estimating a show's actual ending time.

Specifically, be sure to add an extra hour or so to sporting events, awards shows, and other programs that traditionally run long. If you notice that one particular channel doesn't adhere to its listed start/stop times, feel free to pad its beginning and ending times by a few minutes to make up for it.

You can add a few minutes or even hours by choosing Options when scheduling a recording. When in doubt, pad a recording by a few minutes on each end. If the few extra minutes keep TiVo from recording adjacent shows, you may need to set up a manual recording of a particular channel at a particular time.

Automatically Recording TV Premieres

TiVo can't grab shows from the past, but you can hedge your bets. To make sure you don't miss the first episode of that hot new series creating such a media buzz, create an Autorecording WishList for the words "Pilot" or "Premiere" and set to "First Run Only."

When water cooler chatter revolves around TV's latest can't-miss show, TiVo will have it waiting for you at home. If nobody mentions the show or if it's just another dumb bug-eating reality show, delete it or let it die a natural death by scrolling off your list.

Avoiding Overflows from TV Show Marathons

Although Autorecording WishLists come in very handy, they can be dangerous to your storage space, too. If a station runs a 24-hour "Audrey Hepburn" marathon, your Autorecording WishList for the slender gal could push all of your other shows right off your list.

When creating an Autorecording WishList, don't set the "Keep at most" level to more than one or two shows unless you have a good reason. Even then, drop by your WishList and To Do areas to see what shows TiVo will be grabbing.

✔ TiVo's To Do list lives at the bottom of the Pick Programs to Record menu, and it lists all upcoming recordings.

✔ To view all your WishList items, choose View all upcoming WishList programs from your Create new WishList menu.

Navigating Menus More Quickly

When maneuvering through menus, try using the Channel Up/Down button as a Page Up/Down button. When looking at a list of show descriptions, for instance, pressing Channel Down brings up the next show on the list.

Check out the Cheat Sheet in the front of this book for more shortcut keys that quickly jump between menus.

Recording Movies or Shows with Forgotten Names

Can't remember the name of a particular show or movie but want TiVo to record it? If you can remember the show's actors or characters — or even part of the show's title — use the WishLists' "keyword" feature.

Enter in a few words with the actors' names, characters, or any of the words in the title you remember. Choose "View upcoming shows" to see if you can spot it, or simply set it on Autorecord so TiVo will automatically record the show when it airs.

Setting Up TiVo for Vacations

Once you've decided on a vacation destination, let TiVo help with your travel plans. Start by adding your vacation destination to the WishList, so TiVo will grab any shows relating to that particular place.

Take care of this TiVo maintenance before leaving:

- Check TiVo's To Do list, found at the bottom of the Pick Programs to Record option, to see your list of upcoming recordings. You may want to adjust the "Keep at Most" for some favorite shows and delete less popular shows to make sure there's enough room.

- Visit your Season Pass Manager and change the order of your Season Pass recordings. Make sure you list your favorites at the top so TiVo gives them the most attention.

- Find out the favorite shows of your housesitter, if you'll be using one, and add them to TiVo's record list. (That helps ensure your housesitter will actually be sitting at your house while you're gone.)

Recording Sports Events

Sporting events require special care when setting up for two reasons. They usually run longer than the scheduled time, causing TiVo to cut off the ending. Second, because the name of the show often changes depending on the venue, a Season Pass doesn't work well.

To fix the first problem, be sure to "pad" the show's ending time by an hour or so. Described in Chapter 6, this lets you tell TiVo to stop recording after the show's scheduled ending, as insurance against overtime.

As for the second problem, create an Autorecording WishList to catch your favorite sporting teams. When setting up the WishList, use your team's name in the Title. To further filter the results, choose sports in the Category area, and set the Subcategory to the type of sporting event you're after.

To catch all San Diego Chargers games, for instance, I'd create an Autorecording WishList that automatically recorded shows with "Chargers" in the title with the category of "Sports" and the subcategory of "Football."

To test your WishList, choose the View Upcoming Shows option. You might want to change Chargers to "Chargers at," for instance, using the Pause button to create the quote marks. Check your WishList every week or so to see if it needs tweaking.

Chapter 17

Tips for Sharing TiVo with Family or Roommates

● ●

● ●

*L*ike a new carton of ice cream, TiVo instantly becomes a coveted item in any household. And just as the ice cream mysteriously disappears, spoonful by spoonful, TiVo's storage space vanishes — especially when family members or roommates don't share similar viewing interests.

To keep peace in the household, this chapter offers some tips on using TiVo in a family or similar shared setting. A few tips help conserve storage space; others transform TiVo from a toy to a learning tool for children.

Sharing TiVo with a Roommate

A roommate with a TiVo requires special treatment. To keep that roommate for as long as possible, immediately offer to pay TiVo's monthly fee, or offer to discount that amount on the rent. After all, they've made quite an investment in bringing TiVo to the household. (If you're paying the monthly fee, they won't be allowed to keep their TiVo in their room, hogging it for themselves.)

Some landlords, especially in larger cities, toss in a TiVo as part of the rental package. When sharing a landlord's TiVo, try to schedule shows when your roommate's around, so nobody can be considered a space hog. Barter chores to settle the order of shows in Season Pass lineups.

If you want to record a show that repeats fairly often, place it *lower* on the Season Pass list than shows that don't repeat. That lets TiVo grab the shows that don't repeat and then fill in its recording schedule with the shows that do repeat. (You can tell if a show repeats a lot by eyeballing TiVo's "View Upcoming Shows" menu option when choosing to record a show.)

Also, keep an eye on TiVo's To Do list (see Chapter 6) to make sure a roommate's autorecording WishList isn't catching any marathons sure to fill up your TiVo with *South Park* episodes.

Finally, if one of your recorded shows mysteriously disappears, a visit to TiVo's View Recording History option (discussed in Chapter 6) shows the time and date that somebody deleted it — or whether TiVo simply deleted it to make room for incoming shows. It's a good way to avoid arguments.

- ✔ You may be tempted to add a second hard drive to a roommate's TiVo to double its storage. Although this seems logical, the drive can't be removed after installation. TiVo's original and second drive "merge." If you move out, you can't simply remove your second drive and take it with you unless you know advanced Linux computing techniques.

- ✔ TiVo's Home Media Option (HMO, covered in Part III) lets you transfer shows between two TiVos, which sounds nice when you and your roommate have TiVos in separate rooms. In reality, this isn't so nice: You can only transfer shows between TiVos registered under your own name. You can't move them between TiVos with different owners.

- ✔ When several people in the household record their own shows on TiVo, TiVo's Suggestions become a mishmash that rarely appeals to everybody. Leave them turned on, however, simply as a gauge of available free space.

Saving Space When Recording Long Shows

In families or households, TiVo recording space often carries a premium. This trick keeps a particularly long show from hogging TiVo's hard drive.

When recording programs that last several hours — sporting events, long movies, awards shows, and others — don't record the entire show with a single scheduled recording. Instead, use TiVo's manual recording option, and record the show's timeslot in several successive one-block chunks.

For instance, if you want to record the five-hour *Gone With The Wind*, which runs from 5 p.m. to 10 p.m., set up five one-hour manual recordings for the time and channel running the movie. Schedule the first block to record from 5 p.m. to 6 p.m. The second should record from 6 p.m. to 7 p.m. Keep going until you've set up five one hour blocks that cover the movie's air time.

Then, when you're finished watching the movie's first hour, delete the first one-hour block. Repeat with the rest of the blocks until you've finished the entire show.

When you record and delete the program in successive one-hour chunks, TiVo won't hog the entire five-hour chunk of space during the days it takes you to watch the entire movie.

Buy a Second Remote

When more than one person uses a TiVo, the remote often ends up in some pretty strange places. If you're having trouble locating where the last person left the remote, feel free to buy a second one and hide it in a special spot for your own use.

TiVo sells additional remotes at its online store (https://store.tivo.com). They even come in different colors so you can tell when somebody's walking away with your *personal* remote.

Setting Parental Controls Appropriately

TiVo's Parental Controls, described in Chapter 7, can "lock out" adult programming and other channels you don't want your children or visitors to watch. If you think you might need them, remember to turn them on before it's too late.

But even if you *don't* subscribe to adult programming, Parental Controls can be useful for keeping the kids from wasting time in front of the TV set. Simply lock out *every* channel except for educational channels. (If it simply drives the kids over to their friends' houses, change it back. At least you tried.)

Even if you don't use Parental Controls at all, be sure to set a password anyway, and allow access to *all* your channels. That keeps a sneaky kid, prankster, or fumbling visitor from setting their own password, effectively locking you out of your TiVo. (If they do, call TiVo's Customer Support, explain the situation, and convince them that you're the TiVo's *real* owner. DirecTV TiVo owners facing that situation need to grovel before DirecTV, not TiVo.)

Scheduling Children's Shows

Many children enjoy animated shows, and they're not as picky about a show's recording quality. When setting up recordings for animated shows, save hard disk space by setting the recording quality to Basic. (Large TV owners may want to bump the quality to Medium.)

To ensure the kids experience the best that TV has to offer, take the time to create Season Passes for some educational programs. You'll find plenty by setting the Category to Educational when looking for shows to record. TiVo will list upcoming educational shows, letting you choose Season Passes accordingly.

Some cable networks devote all of their programming to educational fare; try the Discovery channels or National Geographic specials, for starters.

Adding Current Schoolwork to WishLists

When the kids study American history, frog dissection, or other subjects in school, add those subjects as keywords for a WishList. TiVo will pluck pertinent educational shows from your flow of channels, ready for your child to watch when taking a break from the pencil and paper.

Delete the Season Passes or WishLists when the homework assignment ends — or leave them turned on, if they've sparked a new interest.

Hiding the Remote from Children and Guests

Because TiVo's always turned on, it never stops listening to the remote. Hide the remote from young children, animals, and guests, or they may play with the remote. A few haphazard key presses usually won't delete shows, but they could change TiVo's settings or assign random Thumbs ratings to shows.

As mentioned earlier in this chapter, be sure to set your own password in the Parental Controls area — even if you don't intend to use that feature. That keeps somebody from accidentally setting a password, effectively locking you out of your TiVo.

Chapter 18

Ten Warning Screens and Their Cures

*O*ccasionally, TiVo interrupts your customary diet of menus and recorded shows. Sometimes, TiVo gives you a gentle attention-getting nudge with a strange icon; other times, TiVo throws a startling, in-your-face intrusion onto your currently watched program.

In either case, TiVo's error messages require your immediate attention. This chapter presents the screen you'll see on TiVo, an explanation of what TiVo's trying to say, and the solution that makes TiVo — and you — happy.

The Show Is Currently Being Recorded . . .

Translation: You're watching a live show that you've also told TiVo to record. But you've suddenly pressed the remote to tell TiVo to change channels, and that would stop TiVo from recording that particular show. (See Figure 18-1.)

Solution: Your best solution is to press the TiVo button twice and watch a recorded show, instead. TiVo will continue to record the live show in the background. When TiVo's through recording it, watch that show's recording. (You should also try to watch less live TV, avoiding these disturbing screens in the future.)

Figure 18-1:
You're trying to change the channel while TiVo's recording the show.

The TiVo DVR Needs to Change the Channel . . .

Translation: You're watching live TV, but TiVo needs to change the channel to record a previously scheduled show. (See Figure 18-2.)

Solution: Stop watching that live TV show and let TiVo change the channel. Then, set up a Season Pass that will catch that show in the future.

If you're incredibly engrossed in the live show, however, tell TiVo to cancel your previously scheduled recording. Then you may continue to watch the live show.

Figure 18-2: You're watching live TV, but TiVo needs to change the channel to record a different show.

The Recorder Is Not Getting a Video Signal

Translation: TiVo isn't receiving any video from your TV provider. (See Figure 18-3.)

Solution: Make sure your cable or satellite box is turned on. If you have another TV, check to see if it's receiving a signal; your cable or satellite service may be experiencing an outage.

Check your video cables, as well. Plugging the yellow RCA cable back into TiVo's Video In jack may fix the problem. (The cable's other end should connect to the Video Out jack of your cable or satellite box.)

If everything seems okay, try restarting TiVo by doing this:

1. **Choose TiVo Messages & Setup from TiVo Central.**
2. **Select Restart or Reset System.**
3. **Select Restart the Recorder.**

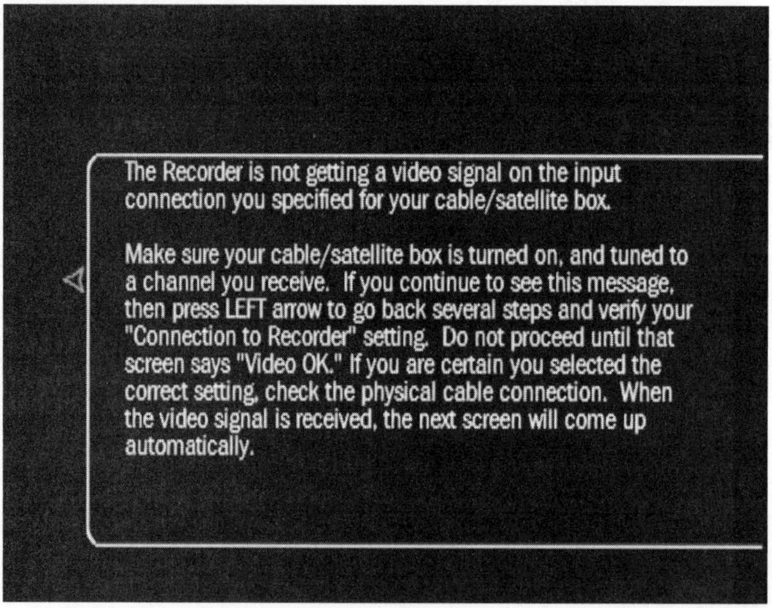

The Recorder is not getting a video signal on the input connection you specified for your cable/satellite box.

Make sure your cable/satellite box is turned on, and tuned to a channel you receive. If you continue to see this message, then press LEFT arrow to go back several steps and verify your "Connection to Recorder" setting. Do not proceed until that screen says "Video OK." If you are certain you selected the correct setting, check the physical cable connection. When the video signal is received, the next screen will come up automatically.

Figure 18-3:
TiVo isn't receiving any video information from your TV provider.

The DVR Cannot Display Live TV

Translation: TiVo can't see *anything* from your TV provider. (See Figure 18-4.)

Solution: Although TiVo lists several solutions on this screen, start by making sure the cable/satellite box is both plugged in *and* turned on.

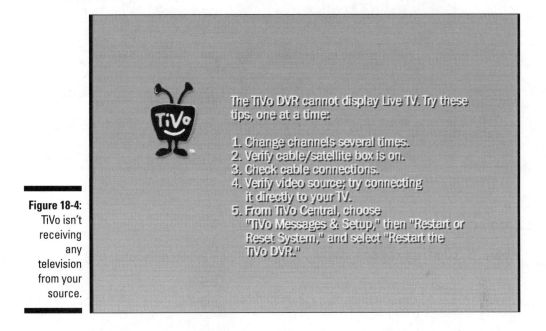

Figure 18-4:
TiVo isn't receiving any television from your source.

The TiVo DVR cannot display Live TV. Try these tips, one at a time:

1. Change channels several times.
2. Verify cable/satellite box is on.
3. Check cable connections.
4. Verify video source; try connecting it directly to your TV.
5. From TiVo Central, choose "TiVo Messages & Setup," then "Restart or Reset System," and select "Restart the TiVo DVR."

Please Activate Service

Translation: You're not yet paying your monthly fees to TiVo. (See Figure 18-5.)

Solution: Activate your TiVo either through TiVo itself, online (www.tivo.com), or by calling TiVo's customer service department. A credit card number chases away the nagging screens.

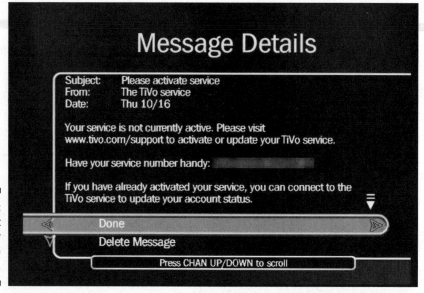

Message Details

Subject: Please activate service
From: The TiVo service
Date: Thu 10/16

Your service is not currently active. Please visit
www.tivo.com/support to activate or update your TiVo service.

Have your service number handy:

If you have already activated your service, you can connect to the
TiVo service to update your account status.

Done

Delete Message

Press CHAN UP/DOWN to scroll

Figure 18-5:
You haven't
yet paid for
your TiVo
service.

A Problem Occurred While Accessing the Server

Translation: Seen only by people accessing their computer through TiVo's Home Media Option, this means TiVo suddenly can't talk with your computer. (See Figure 18-6.)

Solution: Reboot your computer. Then make sure you've published files with the "TiVo Desktop" software (covered in Chapter 9), and make sure TiVo's networking adapter is plugged in.

Read New TiVo Messages and Setup

Translation: TiVo sent you a message describing an event that it wants you to read about. (See Figure 18-7.)

Solution: Select the "You have a message waiting" notice to read the message, then choose to either save or delete the message.

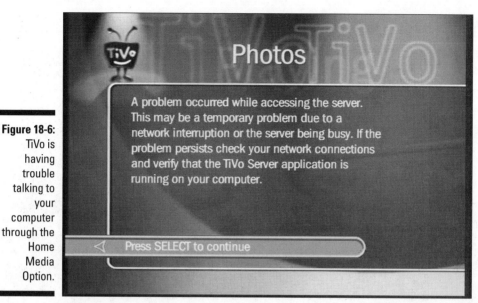

Figure 18-6:
TiVo is
having
trouble
talking to
your
computer
through the
Home
Media
Option.

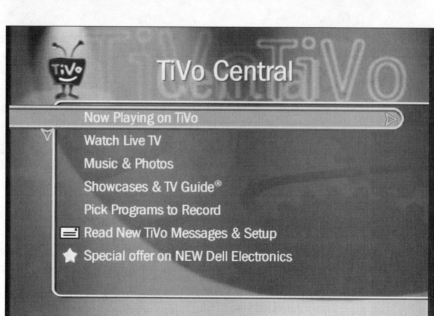

Figure 18-7:
TiVo sent
you a new
message
with
information
about your
service.

Press Thumbs Up to Record

Translation: Usually used as a form of advertising, this message appears onscreen to make it easy for you to record the advertised show by simply pressing the Thumbs Up button. (See Figure 18-8.)

Solution: Press Thumbs Up to record the show; if you don't want to record the show, ignore the message, and it will eventually go away.

Figure 18-8:
Press the Thumbs Up button if you want to record this advertised show.

Error Code: Error #32

Translation: Usually seen when you're searching for shows, this means TiVo's having trouble finding the show information. (See Figure 18-9.)

Solution: Ignore this rarely seen message. TiVo may not have finished completely indexing your shows. If the message continues, tell TiVo to reload its Program Data by doing this:

1. **Choose Messages & Setup from TiVo Central.**

2. **Choose System Reset.**

3. **Choose Clear Program Data & To Do List.**

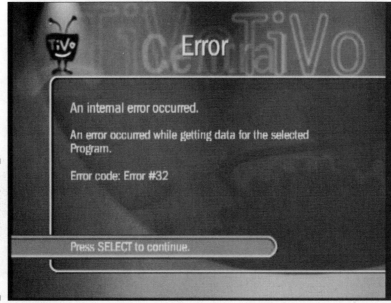

Figure 18-9:
TiVo usually displays this when searching for data about a show.

Black Screen

Translation: Although TiVo thinks it's successfully recording a show, that show isn't being fed to TiVo through your cable or satellite box. (See Figure 18-10.)

Solution: TiVo occasionally presents a black screen instead of a recorded show. Because TiVo recorded a black screen — and didn't present an error message complaining of no video signal — it most likely means you've scheduled a recording on a channel that you don't receive.

To test it, press the Live TV button and tune to the channel TiVo was supposed to record. If it's black — but other live channels come through fine — then you don't receive that channel from your TV provider. Head to Chapter 7's "Weeding out unwanted channels . . ." section and remove that channel from your list.

If the channel does come through when you press the Live TV button, then the station probably experienced technical difficulties while broadcasting.

Figure 18-10:
TiVo
displays a
black
screen
when it tries
to record a
channel you
don't
receive.

Chapter 19

Ten Differences between TiVo and Generic DVRs

*I*nspired by raves about TiVo, many cable and satellite companies now offer their customers digital video recorders (DVRs) for recording TV programs. Most cost about the same amount as renting a cable box or satellite. They're much less expensive than TiVo.

In my own experience with a generic DVR, the old adage "you get what you pay for" really rings true. This chapter lists the biggest differences I found between TiVo and the generic DVR my cable company offered, a Scientific Atlanta 8000 from Cox Communications. TiVo outperformed the DVR in every way.

Scientific Atlanta's DVR will almost certainly improve; the box is using its first generation of software as I write this book. But with TiVo's five-year head start and hefty patent portfolio, the competition had better start scrambling.

TiVo Automatically Searches for Shows

To record an upcoming show on TiVo, you simply type in the show's name. Or, you can search for the show, browsing by category, by actor/director name, or even by entering a few keywords. TiVo locates the show, describes it, and lets you decide how to record it.

The Scientific Atlanta DVR, by contrast, only let me select shows by name from their standard program guide; the guide only listed a few channels on each screen. Only after I spotted the show's name could I select it to be recorded.

Without a search feature, I had to know the show's name, its exact air time, and its channel before I could find it on the guide and record it.

TiVo Offers a Season Pass

TiVo's Season Pass automatically records every new episode of a series. If the network changes an episode's air date or time, TiVo adjusts its recording schedule accordingly. TiVo even recognizes and ignores reruns.

The Scientific Atlanta 8000 DVR offered only to record *every* episode of a show, including repeats of the same episode. (Some models only record by a specific time and date, not by a program's name.)

TiVo Offers a WishList

The WishList keeps TiVo constantly searching for upcoming shows that match what you're looking for — an actor, director, theme, or keyword. When TiVo finds a match — even weeks later — it either automatically records or lists the show, according to your designation.

Because the DVR only records shows you specifically find and select by name, it can't search for and automatically record any shows matching your previously entered search terms.

A Standalone TiVo Won't Record in Dolby 5.1 Sound

Our standalone TiVo can't record in Dolby 5.1 sound, unfortunately, which is what made me try out Cox's DVR in the first place. The DVR definitely had the upper hand here, as it recorded HBO movies that played back in Dolby 5.1 sound.

Unfortunately, the DVR's 5.1 sound feature still had some bugs. Although it played live movies correctly in 5.1 sound, the recorder couldn't play back recorded 5.1 sound. The recorded sound stuttered and skipped, missing bits of dialogue. I swapped it for a different unit, but that one did the same thing. A quick search on the Internet showed several other people with the same problem.

The DirecTV TiVo will record and playback in 5.1 sound, but we subscribe to cable, not satellite, at our home.

TiVo's a Time-Tested Technology

Quite simply, TiVo *works*. TiVo started with the old Series 1 boxes and graduated to the new Series 2 boxes. TiVo has been integrated with a satellite box (DirecTV TiVo), a DVD player, and a DVD recorder (covered in Chapter 1). TiVo has already progressed through five major software versions. Simply put, TiVo has had time to fine-tune everything so it works without problems; its menus are easy to navigate and visually appealing.

DVRs arrived much more recently on the market, so the manufacturers still need time to work out the problems. I'm sure they're improved as you read these pages.

You Own TiVo

When you buy a standalone TiVo, you own it. You can take it with you if you move. You can increase its storage space. If you pay the Lifetime Subscription fee, you don't need to pay monthly rental fees. You can hook a standalone TiVo up to any TV source, including cable, satellite, and plain old rabbit ears.

The DVRs from the cable company come on a rental basis only, and they're never paid off. (Mine even came with a $40 installation fee, although the technician just handed it to me.)

The DVR Lets You Watch One Show Live and Record Another Simultaneously

The Scientific Atlanta 8000 DVR includes two tuners, letting you watch one show live while recording another live show in the background.

Our standalone TiVo can't do this (although we rented a second cable box to get around that problem, as discussed in Chapter 3). DirecTV TiVos come with two tuners, though, so they can do the same thing.

Chapter 20

Ten Big Differences between Series 1 and Series 2 TiVos

*I*n the days of yesteryear, before Series 2 TiVos filled today's store shelves, TiVo sold an earlier model, dubbed a "Series 1" TiVo. Sold from the late 1990s to 2002, the old Series 1 TiVo works very similar to today's "Series 2" TiVos. Nearly everything in this book applies to all TiVo models.

This chapter explores the few key differences between the Series 1 TiVos and the Series 2 models. It explains how to tell them apart at a glance, which comes in handy if you're shopping for a used TiVo. Shoppers should also take note of the Series 2 features not found in Series 1, so they know what they'll be missing.

Series 1 owners should examine the main wording differences in the menus. This book uses the wordings found in Series 2 TiVos. Series 1 owners can compare the Series 1 and 2 menus shown here and substitute their own wordings when following steps in this book.

Differences in the TiVo Central Menu

It's easy to tell if you're looking at a Series 1 or Series 2 TiVo. You don't even have to pull the TiVo off the shelf to look for its missing "USB port." Just pull up the TiVo Central menu for a quick identifier.

The TiVo Central menu on a Series 1 TiVo is *blue*, with a moving "starburst" pattern in the background, as seen in Figure 20-1.

Figure 20-1:
The TiVo
Central
menu on a
Series 1
TiVo is blue
with a
moving
"starburst"
pattern
behind the
words.

The Series 2 TiVo, on the other hand, has a *green* TiVo Central menu with moving gears in the background, shown in Figure 20-2.

Note how the Series 2 TiVo Central menu in Figure 20-2 contains the extra Music and Photos option. Not all Series 2 TiVos sport this menu, as it's part of the TiVo's Home Media Option add-on. But you'll never see that menu option on a Series 1 TiVo — TiVo doesn't offer the Home Media Option for Series 1 TiVos.

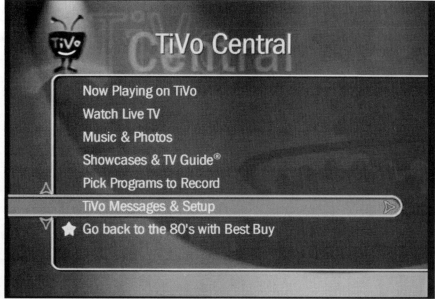

Figure 20-2:
The TiVo
Central
menu on a
Series 2
TiVo is
green with
moving
gears as a
background
pattern.

Note the subtle differences in wording, as well.

- ✔ Series 1 offers the "Now Playing list" as its top menu item. Series 2 TiVos refer to it as "Now Playing on TiVo."

- ✔ Series 1 offers "Showcases." Series 2 refers to that menu item as "Showcases and TV Guide."

- ✔ Series 1 offers "Messages & Setup" compared to Series 2's "TiVo Messages & Setup."

If you're a Series 1 owner, keep in mind these subtle differences when following this book's step-by-step instructions.

Differences in the Now Playing Menu

The TiVo corporation tossed an extra software upgrade onto Series 2 TiVos, giving them several new features not found in Series 1 TiVos. One of the biggest differences appears in the Now Playing menu.

Series 1 TiVos offer only one type of Now Playing menu, seen in Figure 20-3.

Figure 20-3:
The "Now Playing List"
on Series 1
normally
displays
shows in the
order they
were
recorded.

Series 1 TiVos only list shows in the order they were recorded, so the newest shows always appear at the top. It places *every* recorded show on the menu, without an option to manage them or sort them into groups.

Series 2 TiVos, by contrast, allow users to group shows into "folders." Figure 20-4, for instance, shows four folders on the Now Playing menu. The Simply Quilts folder at the top contains five episodes of my wife's "Simply Quilts" show. Two episodes of "The Duke" live in another folder below.

Notice the little star on the folder for Outkast? That star appears on a folder containing two shows caught by an *Autorecording WishList;,* in this case, for the musical group Outkast.

Placing show episodes into folders reduces menu clutter, and keeps users from scrolling down a long list of shows to find the right one. To find a particular episode of "Simply Quilts," for instance, open the Simply Quilts folder, seen in Figure 20-5.

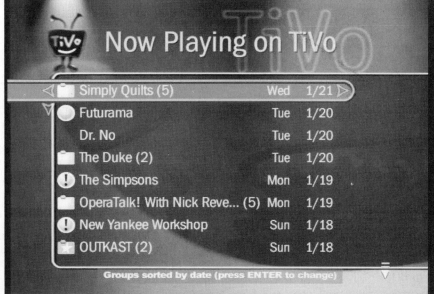

Figure 20-4:
Series 2
TiVos allow
users to
group
shows into
folders.

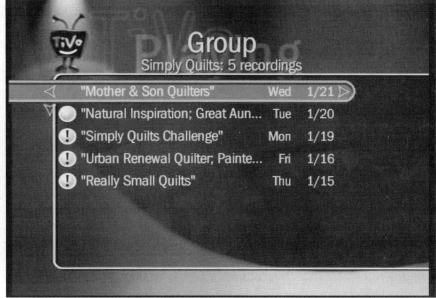

Figure 20-5:
Open a
folder to see
all the
recorded
episodes
of that
particular
show or
Auto-
recording
WishList.

✔ Series 2 TiVos refer to the Now Playing menu as "Now Playing on TiVo;" Series 1 TiVos call it the "Now Playing list."

✔ Pressing Enter on a Series 2 TiVo lets you choose between sorting shows alphabetically or by recording date.

✔ Here's a quick shortcut: From the Now Playing menu, press 1 to toggle between sorting shows by date or by alphabet; press 2 to turn the folder grouping on or off.

Differences in the System Information Screen

The most foolproof way of telling the difference between a Series 1 and Series 2 TiVo comes by looking at the System Information screen. To find the System Information screen on any TiVo, choose Messages & Setup from the TiVo Central menu, then choose System Information.

The Series 1 System Information screen, seen in Figure 20-6, is brown. It doesn't specifically say "Series 1."

The Series 2 System Information screen, seen in Figure 20-7, is not only blue, but the menu says "Series2" on the "Platform" line.

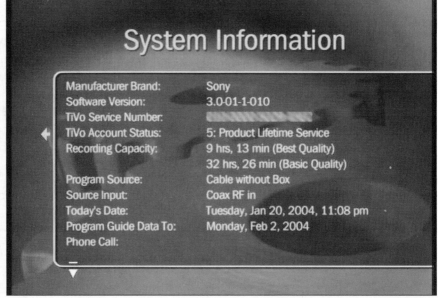

Figure 20-6: The Series 1 System Information screen is brown and doesn't specifically say "Series 1."

System Information

Manufacturer Brand:	Sony
Software Version:	3.0-01-1-010
TiVo Service Number:	
TiVo Account Status:	5: Product Lifetime Service
Recording Capacity:	9 hrs, 13 min (Best Quality)
	32 hrs, 26 min (Basic Quality)
Program Source:	Cable without Box
Source Input:	Coax RF in
Today's Date:	Tuesday, Jan 20, 2004, 11:08 pm
Program Guide Data To:	Monday, Feb 2, 2004
Phone Call:	

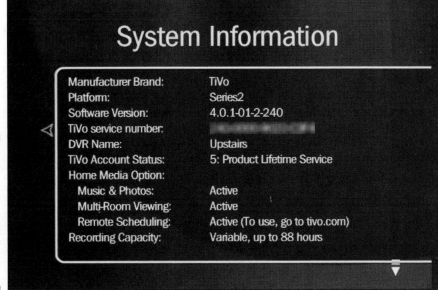

System Information

Manufacturer Brand:	TiVo
Platform:	Series2
Software Version:	4.0.1-01-2-240
TiVo service number:	
DVR Name:	Upstairs
TiVo Account Status:	5: Product Lifetime Service
Home Media Option:	
Music & Photos:	Active
Multi-Room Viewing:	Active
Remote Scheduling:	Active (To use, go to tivo.com)
Recording Capacity:	Variable, up to 88 hours

Figure 20-7:
The Series 2
System
Information
screen is
blue, and
specifically
says
"Series2."

The software version for Series 1 TiVos is never higher than version 3; Series 2 TiVos usually have version 4 software, although the integrated DVD TiVos have version 5 software.

Limitations of Series 1 TiVos

You can usually pick up a refurbished or used Series 1 TiVo from eBay (www.ebay.com) for around one hundred bucks. (You still have to pay the monthly subscription fees to TiVo, although Series 1 TiVos with Lifetime Subscriptions often turn up on eBay, too.) If you buy a used Series 1 TiVo, you *won't* be getting these things:

- **A warranty.** Unless you purchase TiVo from an authorized retailer, it won't come with the standard warranty. You can download a copy of the TiVo's manual from TiVo's Web site (www.tivo.com). Some do-it-yourself replacement parts are available online at WeaKnees.com (www.weaknees.com), PTVupgrade (www.ptvupgrade.com), and other Web sites.

- **A USB port.** Without one, you can't hook it directly to your computer and piggyback on its broadband Internet connection. It will need a phone line.

✔ **The Home Media Option.** Described in Part III of this book, the Home Media Option lets you schedule recordings from any Web site, transfer shows between two of your TiVos, or play MP3 songs and view photos from your computer.

✔ **Speed.** The Series 1 TiVo is a little slower than the Series 2 TiVo. It's certainly usable, but you'll notice a slight speed improvement if you switch to a Series 2 TiVo.

✔ **Menu enhancements.** Described earlier in this chapter, this lets you group recordings into folders, and sort them either by recording date or alphabetically.

✔ **Future enhancements.** TiVo still supports Series 1 TiVos, but they won't be adding new enhancements to this model. New features will only appear on the Series 2 TiVos.

If these things don't really matter to you, a used Series 1 TiVo might be all you need to start living a TiVo lifestyle.

Glossary

Autorecording WishList: A WishList set to record a show or shows automatically. (See Wishlist.)

Backdoor code: A private "developer setting" that enables features primarily of interest to TiVo's engineers, although some users like to play with them, too. (Technically, the 30-second skip feature is more of a hidden feature than a backdoor code.)

Buffer: This 30-minute storage tank for video lets TiVo constantly record the currently tuned channel. TiVo automatically erases the buffer and starts over with each channel change.

Channel Banner: The strip near the screen's top that displays the current channel's name. Press Clear to remove it; press the Right Arrow repeatedly to see it in three different sizes — large, medium, and small.

Component video: A high-quality method of sending video through three separate wires, one each for red, green, and blue color information. HDTV TiVos and DVD TiVos offer component video.

Composite cables: Often used interchangeably with the term *RCA cables*, composite refers to the type of video signal on the yellow (video) cable. (The color and brightness signals both travel through one wire.) The red (right audio), and white (left audio) wires carry audio signals.

Daily call: Although not always daily, nor limited to a phone call, this refers to TiVo's contacting the TiVo corporation to fetch updated show listings.

DirecTiVo: Slang term for "DirecTV Receiver with TiVo Service," meaning a TiVo used with an integrated satellite tuner marketed and supported by DirecTV.

DVR: Digital Video Recorder. A device that records onto a hard drive, like TiVo. (Also called PVR, or Personal Video Recorder.)

Favorite Channels: Channels you've selected as your most frequently watched. Switching the Guide to show Favorite Channels filters everything else, making your Favorites easier to spot.

First Run: Any program that airs within 28 days of its Original Air Date and still hasn't been recorded.

Guided Setup: A series of step-by-step procedures that sets up a new TiVo or reconfigures an old one.

Home Media Option: An add-on sold by TiVo, Inc., allowing TiVo to connect with your computer.

Instant Replay: A remote button that quickly skips back eight seconds and begins playing again.

Live TV: Shows watched through TiVo at the same time the network broadcasts them. (Actually, TiVo displays live TV about a second after its broadcast.)

Now Playing list: TiVo's list of recorded shows ready for you to watch.

Original Air Date: The date that a particular show or episode first debuted.

Padding: Adding some time to a scheduled recording's Start or Stop times to account for shows that start early or end late.

Parental Controls: A password-protection mechanism used primarily by parents to lock children out of unapproved channels.

Peanut: Slang term for TiVo's "peanut"-shaped remote control used on all TiVo models except Sony's.

RCA cables: The design of the plug on the end of the wire often used to carry audio and composite video signals. (See Composite cables.)

Recording History: Found at the top of TiVo's To Do List, this describes what shows TiVo will record in the future, and reasons why it didn't record scheduled shows.

Save to VCR: A way for TiVo to play back a recording into your VCR (or DVD recorder) for recording to videotape.

Season Pass: A way to make TiVo automatically record a TV series or shows featuring a certain actor, director, title, or keyword.

Season Pass Manager: A list of Season Passes or Autorecording WishList items sorted by priority so TiVo knows which one to record if they run simultaneously.

Series 1: The original series of TiVos that are no longer made.

Series 2: The TiVos sold in the stores today. (At the time of this writing, DirecTV TiVos don't have all the features of other Series 2 TiVos, although they're very similar in design.)

Software update: A periodic update sent to TiVo during its Daily Call that adds features or fixes problems.

Standalone: A TiVo without an integrated satellite receiver. (DirecTV TiVos, by contrast, contain an integrated satellite receiver.)

Standby: A menu option that tells TiVo you're no longer playing with it. TiVo subsequently turns off its audio and video outputs; it reinstates Parental Controls (if you've turned them on); and TiVo turns off its front panel lights. But TiVo continues to record your scheduled shows in the background, changing channels whenever necessary. (DirecTV TiVos also stop recording the live TV buffers.) To resume playing with TiVo, press the TiVo button or Live TV button.

Subscription: TiVo's features require a subscription, paid on a monthly basis or, for standalone TiVos, through a single "lifetime" lump-sum payment.

Suggestions: Shows TiVo thinks you'll like, based on your viewing habits. Some Suggestions are automatically recorded (unless you say not to), but you can always see a list of Suggestions from the Pick Programs to Record menu. TiVo always erases Suggestions first when making room for shows you've personally selected to record.

S-Video: A video cable (usually black) carrying separate color and brightness information, which usually makes for a better picture. (The S-Video cable's plug contains four tiny pins arranged in an arc.)

Test call: Making a connection between TiVo and the computer at TiVo's headquarters to make sure they can communicate successfully. Usually done through the phone line, this can also be done through a computer network.

Thumbs Down: Pressing the Thumbs Down button teaches TiVo you don't like that show (and similar shows), and TiVo tailors its Suggestions accordingly.

Thumbs Up: Pressing the Thumbs Up button lets TiVo know you've enjoyed that show (and similar shows), and TiVo tailors its Suggestions accordingly.

UK TiVo: A TiVo built specifically for the United Kingdom and its PAL broadcast format. (No longer sold, UK TiVos won't work in the United States.)

Wireless modem jack: A gadget allowing communications between TiVo and a phone jack without cables. The gadget's "sender" plugs into TiVo and beams signals to the gadget's "receiver," which plugs into your phone jack.

WishList: A list of actors, directors, or topics for TiVo to locate so you can pick and choose which ones to record. (See Autorecording WishList.)

Index

• S •

Notes

Notes

Notes

Notes

Notes

Notes

FOR DUMMIES®

The easy way to get more done and have more fun

PERSONAL FINANCE

0-7645-5231-7

0-7645-2431-3

0-7645-5331-3

Also available:

Estate Planning For Dummies
(0-7645-5501-4)

401(k)s For Dummies
(0-7645-5468-9)

Frugal Living For Dummies
(0-7645-5403-4)

Microsoft Money "X" For
Dummies
(0-7645-1689-2)

Mutual Funds For Dummies
(0-7645-5329-1)

Personal Bankruptcy For
Dummies
(0-7645-5498-0)

Quicken "X" For Dummies
(0-7645-1666-3)

Stock Investing For Dummies
(0-7645-5411-5)

Taxes For Dummies 2003
(0-7645-5475-1)

BUSINESS & CAREERS

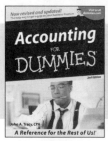

0-7645-5314-3

0-7645-5307-0

0-7645-5471-9

Also available:

Business Plans Kit For
Dummies
(0-7645-5365-8)

Consulting For Dummies
(0-7645-5034-9)

Cool Careers For Dummies
(0-7645-5345-3)

Human Resources Kit For
Dummies
(0-7645-5131-0)

Managing For Dummies
(1-5688-4858-7)

QuickBooks All-in-One Desk
Reference For Dummies
(0-7645-1963-8)

Selling For Dummies
(0-7645-5363-1)

Small Business Kit For
Dummies
(0-7645-5093-4)

Starting an eBay Business For
Dummies
(0-7645-1547-0)

HEALTH, SPORTS & FITNESS

0-7645-5167-1

0-7645-5146-9

0-7645-5154-X

Also available:

Controlling Cholesterol For
Dummies
(0-7645-5440-9)

Dieting For Dummies
(0-7645-5126-4)

High Blood Pressure For
Dummies
(0-7645-5424-7)

Martial Arts For Dummies
(0-7645-5358-5)

Menopause For Dummies
(0-7645-5458-1)

Nutrition For Dummies
(0-7645-5180-9)

Power Yoga For Dummies
(0-7645-5342-9)

Thyroid For Dummies
(0-7645-5385-2)

Weight Training For Dummies
(0-7645-5168-X)

Yoga For Dummies
(0-7645-5117-5)

Available wherever books are sold.
Go to www.dummies.com or call 1-877-762-2974 to order direct.

FOR DUMMIES®

A world of resources to help you grow

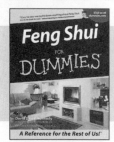

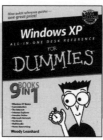

FOR DUMMIES®

Helping you expand your horizons and realize your potential

INTERNET

0-7645-0894-6

0-7645-1659-0

0-7645-1642-6

Also available:

America Online 7.0 For Dummies
(0-7645-1624-8)

Genealogy Online For Dummies
(0-7645-0807-5)

The Internet All-in-One Desk Reference For Dummies
(0-7645-1659-0)

Internet Explorer 6 For Dummies
(0-7645-1344-3)

The Internet For Dummies Quick Reference
(0-7645-1645-0)

Internet Privacy For Dummies
(0-7645-0846-6)

Researching Online For Dummies
(0-7645-0546-7)

Starting an Online Business For Dummies
(0-7645-1655-8)

DIGITAL MEDIA

0-7645-1664-7

0-7645-1675-2

0-7645-0806-7

Also available:

CD and DVD Recording For Dummies
(0-7645-1627-2)

Digital Photography All-in-One Desk Reference For Dummies
(0-7645-1800-3)

Digital Photography For Dummies Quick Reference
(0-7645-0750-8)

Home Recording for Musicians For Dummies
(0-7645-1634-5)

MP3 For Dummies
(0-7645-0858-X)

Paint Shop Pro "X" For Dummies
(0-7645-2440-2)

Photo Retouching & Restoration For Dummies
(0-7645-1662-0)

Scanners For Dummies
(0-7645-0783-4)

GRAPHICS

0-7645-0817-2

0-7645-1651-5

0-7645-0895-4

Also available:

Adobe Acrobat 5 PDF For Dummies
(0-7645-1652-3)

Fireworks 4 For Dummies
(0-7645-0804-0)

Illustrator 10 For Dummies
(0-7645-3636-2)

QuarkXPress 5 For Dummies
(0-7645-0643-9)

Visio 2000 For Dummies
(0-7645-0635-8)

Available wherever books are sold. Go to www.dummies.com or call 1-877-762-2974 to order direct.

FOR DUMMIES®

The advice and explanations you need to succeed

SELF-HELP, SPIRITUALITY & RELIGION

0-7645-5302-X

0-7645-5418-2

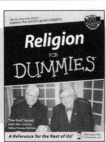
0-7645-5264-3

Also available:

The Bible For Dummies
(0-7645-5296-1)

Buddhism For Dummies
(0-7645-5359-3)

Christian Prayer For Dummies
(0-7645-5500-6)

Dating For Dummies
(0-7645-5072-1)

Judaism For Dummies
(0-7645-5299-6)

Potty Training For Dummies
(0-7645-5417-4)

Pregnancy For Dummies
(0-7645-5074-8)

Rekindling Romance For Dummies
(0-7645-5303-8)

Spirituality For Dummies
(0-7645-5298-8)

Weddings For Dummies
(0-7645-5055-1)

PETS

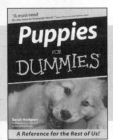
0-7645-5255-4

0-7645-5286-4

0-7645-5275-9

Also available:

Labrador Retrievers For Dummies
(0-7645-5281-3)

Aquariums For Dummies
(0-7645-5156-6)

Birds For Dummies
(0-7645-5139-6)

Dogs For Dummies
(0-7645-5274-0)

Ferrets For Dummies
(0-7645-5259-7)

German Shepherds For Dummies
(0-7645-5280-5)

Golden Retrievers For Dummies
(0-7645-5267-8)

Horses For Dummies
(0-7645-5138-8)

Jack Russell Terriers For Dummies
(0-7645-5268-6)

Puppies Raising & Training Diary For Dummies
(0-7645-0876-8)

EDUCATION & TEST PREPARATION

0-7645-5194-9

0-7645-5325-9

0-7645-5210-4

Also available:

Chemistry For Dummies
(0-7645-5430-1)

English Grammar For Dummies
(0-7645-5322-4)

French For Dummies
(0-7645-5193-0)

The GMAT For Dummies
(0-7645-5251-1)

Inglés Para Dummies
(0-7645-5427-1)

Italian For Dummies
(0-7645-5196-5)

Research Papers For Dummies
(0-7645-5426-3)

The SAT I For Dummies
(0-7645-5472-7)

U.S. History For Dummies
(0-7645-5249-X)

World History For Dummies
(0-7645-5242-2)

Available wherever books are sold. Go to www.dummies.com or call 1-877-762-2974 to order direct.